FWS/OBS-84/02
July 1984

The Ecology of Eelgrass Meadows of the Atlantic Coast: A Community Profile

Fish and Wildlife Service

U.S. Department of the Interior

FWS/OBS-84/02
July 1984

THE ECOLOGY OF EELGRASS MEADOWS
OF THE ATLANTIC COAST:
A Community Profile

by

Gordon W. Thayer
W. Judson Kenworthy
Beaufort Laboratory
National Marine Fisheries Service
Southeast Fisheries Center
Beaufort, NC   28516

and

Mark S. Fonseca
Department of Environmental Sciences
University of Virginia
Charlottesville, VA   22903

Project Officer

Edward Pendleton
National Coastal Ecosystems Team
U.S. Fish and Wildlife Service
1010 Gause Boulevard
Slidell, LA   70458

Performed for
National Coastal Ecosystems Team
Division of Biological Services
Research and Development
Fish and Wildlife Service
U.S. Department of the Interior
Washington, DC   20240

DISCLAIMER

The findings in this report are not to be construed as an official U.S. Fish and Wildlife Service position unless so designated by other authorized documents.

Library of Congress Card Number 84-601046

This report should be cited:

Thayer, G.W., W.J. Kenworthy, and M.S. Fonseca. 1984. The ecology of eelgrass meadows of the Atlantic coast: a community profile. U.S. Fish Wildl. Serv. FWS/OBS-84/02. 147 pp.

PREFACE

This report, one of a series of community profiles produced by the Fish and Wildlife Service, synthesizes scientific literature and data on the eelgrass community of the Atlantic coast from North Carolina to Nova Scotia. It is one of several profiles in the series to deal with seagrass communities and complements a published profile on the seagrasses of South Florida (FWS/OBS-82/25) and profiles being prepared on seagrasses of the Pacific Northwest and the northeast Gulf of Mexico.

Eelgrass, _Zostera marina_, dominates the ecologically important but fragile seagrass communities along the east coast of the United States from North Carolina to Nova Scotia. Grasslike leaves and an extensive root and rhizome system enable eelgrass to exist in a shallow aquatic environment subject to waves, tides, and shifting sediments.

Eelgrass meadows are highly productive, frequently rivaling agricultural croplands. They provide shelter and a rich variety of primary and secondary food resources and form a nursery habitat for the life history stages of numerous fishery organisms. The leaves absorb and release nutrients; provide surfaces for attachment; reduce water current velocity, turbulence, and scour; and promote accumulation of detritus. Rhizomes provide protection for benthic infauna and enhance sediment stability. Roots absorb and release nutrients to interstitial waters.

Because of their shallow, subtidal existence, seagrasses are susceptible to perturbations of both the water column and sediments. Eelgrass meadows are impacted by dredging and filling, some commercial fishery harvest techniques, modification of normal temperature and salinity regimes, and addition of chemical wastes. Techniques have been developed to successfully restore eelgrass habitats, but a holistic approach to planning research and environmentally related decisions is needed to avoid cumulative environmental impacts on these vital nursery areas.

Questions or comments concerning this publication or others in the profile series should be directed to the following address.

Information Transfer Specialist
National Coastal Ecosystems Team
U.S. Fish and Wildlife Service
NASA Slidell Computer Complex
1010 Gause Boulevard
Slidell, LA 70458

CONTENTS

FIGURES

TABLES

CONVERSION FACTORS

Metric to U.S. Customary

Multiply	By	To Obtain
millimeters (mm)	0.03937	inches
centimeters (cm)	0.3937	inches
meters (m)	3.281	feet
kilometers (km)	0.6214	miles
square meters (m^2)	10.76	square feet
square kilometers (km^2)	0.3861	square miles
hectares (ha)	2.471	acres
liters (l)	0.2642	gallons
cubic meters (m^3)	35.31	cubic feet
cubic meters	0.0008110	acre-feet
milligrams (mg)	0.00003527	ounces
grams (g)	0.03527	ounces
kilograms (kg)	2.205	pounds
metric tons (t)	2205.0	pounds
metric tons	1.102	short tons
kilocalories (kcal)	3.968	British thermal units
Celsius degrees	1.8(C°) + 32	Fahrenheit degrees

U.S. Customary to Metric

inches	25.40	millimeters
inches	2.54	centimeters
feet (ft)	0.3048	meters
fathoms	1.829	meters
miles (mi)	1.609	kilometers
nautical miles (nmi)	1.852	kilometers
square feet (ft^2)	0.0929	square meters
acres	0.4047	hectares
square miles (mi^2)	2.590	square kilometers
gallons (gal)	3.785	liters
cubic feet (ft^3)	0.02831	cubic meters
acre-feet	1233.0	cubic meters
ounces (oz)	28.35	grams
pounds (lb)	0.4536	kilograms
short tons (ton)	0.9072	metric tons
British thermal units (Btu)	0.2520	kilocalories
Fahrenheit degrees	0.5556(F° - 32)	Celsius degrees

ACKNOWLEDGMENTS

The development of this community profile took on a larger dimension than any of us had anticipated. The process also went on for a longer period than we imagined. We are indebted to many individuals who kept us going through discussions and encouragement, and, most of all, by providing unpublished data, data reports, submitted or in-press manuscripts, and, in some cases, originals of theses, dissertations, and/or older documents: Steven Bach, Marilyn Harlin, Denice Heller, Michael Kemp, Arthur Mathieson, John Merriner, Robert Orth, David Patriquin, Polly Penhale, Charles Peterson, Fred Short, Hoffman Stuart, Michael Weinstein, Richard Wetzel, and Joseph Zieman. We also recognize stimulation provided by Joseph Zieman, Ronald Phillips, John Ogden, and Peter McRoy during our individual and collective association with the Seagrass Ecosystem Study (SES) Program under the sponsorship of the International Decade of Ocean Exploration Office of the National Science Foundation. We had been working on seagrass systems prior to the inception of SES, but the SES team collectively offered up a challenge which subsequently has been taken up by us and a number of others in elucidating processes that structure seagrass meadows and make them ecologically important yet fragile. Participation in research at the Beaufort Laboratory and co-authorship of this profile by Mark Fonseca was made possible through an Intergovernmental Personnel Action sponsored by Joseph C. Zieman and the University of Virginia where M. Fonseca is a Faculty Research Assistant.

Portions of this profile were written by our colleagues: Denice Heller, Hoffman Stuart, and Jefferson Turner (presently on Intergovernmental Personnel Act assignment to the Beaufort Laboratory). Their insight and ability to extract information on the influence of waves and currents together (part of Section 3.1; Denice Heller), benthic and epibenthic fauna (section 4.5; Hoffman Stuart), and zooplankton (section 4.6; Jefferson Turner) lightened our burden measurably. Special thanks are given to Mark Robertson and Joseph Zieman who allowed us to quote directly the section on Detrital Processing which appears in Zieman (1982) and was written by Robertson.

At one time or another, the entire profile or parts thereof have been reviewed by William Nicholson, Ford Cross, Hoffman Stuart, Jose Rivera, William Lindall, John Merriner, Steve Bach, Polly Penhale, Robert Lippson, Richard Wetzel, and Larry Van Zant. Their advice and constructive criticisms were gratefully received. Edward Pendleton and Wiley Kitchens of the U.S. Fish and Wildlife Service were patient and understanding during the development of the profile, and they and other members of their staff provided extensive editorial assistance.

Perhaps those who labored longest were individuals who typed and provided figures for the profile. Margaret Rose spent many hours over the original draft and its revisions; Jean Fulford typed the final version several times; Herbert Gordy redrew the many figures we employ; Gus Fonseca spent several days assisting in the collection of several of our photographs. The cover collage is composed of photographs taken by Irving and Mark Hooper, Beaufort, North Carolina. Text photographs are by the authors, and Mark Fonseca drew many of the free-hand sketches. We would be remiss were we to not acknowledge Ann Bowman Hall for her monumental effort in searching and obtaining literature and helping to collate and proof the references. To all these people we express our sincere thanks, not only for a job well done, but one done with a smile. Finally, Michael LaCroix, Carolyn Currin, Kathleen Cheap, and Marianne Murdoch kept our research going, reviewed and xeroxed many pages, allowing us the time to work on this profile.

CHAPTER 1
INTRODUCTION

1.1 TAXONOMIC POSITION AND ADAPTATIONS OF SEAGRASSES TO A SHALLOW MARINE EXISTENCE

Two families, 12 genera, and 47 species of monocotyledonous angiosperms have successfully returned to the sea to lead an almost totally submerged existence. These submerged flowering plants, which complete their entire life cycle in seawater, exhibit both vegetative and sexual reproduction. Their ability to flourish, function successfully, and compete with other plants in the shallow marine environment is manifested in their widespread distribution throughout the world (Figure 1). In fact, there are few parts of the world's shallow coastal zone where one or more species of submerged aquatic angiosperms does not grow (den Hartog 1970). In addition to the true seagrasses, other submerged angiosperms have adapted to saline conditions, exhibiting wide salinity ranges and often coexisting with seagrass species in estuarine environments.

Our subject species, <u>Zostera</u> <u>marina</u> L., or eelgrass, and other seagrasses possess two morphological adaptations that are

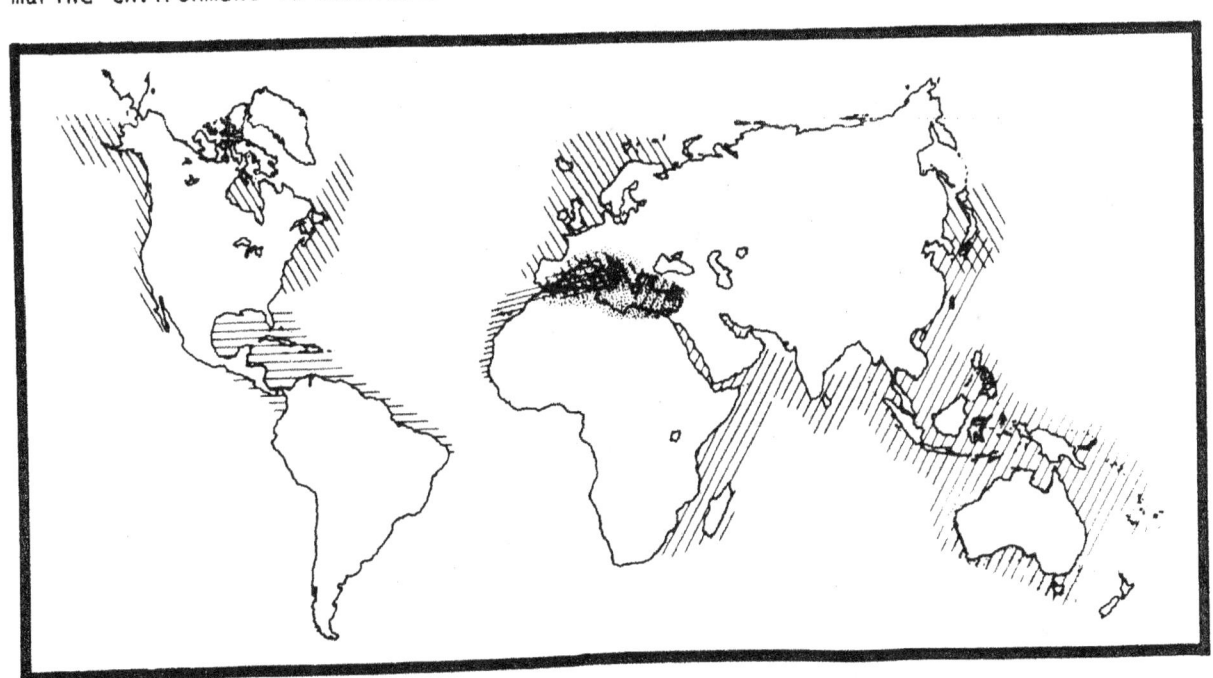

Figure 1. Major geographic distributions of genera of seagrasses: <u>Zostera</u> (\\\ ), <u>Posidonia</u> (▒), <u>Thalassia</u> and <u>Halophila</u> (≡), <u>Cymodocea</u> (▨), and mixed <u>Syringodium</u>, <u>Thalassia</u>, <u>Enhalus</u>, <u>Halodule</u>, or <u>Cymodocea</u> (////). (Modified from Thayer et al. 1979.)

unique for submerged marine plants and that enable them to exist in an aquatic environment subject to wave and tidal action and shifting sediments. These features are linear, grass-like leaves (Figure 2) and an extensive root and rhizome system (Figure 3). In common with their terrestrial relatives, seagrasses also have a functional vascular system.

The leaves of most submerged aquatic plants possess adaptations to facilitate light penetration, diffusion of gases, and buoyancy. The leaves and stems of most species generally are thin, have an extensive system of lacunal air spaces, and possess reduced structural tissue (Figure 4). Diffusion of gases and nutrients is enhanced by thin cellulose walls of epidermal, mesophyll, and cortical cells.

Although chloroplasts exist throughout the undifferentiated leaf mesophyll and outer cortex of the stem, the epidermal layer of seagrass leaves, like that of many shade-adapted terrestrial plants, possesses high concentrations of chloroplasts and is the principal site of photosynthesis (Sculthorpe 1967). This pigment distribution is important to the ability of these plants to grow and survive in turbid coastal estuaries characteristic of temperate areas.

The primary functions of the extensive root-rhizome system of seagrasses are to anchor the plant and to absorb nutrients from interstitial waters of the sediment. Longitudinal sclerenchyma and collenchyma fiber bundles throughout the inner and outer cortex (Figure 5) provide both

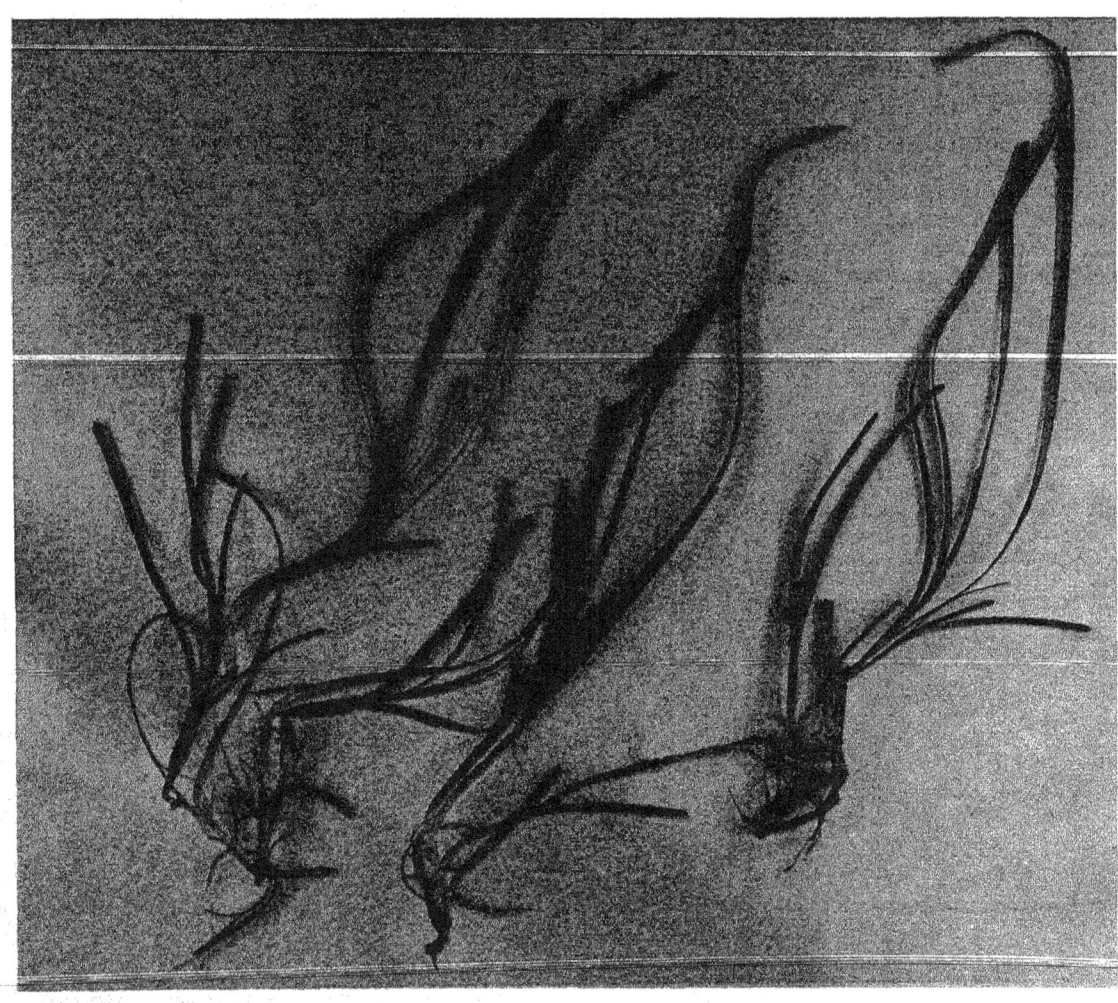

Figure 2. Zostera marina leaves.

mechanical support and absorptive tissues. The lacunal system of the roots and rhizomes are continuous with that of the stem and leaves. Numerous investigators have shown opposing gradients in oxygen and carbon dioxide concentrations in submerged angiosperms, with oxygen decreasing from the leaves to the roots. This observation suggests that the root-rhizome system derives its oxygen supply from photosynthetic activity of the leaves and stems, the gas diffusing to the roots through the lacunar system of the plant (Penhale and Wetzel 1983). The extensive nature of this lacunar system permits submerged seagrasses to anchor oxygen-requiring roots in anaerobic sediments.

Partly because of these features of the root-rhizome complex, seagrasses have been able to colonize successfully in almost liquid mud (Ruppia maritima and Zostera marina) and in rocky intertidal areas (Phyllospadix sp.).

1.2 SEAGRASSES OF THE TEMPERATE ATLANTIC COASTAL ZONE OF THE UNITED STATES

Apart from the naturalists' observations and concerns voiced during the "wasting disease" episode early this century (see Section 1.3), few research papers on the ecology of temperate seagrasses are dated prior to 1970. With the promulgation of NEPA (National Environmental Policy Act) in 1969, the impetus to study eelgrass systems in

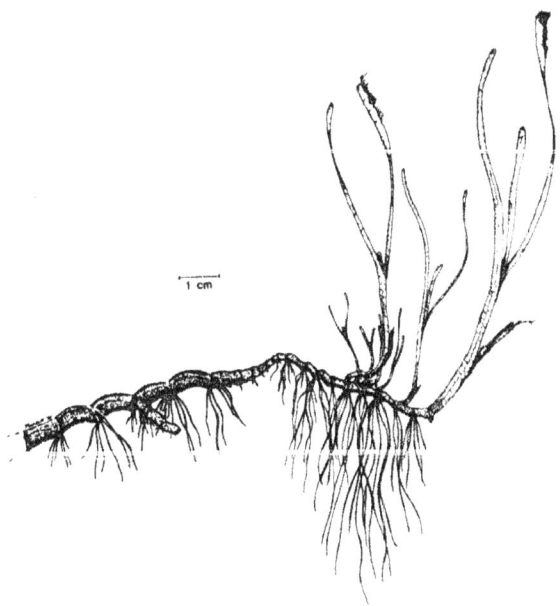

Figure 3. Zostera marina root-rhizome complex.

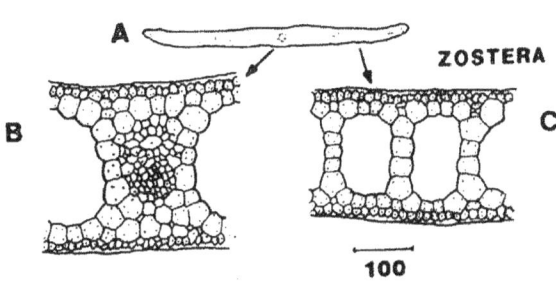

Figure 4. Drawing of a transverse section through an eelgrass leaf (A) and details of the mid-vein (B) and mesophyll (C). (Redrawn from Tomlinson 1980.)

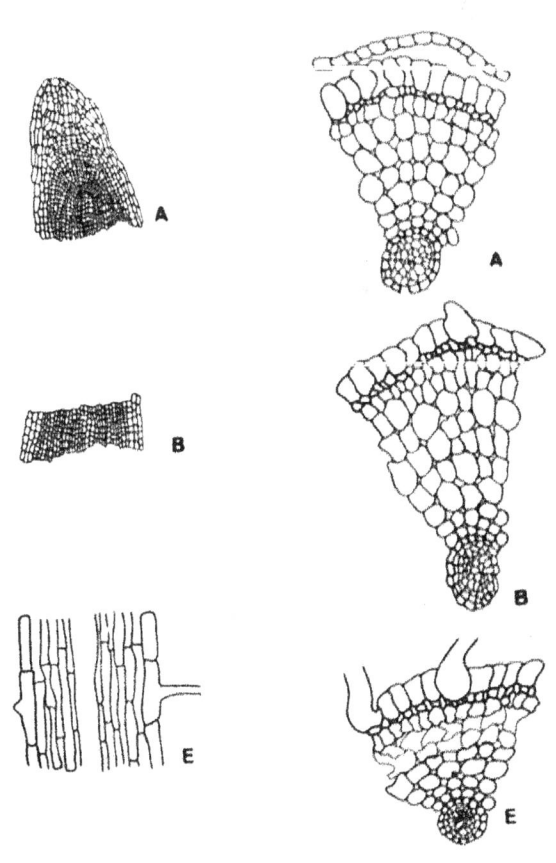

Figure 5. Longitudinal sections of eelgrass root (left) and corresponding cross-sectional views (right). Letters refer to relative distance from root tip (A). (Redrawn from Conover 1964.)

3

response to suspected environmental impacts was established. The establishment of NEPA was coincident with the period of vigorous repopulation by eelgrass after the "wasting disease" (Section 1.3). Widespread, system-level research began only after the U.S. Government began to show interest in the seagrass system through National Science Foundation grants in the 1970's. Our community profile focuses on seagrass ecosystems dominated by eelgrass, Zostera marina L., along the temperate Atlantic coast of North America. Two other species, Halodule wrightii Ascherson (Cuban shoalgrass) and Ruppia maritima L. (widgeon grass), also occur along this coastline and are discussed briefly.

To the casual observer there is little morphological difference between the three species. In fact, prior to the mid-seventies there were few reports of the occurrence of Halodule in North Carolina, where it now occurs in considerable abundance. This species may have been present and mistakenly recorded as a narrow form of Zostera or Ruppia. The astute observer, however, readily distinguishes the three species by leaf morphology (Figure 6) and rhizome coloration. The width of eelgrass leaves normally is 1.5 to 3.0 mm (although there are ecological variants) while the width of shoalgrass

and widgeon grass leaves range from 0.3 to 1.0 mm. The leaf tip is rounded in eelgrass, lancelate in widgeon grass, and bicuspidate in shoalgrass. Finally, the living rhizome is brown in Zostera but is lighter colored for both other species.

Geographic Data Sources/Physical Boundaries

The overall range of eelgrass along the North American east coast is from approximately 33° to 65° N latitude, a distance of about 3,090 km. For our purposes, the range of eelgrass along the east coast may be represented by (1) Nova Scotia to the U.S./Canadian border, (2) the U.S./Canadian border to the Hudson River, (3) the Hudson River to the Virginia-North Carolina border, but primarily the enclosed waters of the New Jersey Barrier Islands and Chesapeake Bay, and (4) the Carolinas, especially the sounds and bays landward of the Outer Banks (Figure 7).

Throughout this range, eelgrass is the dominant species of submerged aquatic marine vegetation. This species successfully inhabits areas that have sediments ranging from soft mud to coarse sand substrates, average salinities of 10% to 30 o/oo, and a water temperature range from less than 0°C to greater than 30°C. On the east coast of the United States alone, annual mean temperatures from north to south range from 7.2° to 17.6°C. The average minimum temperature at the northern extent of the range of eelgrass may be -11.3°C, while the average maximum temperature at the southern limit may be 31.6°C. The occurrence of mean winter temperatures of well below freezing over much of its distribution means that eelgrass exists in or under sea ice part of the year. In the Carolinas, sea ice is not a regular feature of the eelgrass environment.

Incoming solar radiation (insolation) over a 30-year period averaged from 373 langleys (L) m^{-2} day^{-1} at the southern end of eelgrass distribution in the Carolinas area to 285 L m^{-2} day^{-1} in the New England area (75% of the southern maxima) (Blodgett 1980). At the northern limit of eelgrass distribution (circa 65° N lat),

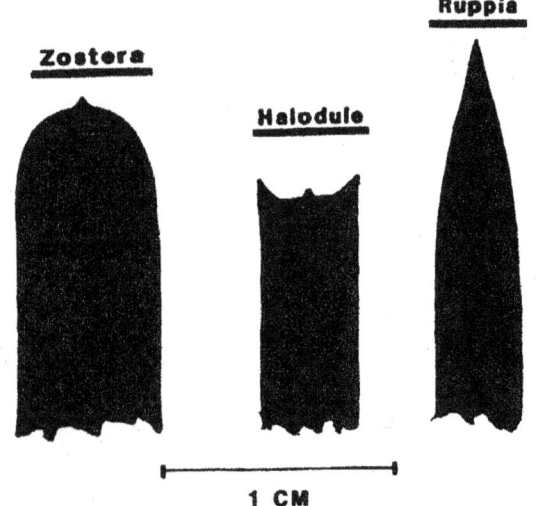

Zostera   **Halodule**   **Ruppia**

1 CM

Figure 6. Sketches of Zostera, Halodule, and Ruppia leaf tips showing the major differences among these genera.

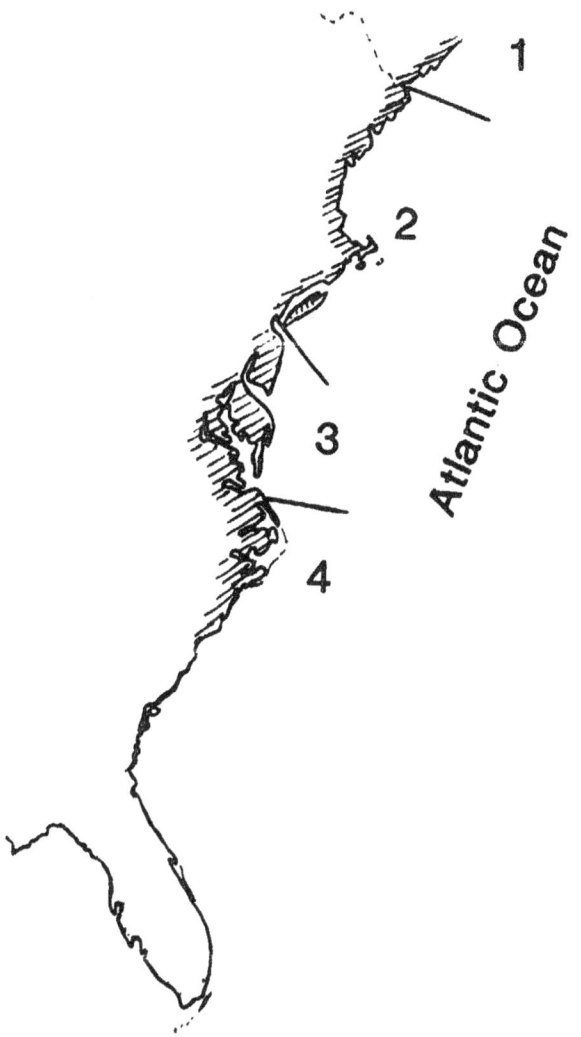

Figure 7. Diagram of the east coast of North America showing major provinces of eelgrass occurrence.

insolation values may be as low as 15% of insolation at the southern limit of eelgrass distribution in the Carolinas.

Light availability appears to be the primary factor limiting both depth and up-estuary penetration of eelgrass within its temperature and salinity ranges. Research on the productivity of eelgrass as a function of insolation and availability of photosynthetically active radiation (PAR) (see Chapter 2), as well as research on changes in standing crops of eelgrass, generally support the hypothesis that light availability, which is a function of

insolation and water clarity, is a primary limiting factor. For example, Backman and Barilotti (1976) reduced ambient light for 9 months by 63% and eelgrass densities relative to controls were reduced by 95%. Nienhuis and deBree (1977) reported an increase in both eelgrass density and depth distribution when a Netherlands estuarine system was closed off from the sea. They suggested that this was the result of increases in overall water transparency.

The depth distribution of eelgrass on the east coast also has a range proportional to tidal ranges characteristic of individual geographic regions. Davies (1964) and Hayes (1975) used tidal ranges to characterize coastal morphologies, and recognized three distinctive types of coastline on the east coast on the basis of tidal ranges and associated morphological features (Figure 8). Tidal amplitude ranges from about 1 m at the southern boundary of eelgrass distribution up to 8 m in the Canadian Maritimes. Although local variations in coastal geomorphology may cause tidal amplitudes greater than those found farther north, the overall gradient is one of increasing tidal amplitude from south to north. From the Carolinas to the midway point of area 3 (Figure 7), the coastline generally is a microtidal region (Figure 8). In the upper portion of area 3 (New Jersey outer banks and generally north of Delaware Bay) up the U.S./Canadian border (area 3), the tidal range is generally mesotidal. Northward through Nova Scotia, meso- and macrotidal systems are interspersed.

Halodule wrightii, shoalgrass, is a pantropical species (Figure 1) which grows over a tidal range similar to that for eelgrass, except that shoalgrass communities extend into the upper intertidal zone and frequently are exposed at low tide. In North America, shoalgrass occurs throughout the Gulf of Mexico and north from the Atlantic coast of Florida to North Carolina. In North Carolina, shoalgrass occurs in areas similar to eelgrass, but it dominates in late summer and early fall whereas eelgrass dominates in winter to early summer (Kenworthy 1981). Shoalgrass reportedly is the most tolerant of all the seagrasses to temperature and salinity variations (McMillan

5

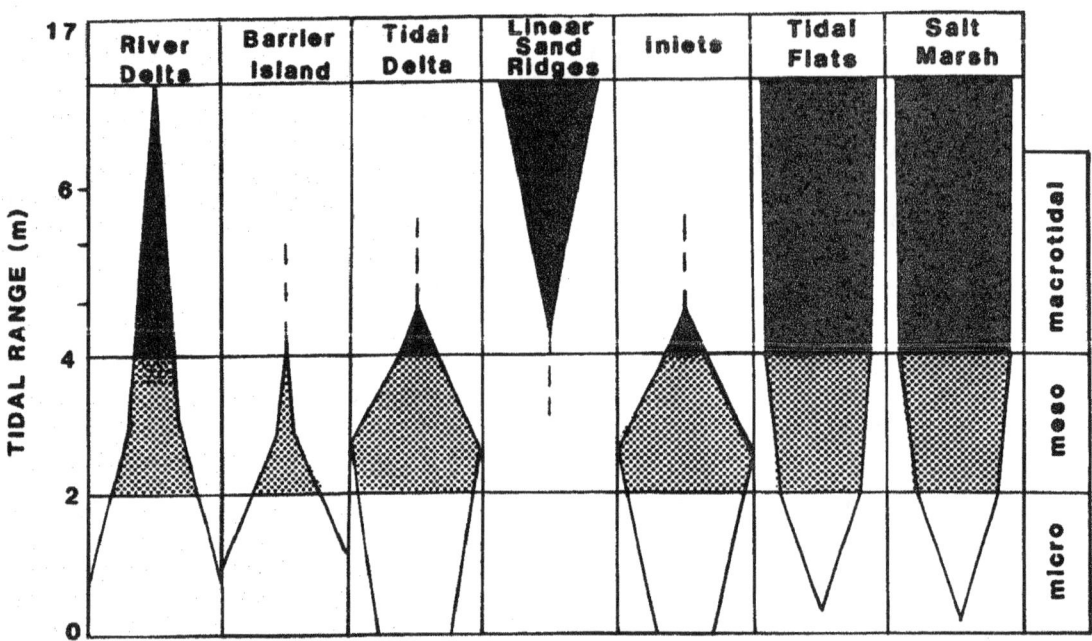

Figure 8. Variations of morphology of coastal-plain shorelines with respect to differences in tidal ranges. (Redrawn from Hayes 1975.)

and Moseley 1967). Since it is one of the few seagrasses that can tolerate extended exposure to air at low tides, shoalgrass frequently occurs in shallow waters on spoil banks and nearshore areas. Trocine et al. (1981) have shown that Halodule has greater tolerance to UV-B radiation between 290 and 320 nannometers than several other species, and this capability may allow the species to exist intertidally.

Ruppia maritima, widgeon grass, is the third species present in the geographic area this profile addresses. Widgeon grass is not considered a true seagrass but a freshwater angiosperm that has a pronounced salinity tolerance (Zieman 1982). This species is both eurythermal and euryhaline and is able to successfully complete its life cycle over a salinity range of 0-45 o/oo (Phillips 1974b). Like eelgrass, widgeon grass depth distribution appears limited by available light. Congdon and McComb (1979) noted that in an Australian estuary reduction of ambient light levels resulted in a reduction of Ruppia biomass.

Except in North Carolina where the three species co-occur, seagrass com-

munities are composed of eelgrass and widgeon grass, usually in pure stands or occasionally in mixed stands. Throughout its temperate range on the Atlantic coast, widgeon grass grows almost exclusively in brackish water and frequently in low salinity pools in salt marshes. Eelgrass, on the other hand, dominates the mid- to high-salinity ranges. In upper Chesapeake Bay, Anderson (1970) noted that where widgeon grass and eelgrass are dominant they grow in mutually exclusive populations, although more recently Boynton and Heck (1982), reported occurrence of mixed beds. Mixed meadows with distinct zonation patterns are characteristic of the lower Chesapeake Bay (Penhale and Wetzel 1983).

In North Carolina one can find relatively pure stands of seagrasses as well as extensive meadows composed of both eelgrass and shoalgrass (Kenworthy 1981) and occasionally of all three species. Eelgrass is dominant in winter and early summer and shoalgrass is dominant in late summer and fall. Because of this bimodal seasonal distribution of dominance, the coexistence of both species in a mixed

6

stand provides a continuous cover of vegetation throughout most of the year.

1.3 EELGRASS "WASTING DISEASE"

The observations of Petersen (1891) and Ostenfeld (1905) initiated a period of relatively intense ecological surveys on eelgrass in Europe, particularly in Danish waters. In 1918, Petersen summarized the bulk of the Danish work and synthesized a trophic model of the Kattegat region of Denmark based almost exclusively on the production of eelgrass (little scientific information was available at that time on phytoplankton production). His model, which postulated that cod and plaice were dependent on the eelgrass community for food resources, was put to the test in the 1930's during and following a natural catastrophy to eelgrass populations along most of the Atlantic coast.

Even with the publication of the hypothesis of Petersen, very little research on the ecology of seagrasses was carried out in North America prior to about 1940. Only after the nearly catastrophic decline in eelgrass stocks over most of its range along the Atlantic Ocean in Europe and North America in 1931 and 1932 did eelgrass systems again became a focus of research. Tutin (1942) reported that between 1930 and 1933 the "wasting disease", as it has been termed, had resulted in the destruction of 90% of all eelgrass throughout its range in the Atlantic. Perhaps no one natural event has centered so much attention on a marine ecosystem type.

The demise of eelgrass resulted in an upsurge in scientific research in both North America and Europe that centered on diagnostic evaluations of changes in the plant and on attempts to trace down its cause. Much of the research was natural history observations and generally lacked quantitative information. These observations, together with studies on the decline of associated faunal populations, particularly those related to fisheries, provoked emotional responses that may even be heard today.

The cause of the massive decline remains unresolved. Initially

Labyrinthula macrocystis was suspected as the causitive agent since it was found associated with dying eelgrass blades (Renn 1934 and many others). This organism originally was considered a slime mold but is now listed in the phylum Gymnomyxia, subphylum Labyrinthulina (Lindsay 1975). Labyrinthula is a saprophyte that apparently penetrates eelgrass leaves only as the leaves become moribund (Porter 1967). Further, Labyrinthula is found commonly associated with healthy stocks of eelgrass (Young 1938; Porter 1967; Phillips 1972). Bacteria, fungi, commercial harvesting of fishery organisms, pollution, and competing species have been implicated as possible causitive agents in the decline, but they have never been conclusively shown to have contributed to the "wasting disease" event. More recently, Rasmussen (1973, 1977) presented evidence that the decline in Denmark (and possibly elsewhere) was associated with a period of warm summers and exceptionally mild winters. Whatever the cause, there is little doubt that the massive decline of eelgrass had both geomorphological and biological consequences. Rasmussen (1973, 1977) discussed both aspects in detail. The most obvious effects were those associated with sedimentary and current regimes. After an eelgrass meadow disappeared, the substrate became coarser, depending on the prevailing current regime, and long, permanent sandbars built up. Sandy beaches that once had been protected by eelgrass became rocky slopes (Figure 9). In addi-

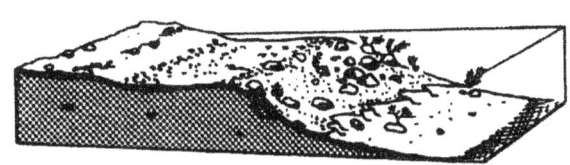

Figure 9. Typical subtidal-intertidal zonation before (upper) and after the depletion of eelgrass from Danish fjords. (Redrawn from Rasmussen 1973.)

tion, deposits of fine muds, which were once adjacent to the eelgrass beds, changed from low oxygen, sulfidic oozes to oxidized sediments. Sediments that had been dominated by burrowing, deposit-feeding invertebrates became dominated by encrusting or fouling, filter-feeding species when there was no longer protection provided by eelgrass meadows.

Similar changes may have occurred in North America. Stauffer (1937, p. 429-430) stated, "The disappearance of the mat of vegetation permitted increased scouring and hence changes in composition of the sediments.... Indirectly, the disappearance of the plant may have caused changes in the water circulation in the lagoon, changes in the amount of dissolved oxygen, in temperature, and in pH. The relative importance of the physicochemical changes compared to the biotic changes remains to be investigated..." The role of eelgrass and seagrasses in general in modifying sediment and current patterns, however, received little further attention until the 1970's.

Along with substrate modifications that resulted from the loss of the seagrass meadow came changes in the faunal community. Near Woods Hole, Massachusetts, Stauffer (1937) noted that species living on or among the grass blades disappeared and that overall species abundance decreased. Similar changes were not reported to have occurred in Denmark (Rasmussen 1973, 1977).

The majority of literature on fauna utilization of eelgrass meadows before the catastrophy is qualitative, but there is consensus among the scientific community that fisheries did change, although slowly at first (Thayer et al. 1975b; Zieman 1982). Whether this change was the result of a loss of food resources (e.g. fauna, epiphytes, and detritus) or refuge is unknown, and present research efforts are attempting to unravel the many roles the system plays. Commercial fisheries did not decline to the degree predicted by Petersen's (1918) calculations, yet Milne and Milne (1951, p. 53) stated, perhaps somewhat emotionally, that the eelgrass catastrophe (which they equated with the Black Death of the 1300's) undoubtedly caused a major decline in fisheries

populations--"Fishermen found that the abundance of cod, shellfish, scallops, crabs, and sea staples fell sharply." Dexter (1947) further reported that lobsters, eels, and mud crabs also declined in abundance.

In general, however, declines in abundance of species important to major recreational and/or commercial fisheries, if they occurred, could not be recognized quantitatively, except for a few species. For example, Patriquin and Butler (1976) reported that residents of the Kouchibouquac region of New Brunswick, Canada, observed no major differences in fisheries between the periods of eelgrass presence and absence. Even though Petersen's calculations predicting large declines in fisheries did not materialize for most recreational and commercial populations (at least within the detection capabilities of recreational and commercial harvest statistics of that time), two notable exceptions (one for waterfowl and one for a fisheries species) have been documented. One was the catastrophic decline of the Atlantic brant (Branta bernicla hrota), that fed at the time almost exclusively on eelgrass, and the more limited decline of the Canada goose, B. canadensis (Cottam 1934; Cottam et al. 1944; Cottam and Munro 1954; den Hartog 1977). The brant population almost disappeared following the decline of eelgrass. The decline in numbers also coincided with a period of poor reproductive success which may have contributed to reduced populations (Palmer 1976). The brant population did not recover until the early 1950's, after which the brant's dietary preference shifted to widgeon grass and sea lettuce, Ulva lactuca. With the reappearance of eelgrass, however, there has not been a concomitant return to an almost exclusive eelgrass diet.

Catastrophic population declines also were documented for the bay scallop, Argopecten irradians, following the decline of eelgrass. The scallop depends on seagrass blades for attachment of the postlarvae (Gutsell 1930; Thayer and Stuart 1974; Fonseca et al. in press). The bay scallop can use detritus derived from the decay of eelgrass leaves (Kirby-Smith 1972; Kirby-Smith and Barber 1974), obtaining up to 30% of its body carbon from detritus (Thayer et al. 1978). Following the "wasting disease", the commercial harvest declined precipitously in both North Carolina and Chesapeake Bay (Table 1a,b). Populations in North Carolina did not return to pre-"wasting

Table 1a. Weight and value of shucked bay scallop meats harvested in North Carolina (Carteret and Onslow Counties) from 1880 to 1972. Taken from Thayer and Stuart (1974, Table 1). Dollar values are for the year in which the catch was taken.

Date	Thousand pounds	Thousand dollars	Date	Thousand pounds	Thousand dollars
1880	16	1	1952	254	126
1890	18	1	1953	65	33
1897	118	6	1954	72	26
1902	13	1	1955	78	39
1918	423	32	1956	125	63
1923	554	46	1957	109	37
1927	835	120	1958	169	58
1928	1,394	126	1959	128	51
1929	686	38	1960	69	27
1930	432	54	1961	106	42
1931	495	50	1962	168	67
1932	91	6	1963	321	122
1934	36	5	1964	340	173
1936	99	14	1965	379	196
1937	62	12	1966	399	184
1938	30	8	1967	387	211
1939	33	6	1968	639	402
1940	34	4	1969	613	383
1945	22	8	1970	130	91
1950	72	38	1971	60	42
1951	183	96	1972	128	110

Table 1b. Weight of shucked bay scallop meats harvested from the Delmarva Peninsula area of Chesapeake Bay from 1928 to 1981. Taken from Orth and Moore (1982b, Table 4.)

Year	Harvested scallops (kg shucked meat)
1928	5,050
1929	16,038
1930	25,549
1931	17,170
1932	9,220
1933	0
1934	0
1981	0

disease" levels until the 1960's (Thayer and Stuart 1974) and have never returned to commercially harvestable quantities in the Chesapeake Bay (Orth and Moore 1982b).

The absence of whole-scale declines in coastal fisheries following the natural "wasting disease" catastrophe may have been a major cause for the 20-year period of relatively inactive research on seagrass communities between 1950-1970, even though the grass began to recolonize areas during this time. Eelgrass in salinities less than 12-15 o/oo apparently was immune to the wasting disease and formed the stocks for eventual recolonization (Rasmussen 1973). Rasmussen (1977) noted that extensive revegetation by eelgrass did not become widespread until after 1945 and that full recovery took 30-40 years. In many areas the seagrass still has not returned (e.g., seaside Chesapeake Bay).

Prior to the 1930's and since the period of recovery, eelgrass and other submerged vascular plant communities have exhibited oscillations in abundance (Orth and Moore 1981), possibly in response to environmental changes, both natural and man-induced. Orth and Moore (1981, 1982b) have documented changes in bedsize and distribution prior to and during the 1930's and again in the 1970's. They noted that the declines in eelgrass in the 1970's in Chesapeake Bay were more severe than the decline in the 1930's "wasting disease" episode. They also noted that recovery has been less. Seagrasses have not exhibited these large oscillations in North Carolina. Kemp et al. (in press) stated that elsewhere in the Chesapeake Bay more than 10 species of submerged aquatics have experienced significant population and distributional declines: primarily Ruppia maritima, Potamogeton perfoliatus, P. pectinatus, P. crispus, Vallisneria americana, and Zannichella sp.; all are freshwater-low salinity plants.

With the general recovery of eelgrass after the wasting disease, scientific interest in seagrass systems as major contributors to the productivity and stability of coastal marine ecosystems was renewed. Quantitative evidence documenting the overall importance of seagrasses in estuarine and nearshore marine systems has increased within the past 10 years. Evidence also abounds that man does alter environmental conditions, both locally and globally, and that these alterations are having an increasingly detrimental effect on submerged aquatic macrophyte communities, frequently causing them to decrease in areas where industrial or urban development has been extensive. Man can and does exert an influence on seagrasses (Thayer et al. 1975b; Thayer et al. in press b; Orth and Moore 1981, 1982b; Zieman 1982) which potentially can exact a toll on commercially and recreationally important fishery organisms, although possibly on a smaller scale than the two documented examples noted earlier.

The processes associated with the growth and development of seagrass systems and the contribution of these systems to marine fisheries must be recognized by both scientific and management sectors of our population. Unless a holistic approach to environmentally related planning decisions is adopted, the potential will continue to exist for man to be a major contributor to large-scale environmental changes comparable to the eelgrass catastrophe in the 1930's.

1.4 SEAGRASS MEADOWS AS ECOSYSTEMS

Worldwide, seagrass beds constitute one of the most conspicuous and common coastal habitat types, frequently contributing a large portion of the total primary productivity of the ecosystem of which they are a part (Thayer et al. in press b). Under optimum conditions some seagrass species fix carbon at rates equivalent to or exceeding the rates of the most intensively farmed agricultural crops. Organic matter produced by seagrasses is transferred to secondary consumers through three pathways: herbivores that consume living plant matter, detritivores that exploit dead material and its associated microorganisms as particulate organic matter, and microorganisms that use seagrass-derived particulate and dissolved organic compounds. Leaves of submerged angiosperms also provide a substrate for the attachment of epiphytic organisms, including

bacteria, fungi, meiofauna, micro- and macroalgae, macroinvertebrates, and detritus. Total biomass of this epiphytic community can exceed that of the leaf (Harlin 1980). The primary productivity of this component can be 20-35% of the productivity of seagrass leaves (Penhale 1977; Penhale and Smith 1977). Phytoplankton also are present in the water column, and macroalgae and microalgae are associated with the substrate.

Thus, a variety of primary and secondary sources of organic carbon are present in these communities that provide multiple food resources for invertebrates and vertebrates. No less important is the protection afforded by the variety of living spaces in the vertical and horizontal structure of the grass bed itself. Together, food and shelter afforded by seagrasses result in a complex and dynamic system that provides a primary nursery habitat for various life history stages of organisms that are important both ecologically and to commercial and recreational fisheries. Although this basic theme is common throughout much of the seagrass ecological literature, not all seagrass systems provide equivalent habitat utilization potential. The differences exist because leaf surface area varies by species, the bottom area covered by plants varies by species and season, and hydraulic regimes may differ (Thayer et al. in press b; and references cited therein).

Accompanying these attributes of the seagrass ecosystem are interactions between the grass meadow canopy, the root-rhizome complex, and the aquatic and sedimentary environments that further enhance the role and value of seagrass ecosystems. The grass blades, by exerting drag forces on the overlying water, reduce current velocity within and across the meadow (Fonseca et al. 1982b). Velocity reduction promotes net sedimentation of inorganic and organic material and reduces both turbulence and scouring. These processes significantly influence trophic interactions, distribution of flora and fauna, and habitat utilization potentials of these systems. The well-developed root-rhizome complex enhances sediment stability, absorbs inorganic nutrients from interstitial water in the sediments, and releases both inorganic and organic nutrients into the interstitial water. Leaves absorb nutrients from and excrete nutrients into the overlying water column. Therefore, these systems, where they are prevalent, modify mineral cycles of shallow water environments.

Attributes of eelgrass meadows along the temperate Atlantic coast of North America are discussed in detail in the succeeding chapters. In addition to work on the east coast, we also draw upon pertinent information from research on temperate seagrass elsewhere in the world, as well as research on tropical species.

CHAPTER 2
BIOLOGY OF *ZOSTERA MARINA*

2.1 MORPHOLOGY

Gross Anatomy

Zostera marina L. is an angiosperm belonging to the family Potamogetonaceae, which consists of several genera of both annual and perennial aquatic plants (den Hartog 1970). The vegetative growth form of an individual plant consists of a rhizome which bears linear strap-shaped leaves (usually 2-5 leaves per shoot) enclosed at the base in a sheath that forms a stem-like structure (Figure 10). Each leaf has a basal meristem produced dichotomously on the rhizome. The younger leaves are subtended by older leaves giving the shoot a laterally flattened appearance. For each leaf there is a node and usually two bundles of unbranched roots. A rhizome is formed from the elongation of the internodes which pushes the shoot through the sediment.

Organismal and Cell Structure

The fine anatomical structure of the strap-like leaves (Figure 4) is somewhat modified from terrestrial plants. Cells have a minimum of supporting structure, no stomata, very thin cell walls, and little cuticular development (Sauvageau 1891). These features are an adaptation to total submergence. The leaves must be pliable in a viscous fluid, and the thin cell walls allow for gas diffusion which is generally two or three orders of magnitude slower in water than in air.

Chloroplasts are most abundant in the epidermis which is the major site of photosynthesis (Tomlinson 1980). This is also an important adaptation to life underwater. Distribution of chloroplasts in the outer layer of the cells increases photosynthetic efficiency in a medium where light is attenuated selectively and quite rapidly.

The chlorophyll concentrations in leaves and the chlorophyll a to b ratio are low relative to other plants but similar to many aquatic species (Dennison 1979). Under a given light intensity the absolute amount of chlorophyll is relatively constant throughout the leaf (Dennison and Alberte 1982), but the ratio of chlorophyll a to b declines from the tip of the leaf to the base (Stirban 1968). There is very little chlorophyll in the sheath (Dennison 1979).

Large, longitudinally extended lacunae facilitate gas diffusion (Sculthorpe 1967; Tomlinson 1980; Penhale and Wetzel 1983). When filled, the lacunae help maintain the erect position of the leaves thereby increasing the efficiency of light interception in a diffuse light field (Dennison 1979). The sheath is principally a supporting structure without significant assimilative functions, and differs from the leaf in having relatively more structural tissues consisting mostly of lignified fibers (Tomlinson 1980). At the transition between the blade and sheath there is a noticeable weakening in structure which is frequently the site of leaf abscission (Tomlinson 1980).

Conducting tissues, including phloem and xylem, are present but reduced to some degree (Sauvageau 1891; Sculthorpe 1967). Histological studies indicate that the phloem is somewhat narrow, but is far more

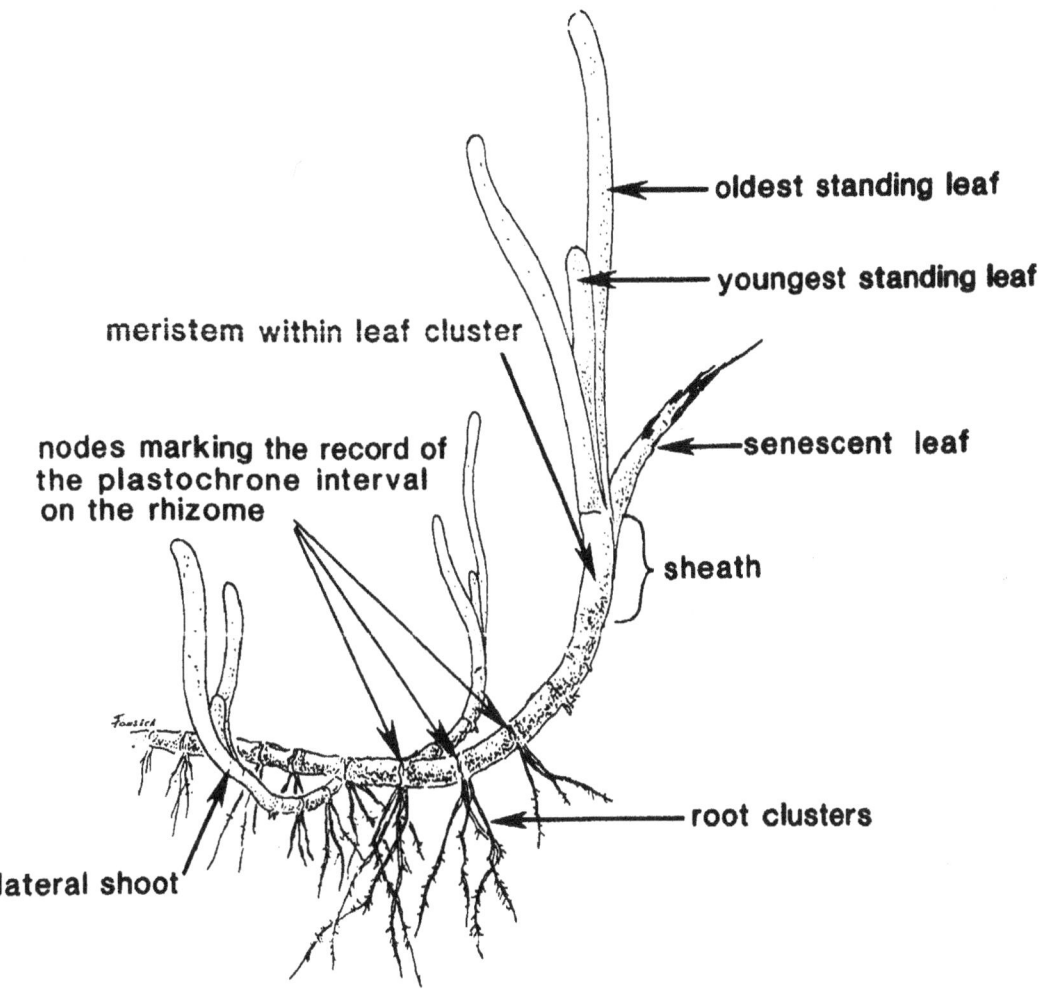

Figure 10. Major features of the morphology of _Zostera marina_.

developed than the xylem. Although structurally modified, these conducting elements are quite functional (Penhale and Wetzel 1983).

Anatomically, the roots and rhizomes are marginal in structure and form relative to land plants (Sculthorpe 1967). Functionally, they anchor the plants in soft substrates and absorb nutrients and gases for translocation to stems and leaves (McRoy and Barsdate 1970; McRoy and Goering 1974; Penhale and Thayer 1980; Short 1981; Thursby and Harlin 1982). Oxygen in excess of respiratory needs diffuses from the leaves to the roots and is released into an oxidized microzone around the roots (Iizumi et al. 1980; Penhale and Wetzel 1983).

The rhizome is strengthened by schlerenchyma fibers (Figure 5) running longitudinally through the inner and outer cortex (Sculthorpe 1967). There may be several rhizome nodes associated with an individual shoot. Usually, the most distal nodes are in the process of decay, while new nodes are continually formed at the base of the shoot.

Beneath each node are two bundles of unbranched roots which anchor the rhizomes in the sediment. The roots are usually 5-10 cm long at maturity and are covered with root hairs (Smith 1981). According to Conover (1964), Smith et al. (1979), and Smith (1981), nearly 23% of the root surface is covered by root hairs, and the total surface area of hairs is over three

13

times the surface area of the root alone. The vascular system of roots contains very large lacunae (Conover and Gough 1964; Penhale and Wetzel 1983).

2.2 GROWTH

Since eelgrass is capable of sexual and asexual reproduction, both processes must be considered in the context of plant growth. Most eelgrass meadows persist to a large degree by vegetative growth (Tomlinson 1980); however, the production and dispersal of seeds are an important mechanism to maintain eelgrass populations. Seeds are especially important in meadows that suffer recurring seasonal perturbations, for general plant dispersal in uncolonized areas, and for continual genetic adaptation.

Life History

Setchell (1929) described a generalized life history model of Z. marina. Even though some of his work regarding environmental influences on growth (especially temperature interactions) has been disputed, his life history model, with some modifications, remains accurate. Setchell suggested that growth occurs in several stages (Figure 11). The first stage extends from seed germination to development of the first shoot. Setchell and many other authors, even in the very recent literature, refer to a shoot of eelgrass as a turion. Sculthorpe (1967), however, defined a turion as having leaves which are specialized in form and quite unlike the normal foliage leaves. We will not use the term turion since there is no morphological evidence of such a

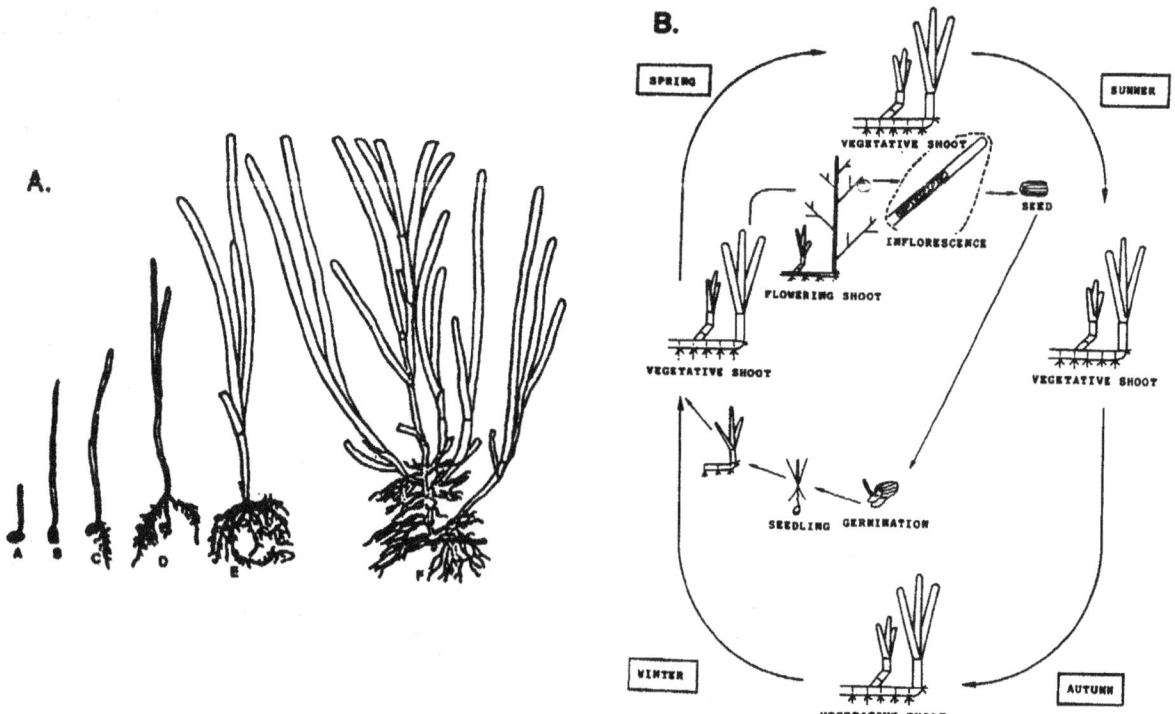

Figure 11. The life history of Zostera marina. Part A shows the vegetative growth of a shoot beginning with a recently germinated seedling (A-E) and ending with a mature shoot and several lateral branches (F). (Redrawn from Setchell 1929.) Part B shows the major aspects of the life cycle of eelgrass. (Illustration in part B was provided by Yasuo Kawasaki. Biology Laboratory, Central Research Institute of Electric Power Industry, Abiko City, Japan.)

specialization in eelgrass. Recently Churchill (1983) has elaborated on further dividing seedling germination into three distinct intervals. The second stage extends through the development of the first shoot, including the addition of new leaves to the formation of a rhizome and roots at the nodes.

The foundation for growth at the beginning of stage two is the meristem located in the basal area of the leaf. The meristem differentiates as either an erect leafy shoot or as a rhizome (Tomlinson 1980). Leaf growth and elongation of rhizome internodes occur as the meristem separates from the node by intercalary growth. The growth and development of individual leaves exhibit a remarkable periodicity (Jacobs 1979). The growth rate of a leaf is fastest just after it emerges from the sheath and decreases with age, nearly ceasing with the emergence of two additional new leaves. Eventually, the oldest leaf is sloughed off and replaced by a young, rapidly growing leaf. The pattern of growth resembles a conveyor belt of organic matter with new leaves emerging within older and senescent ones.

Accompanying the second stage is the development of new shoots. The meristem divides vegetatively forming a shoot rather than a leaf. The new meristem repeats construction of the parent axis with an identical shoot. These new lateral shoots are much smaller than the parent but grow progressively larger with time (Figure 10). The first two stages of growth were graphically illustrated by the results of a study of the growth and development of seedlings in Chesapeake Bay (Figure 12: Orth and Moore 1983). Growth is shown by an increase in the length of the primary shoot, the number leaves per shoot, and the number of shoots per original seedling.

The third stage of growth consists of further development of all existing shoots and continued formation of new shoots by vegetative reproduction. During the fourth stage of growth some of the oldest shoots develop into erect flowering stalks (Figure 13). At this point a simplistic growth model is no longer appropriate, in part because it is difficult to define a

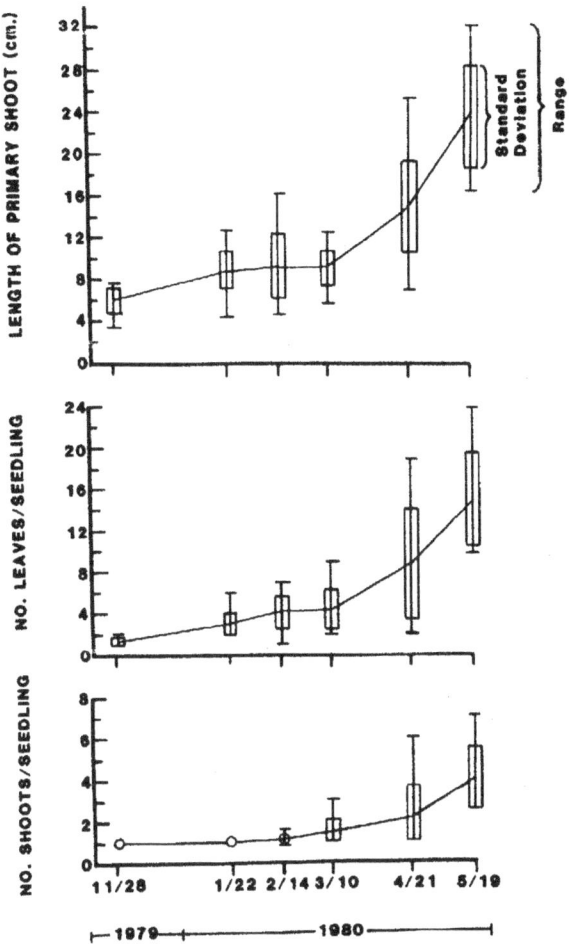

Figure 12. Mean length of primary shoot, number of leaves per seedling, and number of shoots per seedling, demonstrating the growth of eelgrass seedlings in the Chesapeake Bay, Virginia. (From Orth and Moore 1983.)

single eelgrass plant. Structurally, the original plant develops into an assemblage of vegetative and flowering shoots interconnected by rhizomes. The flowering shoot is a determinant type in the life history of this plant and dies after it flowers. The remaining vegetative shoots continue to propagate.

According to Setchell (1929), flowering shoots develop from vegetative plants in the second season of growth; thus he described eelgrass as a perennial plant with an apparent biennial life history. Recent evidence suggests some

15

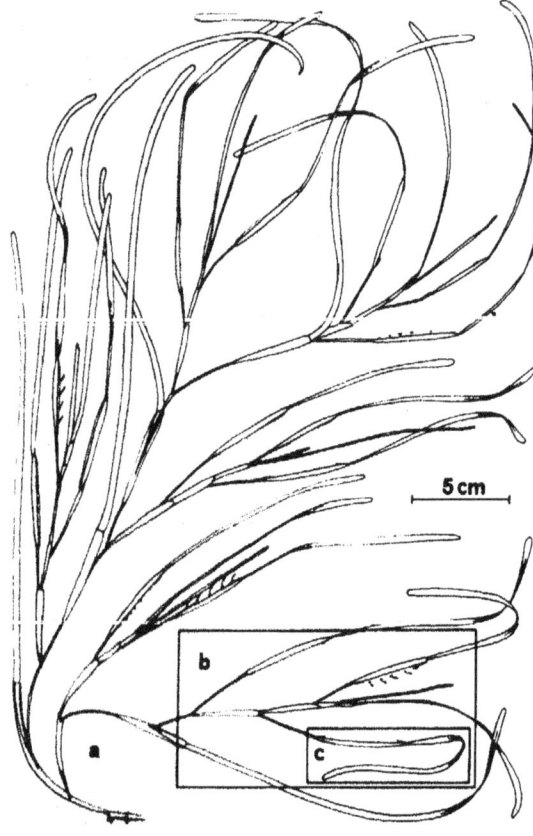

Figure 13. A flowering shoot of _Zostera marina_: (a) flowering shoot, (b) rhipidium, and (c) inflorescence. (From DeCock 1981a.)

taxonomic characters, phenology, and distribution of annual and perennial forms must be ascribed to nongenetic factors. Evidently, eelgrass has the potential to yield seeds of both annual and perennial forms, a reproductive strategy which certainly must assist in dispersal and overall reproductive success of the species.

Sexual Reproduction

An individual flowering shoot forms from the metamorphosis of a mature vegetative shoot. The shoot is easily recognized by its erect stems that are terate, brown, and have lateral inflorescences (spadices enclosed in spathes) (Figure 13). The entire flowering shoot usually is branched several times, each branch alternating with a normal vegetative leaf. The rhipidum is a compound inflorescence consisting of several spadices. Both male and female flowers are located on one side of a spadix. During the flowering sequence, only one inflorescence per branch flowers at a given time. Typically, while one inflorescence is flowering, another is developing on the same branch that will flower several days later.

According to DeCock (1981a), a large degree of variation between habitats and geographical locations exists in both the number of rhipidia and inflorescences formed on a flowering stalk. The extent to which flower development is governed by specific environmental factors such as light (DeCock 1981b), salinity (Phillips et al. 1983a), temperature (DeCock 1981a; Phillips et al. 1983a,b), nutrients (Churchill and Riner 1978), and water depth (Jacobs and Pierson 1981) remain to be determined. Generic factors alone or in combination with specific environmental parameters may control the extent of floral development (DeCock 1981 a; Phillips et al. 1983 a,b).

flexibility is needed in the life history model since at some times and in certain locations all shoots develop into flowering stalks (Felger and McRoy 1975; Keddy and Patriquin 1978; Bayer 1979; Gagnon et al. 1980; DeCock 1981a; Harlin et al. 1982; Harrison 1982a; Jacobs 1982).

In Atlantic coastal areas (Nova Scotia, Maine, and Rhode Island) an annual form of eelgrass has been described. The annual growth form reproduces asexually, and all shoots develop into flowers and die during the first growing season. In Canada, Keddy and Patriquin (1978) found that flowers from individual annual and perennial plants produced seeds that express themselves both as perennial and annual plant forms. Gagnon et al. (1980) compared annual and perennial forms and concluded that differences in the

Pollination occurs entirely underwater and since female flowers on the same inflorescence mature before male flowers (DeCock 1980), cross pollination is normal. Under certain conditions, however, self pollination occurs when male and female flowers mature coincidently. The pollen grains are assembled in a long, very sticky threadlike mass with a specific weight slightly greater than water (DeCock 1981a,b). The pollen grains depend to some degree on water movement to prevent sinking and to promote their dispersal. Sometimes the pollen threads will adhere to practically any object they contact, or will get trapped in quiescent areas by surface tension. Since pollen grains probably live only 2 or 3 days (DeCock 1981a), their adherence to maturing female flowers should improve pollination success. If fertilization is successful, a single seed forms in each fruit.

Evidently, fertilization is not always successful. Churchill and Riner (1978) estimated that 72% of the ovaries on the shoots of reproductive plants in Great South Bay, New York, produced seeds. Orth and Moore (1983) estimated that 68% of the ovaries were fertilized on reproductive shoots in the Chesapeake Bay, Virginia. In a North Carolina estuary Kenworthy et al. (1980) estimated that only 14% of the ovaries on reproductive shoots were fertilized.

The extent to which seeds contribute to the abundance of eelgrass from year-to-year depends on three principal factors: the abundance of flowering shoots, the number of seeds produced, and the rate of seed germination. Predation or eelgrass seeds by birds, crustaceans, and/or fish may damage seeds, but very little is known about the overall impact of this process (Cathleen Wigand, Dept. Biology, Adelphi University, Garden City, New York; pers. comm.).

The number of flowering shoots varies both temporally and spatially. Silberhorn et al. (1983) estimated that 11%-19% of the eelgrass population in part of Chesapeake Bay had flowering shoots and that the density of flowering shoots ranged between 303-424 m^{-2}. Similar densities reported for Rhode Island ranged from 78 to 498 m^{-2} (Thorne-Miller et al. 1983). In Great South Bay, Long Island, flowers constituted less than 10% of the total shoots and average density was 53 flowering shoots per square meter (Churchill and Riner 1978). In North

Carolina the relative abundance of flowering shoots ranged between 13.4% and 32.3% and averaged approximately 27.7% of the total shoot population at peak abundance (Fonseca et al. 1982a). Since all the shoots flower in an annual population, flowering shoot densities usually will be quite large. For example, Harlin et al. (1982) reported densities of about 1000 m^{-2} for an annual population in Rhode Island.

Recently, studies addressing the reproductive strategy of eelgrass have drawn attention to environmental variables that might control flower abundance (Jacobs 1982; Phillips et al. 1983 a,b). One study (Phillips et al. 1983a) suggested that flower abundance is related to seasonal temperature extremes and environmental fluctuations in the intertidal habitat. For example, eelgrass growing at its southern most range on the west coast in the Gulf of California cannot survive the warm summer temperature. The entire population is replaced annually by seed with a very high incidence of germination. This is the only example we know of where there is such a large-scale distribution of what is apparently an entirely annual population. At the opposite temperature extreme the incidence of flowering in Alaska is considerably higher in populations that are disturbed annually by ice scour, while subtidal populations have an intermediate abundance of flowers.

Phillips et al. (1983a) argue that intertidal populations are exposed to wider fluctuations in temperature and salinity as well as being subject to grazing waterfowl, wave disturbances, and erosion. The populations respond to these disturbances by producing more flowers. In the middle portion of the species range the subtidal populations allocate far less energy to sexual reproduction and persist largely by vegetative reproduction. The authors argue further that increased incidence of flowering in the intertidal zone coincides with areas of low salinity which, according to lab studies, enhances seed germination (Phillips et al. 1983a; Lamounette 1977). Exceptions to the general trend in flower abundance were noted at nonestuarine sites where the authors believed that reduced salinities

17

did not occur. Unfortunately the arguments for a strict salinity control remain unresolved. Phillips et al. (1983a) did not report salinities, therefore, we assume it was not measured and that the authors merely speculated on its possible role.

The incidence of increased flowering in association with disturbed sites and extremes of salinity are supported by a number of studies. Jacobs (1982) reported that the annual form of eelgrass was restricted to the upper eulittoral and brackish inland waters. The annual growth form in Rhode Island (Harlin et al. 1982) occurred on a highly disturbed flood tide delta, while Keddy and Patriquin (1978) reported having found the annual restricted to mud flats near Spartina marshes. In Nova Scotia, the annual growth form occurs in shallow subtidal and intertidal areas where frequent winter ice scour denudes the grass beds (Robertson and Mann 1984). In Maine, Gagnon et al. (1980) reported an annual form growing in the intertidal areas of an estuary. In Yaquina Bay, Oregon, Bayer (1979) reported that 91% of the plants located above mean low water had flowered and most of those plants were the annual growth form. In subtidal areas only 17% of the plants were flowering. Exceptions to these generalizations are reported in Phillips et al. (1983a). Most notable is the fact that in North Carolina, at the southernmost limit of eelgrass distribution on the Atlantic coast, the incidence of flowering and the occurrence of the annual life form do not seem extraordinary compared to the rest of the Atlantic coast.

The need to understand the environmental factors controlling flower abundance results from our efforts to develop accurate population models. According to our present understanding of the life history of eelgrass the age structure of a population should have a substantial influence on sexual reproduction in subsequent years. Since the age class structure of a population in a given year is a direct result of the formation and survival of vegetative shoots from a previous growing season (Bak 1980) a key to understanding flower abundance may actually be an evaluation of factors controlling vegetative repro-

duction. Flowering influences the numerical abundance of plants positively by enhancing recruitment, as well as negatively, by mortality. Since the flower dies, the population is subject to losses directly proportional to the number of flowers, a parameter of special importance in any population model.

The number of seeds produced also varies widely. On the basis of flower abundance and estimates of fertilized embryos, Silberhorn et al. (1983) reported that 8,127 seeds m^{-2} were produced in a Chesapeake Bay meadow, while in Great South Bay, Long Island, Churchill and Riner (1978) estimated that flowers produced 1.800 seeds m^{-2}. Since estimates of seeds per flowering shoot were similar for both areas (23 and 34, respectively), the large differences resulted from differences in shoot density. Kim Gates (Department of Biology, Adelphi University, Garden City, New York; pers. comm.) estimated that the potential seed crop in Great South Bay ranged between 2,000 and 4,000 seeds m^{-2} and the measured seed crop was 570-828 m^{-2}. Further evidence for the large variation in seed production is supported by other studies on the U.S. west coast. Phillips et al. (1983a) reported the number of seeds per plant ranged from 11.2 to 2,061 (mean = 60). Large variations occurred in all flower components, including total shoots, spathes per shoot, and seeds per spathe. Estimates of the density of seeds on flowering shoots ranged from 392 to 36,936 seeds m^{-2}.

The third variable, seed germination, is the final step in determining the overall contribution of sexual reproduction to developing and maintaining populations of eelgrass. Mature seeds are dispersed by three principal mechanisms: (1) by sinking, (2) by free floating stalks (DeCock 1980), and (3) by passage through the digestive tract and feces of waterfowl (Lamounette 1977). The seeds are negatively buoyant, but may be prevented from sinking by gas bubbles (A.C. Churchill, Dept. Biology, Adelphi University, Garden City, New York; pers. comm.) or resuspended by turbulence.

Even though the number of seeds produced can be quite large, seed viability is less than certain. Field and laboratory studies have yielded variable results for germination success and specifically for those environmental factors controlling germination. Under controlled laboratory conditions in full strength seawater, only 9% (Lamounette 1977) and no more than 10% (Phillips 1972; Phillips et al. 1983a) of the tested seeds germinated. Based on laboratory experiments the general impression is that seed germination is lowest at the highest salinities.

Orth and Moore (1983) reported that 70% of the seeds from Chesapeake Bay study sites germinated in flowing seawater, but that only 3% to 40% of the seeds held in acrylic tubes in the field germinated. Churchill (1983) reported that a high percentage of seeds (76% and 93%) tested in the field germinated. Reduced salinities seem to greatly enhance germination (Tutin 1938; Phillips 1972; Lamounette 1977; Churchill et al. 1978; Keddy and Patriquin 1978; Philips et al. 1983a). But it would appear that many seeds do not germinate, and potentially sizeable seed banks may exist in the sediment (Bigley 1981; Robertson and Mann 1984). Non-germinated seeds may be retained in the sediment to germinate in later years. Phillips (1972) and Orth et al. (1982a) reported that seeds remain viable for at least one year. Churchill (1983) successfully germinated seeds that had been held in sediments at 30 o/oo for 22 months and concluded that viable seeds from two or three prior years may be present in the sediments.

Estimates of seedling abundance indicate that there are large variations. Seedling densities in South Oyster Bay, New York, exceeded 100 m^{-2} (Kim Gates, pers. comm.). In North Carolina, seedling abundance ranged from 0 to 5 m^{-2} in several representative estuarine habitats (Fonseca et al. 1982a). The greatest number occurred in a semi-enclosed embayment and none were found on an open water meadow located on a high-energy shoal. Orth and Moore (1981) reported seedling densities of 66 m^{-2} in a Chesapeake Bay meadow, which represented 0.8% of their estimated average number of seeds produced. Conover (1964) reported seedling densities of 0 to 11 m^{-2} in a coastal lagoon in Rhode Island

and argued that the dispersal of seeds into well-delineated regions depended upon current regime. He reported that the largest number of seedlings were in the quiescent basins, and few were on sandy shingles of windward shores, sand bars under the influence of strong tidal currents, and current-swept channels. In quiescent areas of the same Rhode Island lagoon seedling densities averaged between 298 and 726 m^{-2} (Thorne-Miller et al. 1983). In Nova Scotia, seedling abundance was greatest in late fall and early summer with densities as high as 800 m^{-2} (Robertson and Mann 1984).

Kentula (1983) estimated a maximum of 86 seedlings m^{-2} for a location in Netarts Bay, Oregon. Kentula's survey revealed an important aspect of the sampling problem. She conducted surveys on three line transects and made observations during several months in two different years. On a given transect, the month of peak abundance was different in each year. Also, on a given transect, there was considerable month-to-month variation. The recognition of seedlings is masked by the continual emergence of new seedlings over an extended period and there is considerable difficulty recognizing individual seedlings which have vegetatively reproduced.

Finally, seedling mortality, export, or herbivory may be significant factors in the overall contribution of seed reproduction (Robertson and Mann 1984; Cathleen Wigand, pers. comm.). Loss of seedlings by these mechanisms has not been studied in any detail.

Phenology

Water temperature has a strong influence on timing of the reproductive cycle. The flowering sequence along a latitudinal gradient on the Atlantic coast occurs increasingly later at more northern latitudes (Phillips et al. 1983b). According to Silberhorn et al. (1983) (Figure 14), all stages in the phenological sequence occur at approximately similar temperatures on the Atlantic coast but, due to latitudinal differences in temperature, each stage occurs progressively later as one moves from south to north.

19

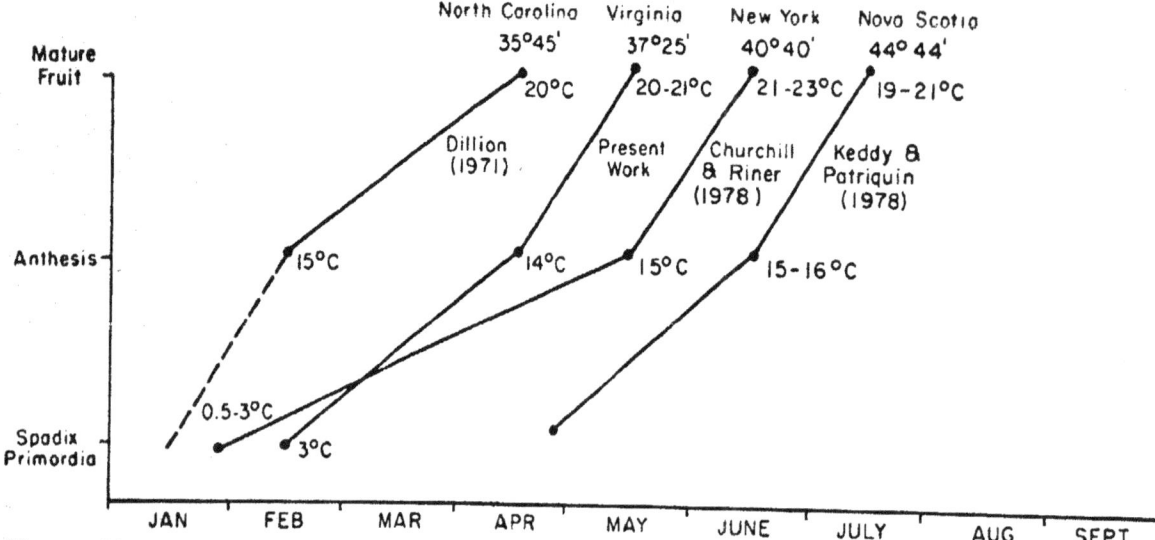

Figure 14. Reproductive phenology of eelgrass at different latitudes along the east coast of North America. The approximate temperature that was recorded for each event also is shown. Keddy and Patriquin provided data for areas that only had an annual form of eelgrass; temperatures were assumed to approximate those of nearby beds of perennial eelgrass. (From Silberhorn et al. 1983.)

The length of time over which the rise in water temperature occurs also influences the length of each phase in the reproductive cycle. Silberhorn et al. (1983) noted the average number of spathes per shoot increased from Virginia to New York and to Roscoff, France. They argued that in northern latitudes, where water temperatures averaging 9°-15°C extend over a prolonged period, there is a more favorable environment for floral development. In more southerly locations, such as Virginia, the seasonal temperature maxima are reached more rapidly and the duration of the favorable time period for initial flower development is shortened (Silberhorn et al. 1983). Although temperature appears to be critical for all phases of the flowering process, interacting factors, such as nutrient stress (Churchill and Riner 1978; DeCock 1981a), irradiance (DeCock 1981b; Phillips et al. 1983b; Silberhorn et al. 1983), day length (DeCock 1981b; Phillips et al. 1983b) and genotypic variation (Phillips 1983a,b) also may influence the timing and characteristics of the flowering process.

The entire flowering process requires approximately 30-60 days and is longest in more northern latitudes. Seeds are released between May and August.

Depending on the geographical location and rate of floral development, they may germinate as early as August or September. Germination continues through winter and spring (Addy 1947b); Taylor 1957; Lamounette 1977; Orth and Moore 1983; Churchill 1983; Phillips et al. 1983a; Robertson and Mann 1984). In Virginia, substantial growth and asexual reproduction resulting after germination of seeds in early autumn is important in maintaining the meadows through the winter (Orth and Moore 1983). The results of field experiments in New York showed that most of the seeds that were tested germinated in autumn, 3 to 4 months after they were released (Churchill 1983). Likewise, Phillips et al. (1983a) reported that the maximum rate of seed germination in the laboratory study occurred during the first four months, at a time when little or no germination was observed in nature. Thus, culture conditions, in either the field or laboratory, seem to accelerate the onset of germination; however, it is also possible that the very early stages of germination in the field go unnoticed by a casual observer. Germination occurring in the latter part of the fall is probably not recognized until after late winter and early spring growth.

20

Population Growth

As part of this effort to synthesize the information concerning the growth and life history of eelgrass we are developing a population growth model (Kenworthy et al., manuscript in preparation). The model is a tool designed to serve as the conceptual framework for a more refined version which could be used for the management and restoration of eelgrass meadows. Sources of information used in this model were obtained from surveys of plant distribution and abundance, measurements of vegetative and areal growth rates in natural and transplanted populations, observations on the characteristics of sexual reproduction, and seedling distribution and abundance. Our data base is mostly derived from studies in North Carolina, but in order to develop a more comprehensive understanding of the population biology of eelgrass we have drawn upon a large literature base.

Eelgrass transplants were done under a range of environmental conditions in several habitats and confirm that vegetative reproduction is important in maintaining the meadows (Figure 15) (Fonseca et al. 1984). These data illustrate the seasonal cycle of population growth in North Carolina attributed to vegetative reproduction. Growth is initiated in early October during which asexual reproduction adds new shoots relatively slowly through the winter. Approximately 150 days later, in late February and early March, growth accelerates, and the number of additional new shoots may be five to ten times the original number planted. Growth slows dramatically during summer (Figure 15 B), especially in shallow, intertidal meadows where shoot mortality may be substantial (Figure 15D). Mortalities of the transplants and in the natural meadows coincide with the onset of excessive warm summer temperatures and periodic low tides. Nearly all transplants on a semi-enclosed embayment died (Figure 15D) while transplants in open-water shoal environments experienced reduced growth, but not a serious mortality (Figure 15 B,C). A continuous flow of water maintains cooler temperatures over the shoals, while in the embayment poor circulation enables the water to be heated to excessively high temperatures frequently exceeding 30°C. In natural eelgrass meadows at their southern range limits, cooler fall temperatures initiate a period of renewed growth which is especially important in maintaining shallow embayment and intertidal populations that normally experience summer heat stress and large mortalities. Transplanted populations in the Chesapeake Bay undergo a seasonal cycle of growth similar to North Carolina and coincide closely with growth cycles in natural meadows (Orth and Moore 1981).

In the northern portion of the geographical range, Zostera abundance peaks later in the summer and declines sharply in winter. This shift in the growth cycle corresponds to the thermal tolerance of the species. The large vegetative growth potential of eelgrass was demonstrated in a spring transplant study in Long Island, New York, where after planting, the number of new shoots increased five fold in just 4 months (Riner 1976).

Data from transplants were used to estimate part of the growth potential for this eelgrass model since the seasonal growth cycle in natural populations corresponds to the observed growth response of transplants (Churchill et al. 1978; Fonseca et al. 1982a). We also compared vegetative reproduction to the potential for growth by seed reproduction. For five transplant experiments and one control area that was revegetated naturally by seed, the area revegetated by seed had the highest growth rate (Table 2). Similar rates of growth for transplants of mature shoots were reported for the Chesapeake Bay (Orth and Moore 1981) and Long Island (Riner 1976). Note, in Table 2, that the value for r ranged by more than a factor of two, 0.00530-0.01365, and was generally less than the naturally occurring population of seedlings, 0.0185. Since the exponential model is very sensitive to the coefficient, r, large annual variations in the abundance of eelgrass can be attributed to factors which cause the value of r to fluctuate. The fact that the estimated r value for seedlings was much higher than for the transplants is consistent with the observed growth rates

ZOSTERA MARINA

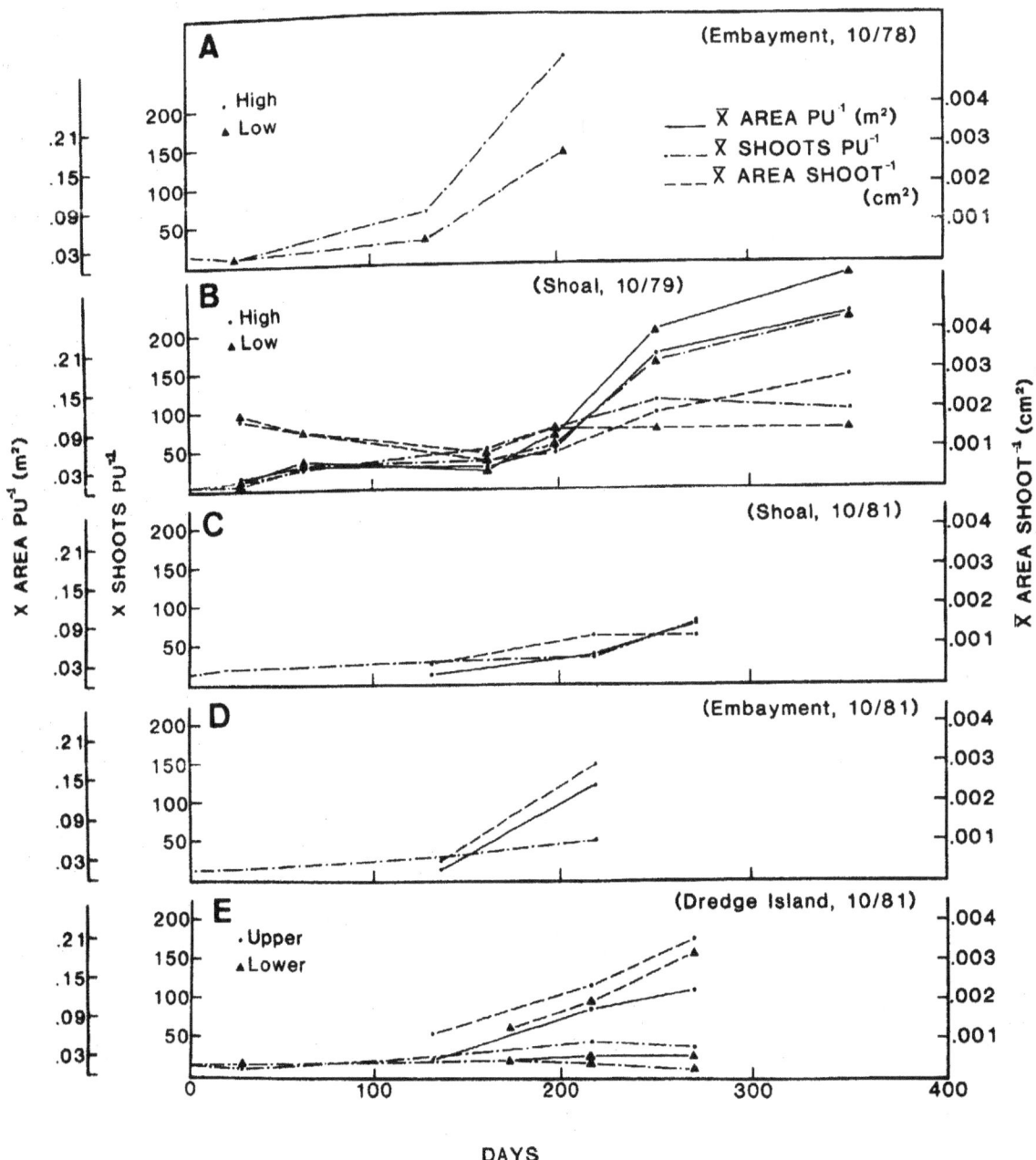

Figure 15. Data for the growth of <u>Zostera marina</u> in five transplant experiments (A-E). Growth is shown as the change in the average number of shoots per planting unit ($\bar{x}$ shoots PU^{-1}), the average bottom area covered per planting unit ($\bar{x}$ area PU^{-1}), and the average bottom covered per individual shoots (x area covered shoot^{-1}). High and low refer to planting stock which originated in high and low energy environments. The location of each transplant is shown in parentheses on each graph. Day 0 is approximately October 1 in each of the years for which a planting was done. (Data from Fonseca et al. 1984.)

22

Table 2. Instantaneous coefficient of growth (r) for transplants and seedlings of Zostera marina calculated from the equation $Y_t = Y_0 e^{rt}$, where Y_t = number of shoots at time t, Y_0 = initial number of shoots, e = base of natural logarithm. (Data from Fonseca et al. 1984.)

Transplant site with planting month and year	t (days)	r (Calculated from no. shoots/PU)
Shackleford Shoal 10/81	271	0.00533
Middle March Embayment 10/81	218	0.00618
Dredge Island 10/81	269	0.00530
Shackleford Shoal 10/79	350	0.00964
Middle Marsh Embayment 10/78	203	0.01365
Z. marina seedlings 10/78	203	0.01850

of plants in general. The youngest plants in a population usually grow faster, and since the transplants had older, vegetative shoots, the data agree with the generalized trend. In addition, this points out the great potential seedlings have for natural recolonization.

Although the growth rate of plants established from seeds can be quite high, the abundance of seeds and seedlings can be drastically affected by a number of biotic and abiotic variables. Seeds can be deposited quite readily in quiescent, depositional environments (Fonseca et al. 1982a), but in open-water, high-energy habitats, with strong currents or considerable wave action, seedlings may not be able to establish. In high energy habitats, growth of meadows is restricted to vegetative reproduction, while in less turbulent areas eelgrass growth can result from a combination of vegetative and sexual reproduction. Refinements of this growth model should account for habitat and geographic differences as well as the timing and duration of reproduction. Plants reproduce sexually over a relatively short duration and release mature seeds during a discrete period. Except for the most stressful circumstances, vegetative reproduction is a relatively continuous process. In

northern latitudes shoots that were produced in early spring will reproduce vegetatively from late spring and through the summer and early fall. Farther south, for example, in North Carolina, vegetative reproduction occurs over a period of 250 days beginning in October and ending in June.

As a first approximation, eelgrass population growth resembles a sigmoid curve (Figure 15 B) and may be represented by a simple logistic model. The model should have parameters that account for vegetative growth, seedling growth, length of growing season, losses due to death of flowering shoots, and losses from other sources of mortality as yet unknown. The form of the model could be illustrated by several variations of the simple logistic growth equation. For example, growth in an intertidal embayment near the southern edge of the geographical range of eelgrass is likely to take the form of Line A in Figure 16, where mortality induced by summer heat stress is quite substantial. In this case the initial number of seedlings, year-to-year, is an important parameter, and any future refinement of the model should take seedlings, as well as environmental factors that influence sexual reproduction, into account. Line B (Figure 16) illustrates eelgrass growth in an open-water, high-energy meadow where summer mortality is relatively low. In this case, there either must be a drastic year-to-year fluctuation in vegetative growth, a large degree of mortality, or there must be some other density-dependent factor controlling growth; otherwise, these populations would reach unrealistic densities. Line C (Figure 16) conceptually illustrates growth in the north Atlantic coastal area. In this model the annual peak is shifted to a point later in the year and illustrates a more amplified winter decline as well as the influence of annual temperature and insolation cycles on growth.

The data in Figure 15 and Table 2 show a substantial year-to-year variation in the growth coefficient as well as differences between habitats. Thus, in the conceptual model the growth rates represented by the curves are an oversimplification of the potential variation in population growth. Future

23

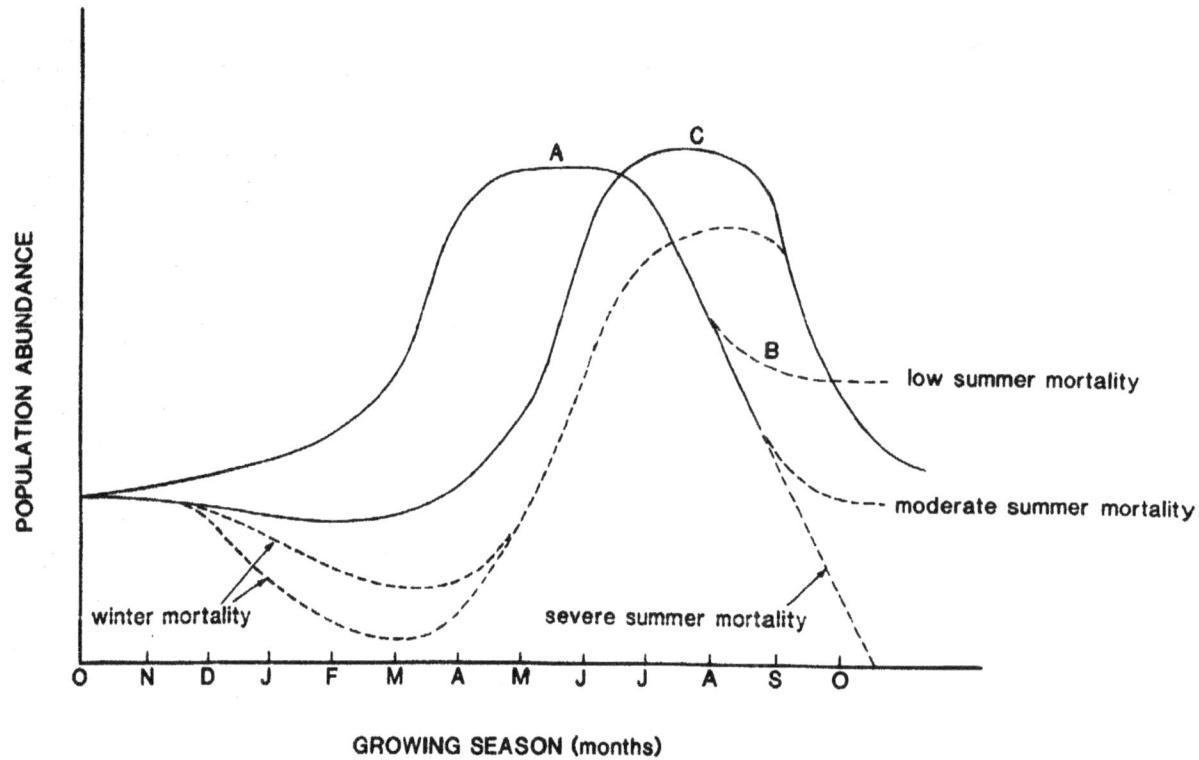

Figure 16. Conceptual growth model of eelgrass, Zostera marina. Line A illustrates model where plants experience severe heat stress; Line B illustrates growth without summer heat stress; Line C illustrates growth in northern latitudes.

research into the population dynamics of this plant should address the factors responsible for controlling the variation. Since many aspects of the growth cycle of eelgrass have been identified, we believe a quantitative population model can be constructed that will be useful in studying the dynamics of the growth, abundance, and distribution of eelgrass.

2.3 ASPECTS OF THE PHYSIOLOGICAL ECOLOGY OF EELGRASS

The most notable feature of eelgrass is its ability to grow in a remarkably wide range of coastal habitats. Its circumglobal distribution in the northern hemisphere (Figure 1) is due, in part, to its ability to tolerate a wide range of environmental parameters. The roots and rhizomes are a well-developed anchoring system that not only help to maintain the plant securely in place, but also gives it access to the interstitial sedimentary environment that is rich in nutrients. Several of the important environmental factors which have a measurable influence on its growth, reproduction, and distribution are addressed in the following discussion.

Light

Since a source of radiant energy is necessary to activate chlorophyll molecules and drive the reactions of photosynthesis, sunlight is a fundamental requirement for plant growth. Seasonal changes in the sun's altitude and daily changes in clouds cause large variations in the solar radiation reaching the water. Light penetrating the water is rapidly attenuated by absorption, scattering, and reflection. The quality or spectrum of light is also altered. The longer wavelengths are rapidly absorbed causing substantial shifts in the depth of penetration by specific wavelengths that

24

are photosynthetically important. In shallow, well-mixed estuaries, like many of those along the east coast of the United States, turbidity from suspended sediments and dissolved and particulate organic matter can be quite high, further altering light quality and quantity. Since eelgrass often grows at very high densities, the leaf canopy itself absorbs, reflects, and diffuses light. Light penetration through the canopy may be reduced by as much as 25% of ambient (Short 1980; Dennison and Alberte 1982).

Studies of the response of eelgrass photosynthesis and growth to radiant energy have taken a number of approaches. From a population standpoint, reductions in light levels with in situ experiments caused significant decreases in plant density. For example, Backman and Barilotti (1976) used shading devices to reduce the ambient light level by 63% and found that after 9 months, plant densities in shaded treatments were only 5% of those in unshaded controls. Declines in density as a result of shading also were reported by Burkholder and Doheny (1968) and Short (1975). These decreases suggest that asexual reproduction declined and plants died from the near cessation of primary production. Dennison and Alberte (1982) reported that shading had a far greater effect on plants growing at stations located near the lower limits of their depth distribution than it did on plants growing in shallower areas. These studies illustrate that light intensity has a dramatic influence on the lower limits of depth distribution of eelgrass.

Shading by a mature canopy of eelgrass has a substantial influence on seedling growth and morphology (Robertson and Mann 1984). Seedlings growing under mature canopies exhibit a lower rate of vegetative reproduction, decreased overall net production, and a light-stressed morphology.

In turbid coastal plain estuaries, such as those in North Carolina eelgrass is usually limited to depths less than 2 m (Thayer et al. 1975b; Fonseca et al. 1982a; Stuart 1982). Wetzel and Penhale (1983) concluded that light is the single most critical factor in the survival and growth of eelgrass in Chesapeake Bay and that nearly all plants are light stressed for a large portion of the year. Farther north, for example, New England or Nova Scotia estuaries are less turbid, and sufficient light penetrates to greater depths so that eelgrass may grow to depths exceeding 10 m (Harrison and Mann 1975b).

The influence that the quantity of photosynthetically active radiation (PAR) has on eelgrass growth was illustrated in a year-long survey of transplant sites in North Carolina (Fonseca et al. 1984). The instantaneous coefficient of growth for eelgrass transplants was zero at 1.17% PAR, but increased dramatically with only a slight increase in the PAR (Figure 17). At the highest PAR value, growth rate was depressed, suggesting the possibility that high light intensities may limit growth of the transplants. The negative influence of high light intensity may have been confounded by periodic exposure to air and wave stress since a high PAR occurred at the shallowest transplant site, a situation which may be quite common in many natural meadows.

Seasonal cycles in production of eelgrass have been attributed to annual

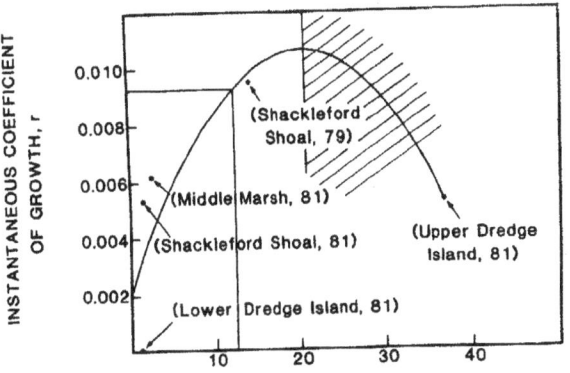

Figure 17. The relationship between average annual photosynthetically active radiation (PAR) and the instantaneous coefficient of growth (r) for eelgrass in five transplant experiments in North Carolina. A second degree polynomial is drawn, and the intersecting line illustrates the 12.5% light level. (Redrawn from Fonseca et al. 1984.)

25

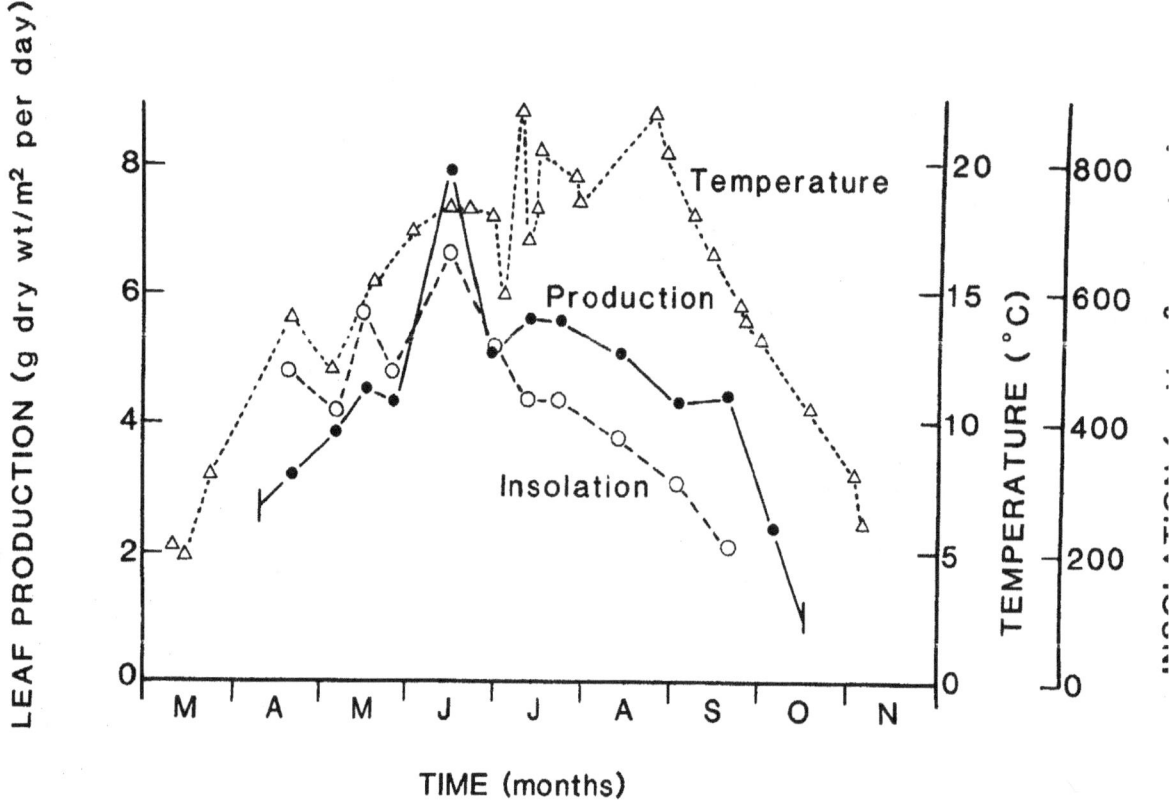

Figure 18. Leaf production of eelgrass in Denmark in relation to insolation an temperature. (From Sand-Jensen 1975.)

cycles of light intensity. For example Sand-Jensen (1975), Jacobs (1979) and Kentula (1983) showed a close correspondence between leaf production and insolation (Figure 18). Investigations of eelgrass photosynthesis-light relationships (P-I) illustrate some of the effects that light, and the interaction of light and temperature, have on eelgrass growth. Light saturation of eelgrass photosynthesis in Alaska occured at just about 50% transmittance, and carbon uptake decreased linearly below 50% surface light intensity (McRoy 1974).

Zostera photosynthesis is also subject to temperature effects. In Chesapeake Bay in January, at water temperatures of 10°C the P-I relationship (Wetzel 1982; Penhale and Wetzel 1983) (Figure 19) is similar to that in Alaska (McRoy 1974), but at a typical August water temperature of 28°C saturation occurs at around 10%. On the basis of these data, Wetzel and Penhale (1983) concluded that eelgrass in

Chesapeake Bay is characterized by: (1) temperature optimum for photosynthesis o between 22° and 28°C, (2) hig photosynthetic efficiency at low-ligh intensity, and (3) a P_{max} (photosynthesis and light response that is characteristi of shade or low-light tolerant plants.

Wetzel and Penhale's (1983 conclusions were corroborated by detaile investigations of the photosyn thetic, chromatic, and morphologica characteristics of eelgrass (Denniso 1979; Mazzella et al. 1981; Dennison an Alberte 1982). The conclusions of Dennison and Alberte (1982), who estimate light saturation and light compensatio points for eelgrass plants near Wood Hole, Massachusetts, were similar t Wetzel's (1982). Dennison and Albert (1982) also concluded, based on this worl and a previous study (Dennison 1979), thai eelgrass can alter its leaf area inde) (LAI = m² of leaf area per m² of botton area) to capture light more efficiently.

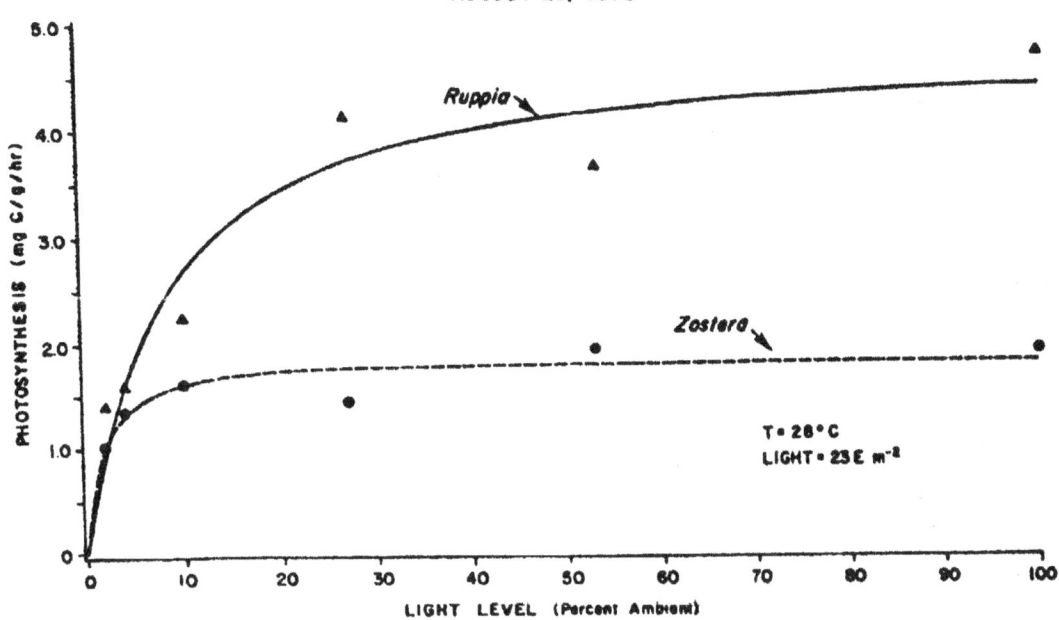

AUGUST 29, 1979

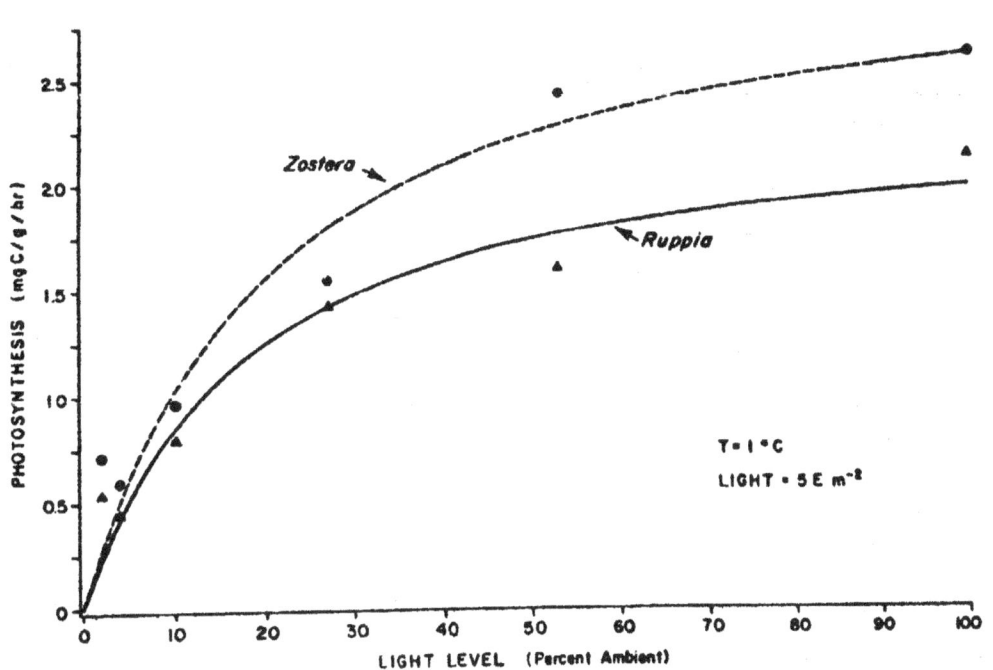

JANUARY 29, 1980

Figure 19. Photosynthesis-light (P-I) relationships for Zostera marina and Ruppia maritima at two temperature regimes in the Chesapeake Bay, Virginia. (From Wetzel 1982.)

27

Changing LAI may not be the entire adaptive mechanism. There are other features that distinguish plants growing at different water depths. Eelgrass plants in shallow water had significantly greater photosynthetic rates, respiration rates, chlorophyll a/b ratios, less chlorophyll per leaf area and a denser leaf canopy (LAI of 3 compared to an LAI of 2) than plants in deeper water. Even though shoots were much smaller, areal production rates in shallow water where light intensity was high were double the rates in deep water. Apparently, eelgrass can adjust to low-light intensity in deep water by partitioning more energy into the formation of longer and wider leaves at the cost of shoot density. In deeper water, larger leaves grow higher into the water column thereby accessing the highest light intensities. This response was manifested in a higher rate of production per individual shoot for the deeper water station (Dennison and Alberte 1982).

There is a positive feedback to this adaptation of changing morphology. Dennison and Alberte (1982) demonstrated that in shallow water where the grass was dense the canopy attenuated 90% of the light, but that the deep water canopy attenuated only 75% of the light and permitted more light to penetrate through the deep water canopy for use by the smaller, very young shoots. As a consequence of canopy attenuation, eelgrass meadows in both shallow and deep water are rarely, if ever, completely light-saturated for photosynthesis during the summer in Massachusetts (Dennison and Alberte 1982). In addition, Mazzella et al. (1981) reported that the light saturation point for the base of eelgrass leaves was lower than leaf tips. These features suggest a remarkable ability of eelgrass to adjust to existing light gradients within the meadows.

An interesting example of the light-plant interaction has been reported for mixed beds of eelgrass and Ruppia in Chesapeake Bay (Wetzel 1982; Wetzel and Penhale 1983). Ruppia has a high light and temperature optimum (Figure 19), a low photosynthetic efficiency at low-light intensity, and a P_{max} and light response, typical of sun- or high-light tolerant plants. In mixed communities, depth

distributions and seasonal abundances of both species are consistent with our knowledge of photosynthesis from physiological studies. In the Chesapeake Bay, Zostera grows best during the spring and early summer, and in late fall when both water temperatures and light intensities are at optimum levels. Ruppia grows best in the mid-summer at higher temperatures and reduced light intensities. Distribution surveys (Orth and Moore 1982a; Wetzel and Penhale 1983) clearly illustrate that Zostera is more abundant in the deeper water where conditions are favorable for its growth.

Wetzel and Penhale (1983) measured canopy structure of a mixed bed in Chesapeake Bay and noted that the leaf areas of both species were concentrated in the lower portion of the canopy. They concluded, as did Dennison (1979), that the concentration of leaf area in the lower portion of the canopy provided plants with a greater surface for capturing light when light levels are reduced. Furthermore, Ruppia exhibited a relatively greater stratification and a greater concentration of chlorophyll in the lower canopy. The authors reasoned that these photosynthetic and morphological characteristics contributed to the success of Ruppia in mixed stands of Ruppia and Zostera. Evidently, the photosynthetic systems in these two species differ in a manner which allows optimal exploitation of certain habitats during specific seasonal thermal cycles.

Temperature

Temperature influences all facets of the life cycle of eelgrass. For example, when plants are light saturated the photosynthetic enzymes are temperature sensitive. Biologically mediated nutrient remineralization is influenced by temperature. Elevated temperatures may enhance respiration thereby increasing a plant's maintenance costs. Setchell (1929) argued that temperature was the primary regulator of growth and development of eelgrass and he even went so far as to state that eelgrass growth and reproduction were not dependent on a photoperiod. Many discussions have centered on the pros and cons of that temperature model. Using several Atlantic coast locations and one Pacific coast location, Setchell argued that eelgrass displayed five discrete growth periods governed by 5°C temperature intervals: (1) no growth between 0° and 10°C, (2) vegetative growth between 10° and 15°C, (3) sexual reproductive development between 15° and 20°C, (4) heat rigor and no growth at temperatures exceeding 20°C, and (5) seed and leaf loss with little or no growth during falling temperatures.

Setchell's model with discrete thermal boundaries is incorrect. Eelgrass growth occurs at temperatures well below 10°C and, in fact, in Hudson Bay, Canada, the entire life cycle probably occurs at temperatures between 2°C and 4°C (Hout 1962, cited in Phillips 1974b). In Rhode Island, growth continues at temperatures less than 10°C (Brown 1962) and sexual reproduction occurs at temperatures around 5°C (Short 1975). Within limits, neither warm nor cold appears to stop photosynthesis. McRoy (1969) found eelgrass living under 1 m of sea ice in the Arctic, and good growth of eelgrass has been reported at temperatures exceeding 20°C. Wetzel (1982) reported that the likely optimum range for photosynthesis of eelgrass in Chesapeake Bay was somewhere between 22°C and 28°C, a temperature that is considerably higher than would be expected from Setchell's model. According to Biebl and McRoy (1971), gross photosynthesis of *Zostera* increases steadily as temperature rises between 0° and 30°C, but drops off sharply between 30°C and 40°C. We cannot avoid the conclusion that eelgrass is far more eurythermal than Setchell suggested.

Extreme temperatures in combination with other factors (e.g., exposure and desiccation), however, can have dramatic effects on eelgrass populations (Figure 20). At the colder end of the temperature scale, situations exist in shallow water where long periods of sub-freezing temperatures may produce a thick ice cover. As the ice thaws, wind and tides cause ice floes that scour the bottom, uprooting most of the eelgrass. Shoot density in a stand of eelgrass in a coastal lagoon in Rhode Island declined from 4,000 to 400 shoots m^{-2} in one winter due in part to ice scour (Short 1975). This type of situation is probably common

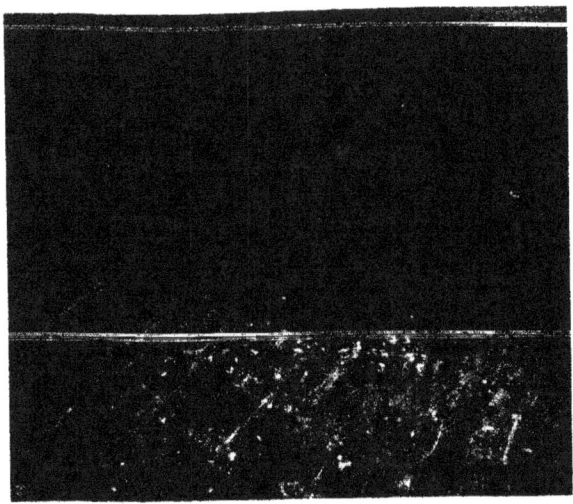

Figure 20. An eelgrass bed in North Carolina exposed at low tide during warm summer temperatures which frequently exceed 30°C.

in shallow water throughout the north Atlantic region. Likewise, Robertson and Mann (1984) reported that seasonally recurring disturbance by ice scour in shallow subtidal eelgrass meadows in Nova Scotia has a strong influence on the life history characteristics of the eelgrass populations.

At the southern end of its distribution in North Carolina, intertidal and shallow subtidal grass beds experience mid-summer temperatures that may exceed 30°C. In late winter and spring when temperatures are optimum for growth, the plants achieve very high biomass; however, summer heat stress causes excessive mortalities. These beds recover annually by recruitment of seedlings and when viewed during a single year they may appear ephemeral, but they are actually quite persistent over a long period.

Sometimes the combined effects of temperature and exposure (desiccation) may be difficult to separate. The accretion of sediments may elevate shallow water beds and they undergo increasingly longer periods of exposure (Figure 20). A measurable decline of an intensively studied eelgrass meadow in North Carolina was attributed to this process (Thayer et al. 1975a).

Salinity

Eelgrass should be considered euryhaline since it has been reported growing at salinities ranging from nearly fresh water (Osterhout 1917) to full-strength seawater (Uphof 1941; Arasaki 1950) or even higher salinities (Tutin 1938). Biebl and McRoy (1971) found that eelgrass exhibited a net production within a salinity range of 0-56 o/oo. An optimum salinity has never been determined.

Salinity may affect seed germination (Arasaki 1950; Burkholder and Doheny 1968). In laboratory studies, Lamounette (1977) and Phillips et al. (1983a) determined that seed germination increased as salinity declined. The germination rate at 10 o/oo was double that at 19 o/oo, and at 19 o/oo it was double that at 28 o/oo. Phillips et al. (1983a) reported that the percentage of germination for seeds tested at o/oo was 57%, at 10 o/oo it was 42.5%, and at 28-30 o/oo only 5.2%. Lamounette (1977) reasoned that as salinity declined there is increased imbibition of water by the embryo. When water enters the embryo it swells, creating increased pressure within the seed that assists in cracking the seed coat. Although this seems to be a good explanation, no one has actually quantified the imbibition (A.C. Churchill, pers. comm.).

From a distributional standpoint, long-standing differences in salinities may determine the differences in species composition between nearby bodies of water. Adjacent coastal lagoons on the south shore of Rhode Island provided an excellent case study of salinity (Thorne-Miller et al. 1983), since the primary difference among the physical characteristics of the lagoons was the exchange with oceanic waters from Rhode Island Sound. The lagoons with a long standing continuous connection to the open ocean had the highest salinities and were dominated by eelgrass, while lagoons just a few kilometers away with more restricted connections to the open ocean were dominated by *Potamogeton* *pectinatus* and *Ruppia*.

Water Motion

Forces generated by water motion originating from tides and wind have measurable effect on growth and distribution of eelgrass. Waves and currents, by scouring the bottom, erode sediments, mature plants and seeds, and prevent deposition of material. In some cases large quantities of sediment may be transported and deposited, burying substantial portions of existing meadow (Blois et al. 1961; Christiansen et al. 1981; Kenworthy and Fonseca unpubl observ.).

From a physiological standpoint investigators have hypothesized that water motion stimulates molecular diffusion of dissolved gases and nutrients to the surface of a plant by decreasing the boundary layer (Neushall 1972). Conover (1964, 1968) argued that increased velocities should make more nutrients available to the leaves, since the volume of water passing the plant surface is a function of velocity. The most luxuriant stands of eelgrass are usually in areas of moderate to high current speeds (Phillips 1972; Conover 1964; Short 1975). As suggested by Conover (1964) and Fonseca (unpubl. data), there may be an optimum current speed between 20 and 40 cm sec⁻¹ below which metabolism may be limited by diffusion, and above which growth may decline as a result of physical disruption of the plants. Further studies are needed to determine the interrelationships between physiological aspects of the plant and water motion.

Since eelgrass slows water flow, an established meadow can have a substantial influence on the physical, chemical, and biological characteristics of sediments by retaining organic matter and nutrient resources within the meadow (see Chapter 3 for a detailed discussion of these aspects).

Substrate

Eelgrass grows on substrates varying from pure, firm sand to fine, soft muds (Ostenfeld 1908; den Hartog 1970). Isolated occurrences of eelgrass in sediment-filled depressions on open shorelines and in fjord-like embayments among cobble have been observed in New

England (Riggs and Fralick 1975; Kenworthy and Fonseca, pers. observ.). In North Carolina, eelgrass grows in fine muds, silts, and sands, and Kenworthy et al. (1982) concluded that there was no evidence that substrate type limited eelgrass distribution, except where the substrate was too firm for roots and rhizomes to penetrate and in areas of unstable sediments. However, growth rates and plant morphology may be influenced by the physicochemical characteristics of the sediment (Ostenfeld 1908; Kenworthy and Fonseca 1977; Orth 1977; Short 1981, 1983a,b,).

Nutrients

Most research on seagrass-nutrient interactions has centered on nutrient cycling processes (see Chapter 3) rather than the specific physiological nutrient requirements of the plants. Few studies of micronutrient physiology and biochemistry are available. The plants are rooted and can obtain the major macronutrients (McRoy and Barsdate 1970; Penhale and Thayer 1980; Short 1981; Thursby and Harlin 1982) and micronutrients (Brinkhuis et al. 1980) from both sediment and water column.

The concentrations and regeneration rates of major macronutrients are largest in the sediments, but the extent to which eelgrass plants utilize water or sediment nutrient sources remains unresolved. In the laboratory Thursby and Harlin (1982) reported that root uptake of ammonium was affected by nutrient concentrations in the water surrounding the leaves, but leaf uptake was not affected by roots. Thus, if sediment nutrients fluctuated, leaves should still be able to continue exploiting the lower concentrations of nutrients in the water column, unaffected by root zone concentrations. Considering that the range of fluctuation in the interstitial water concentrations is far greater than in the water column (Kenworthy et al. 1982; Short 1981), this observed response would be beneficial to the plants.

Eelgrass may be nutrient limited under certain circumstances. Application of fertilizer to sediments (Orth 1977) and to the water column (Harlin and Thorne-Miller 1981) appeared to stimulate growth.

Unfortunately, however, design weaknesses in these studies leave many questions unresolved. Orth (1977) applied a mixed fertilizer to the sediment and was unable to determine if it was nitrogen, phosphorus, or some other mineral in the fertilizer that enhanced growth. He was also unable to trace the ultimate disposition of the elements in the fertilizer-sediment-plant complex. Harlin and Thorne-Miller (1981) dispensed individual fertilizers into the water column and reported substantially less growth than Orth (1977). They could not ascertain whether this lesser growth resulted because the plants could not utilize the nutrients in the water column as efficiently or because there was an untested nutrient combination effect. Neither study accounted for the utilization of nutrients by other components of the community, a problem typical to many field studies that lack proper controls. In fact, Harlin and Thorne-Miller reported that the growth of a dense algal mat probably utilized considerable amounts of nutrients.

Short (1981, 1983a,b) and Iizumi et al. (1982) suggested that nitrogen may limit the growth of eelgrass. Iizumi et al. (1982) measured nitrogen regeneration and concluded that water column regeneration was of little significance in meeting the nitrogen requirements of the plants. Approximately 41% of the ammonium regenerated in the sediments was assimilated by microorganisms, suggesting a competition between the plants and heterotrophs for the available nitrogen in the sediments. Based on estimates of net production, the remaining ammonium just met the demands of the plants. Nitrogen availability, in fact, may be limited by the requirements of the heterotrophic community responsible for the decomposition of organic matter in the sediments.

Short (1983a) compared uptake rates and nitrogen pools in organic-rich and organic-poor sediments and concluded that nitrogen regeneration in organic-poor sediments was inadequate to supply nitrogen required for plant growth. There was a larger discrepancy between calculated N:P ratios for uptake relative to the N:P of plant tissues in organic-poor sediments.

31

The matter of nutrient sources and availability, as well as the general nutritional requirements of the plant, is open to more research. Since eelgrass constitutes such a large portion of the autotrophic production and biomass of temperate shallow water areas, the flux of nutrients through it must be quite large (Thayer et al. 1975b; Zieman and Wetzel 1980; Sand-Jensen and Borum 1983).

2.4 CHEMICAL COMPOSITION

Estimates of the chemical composition of eelgrass listed in Table 3 come from a very diverse literature base. We recommend use of the original citations for specific information regarding sampling and analytical techniques. It is difficult to present this information without noting that potential interpretation problems exist, and spatial and temporal variations are inherent in the data. Most of the data represent pooled samples or averages of a number of samples, as well as samples taken in different habitats and at different times. For example, Thayer et al. (1977) reported distinctive seasonal variations in the organic matter content of all components of eelgrass and attributed the variations, in part, to increases in carbonates from encrusting organisms that occur during senescence of the plant tissue. Both organic carbon and nitrogen levels had distinctive seasonal maximum and minimum values. Seasonal variations in nitrogen and carbon also were reported by Harrison and Mann (1975b). Lyngby and Brix (1982) reported seasonal variations in ash and heavy metal content, with maximum concentrations occurring in late winter and early spring and minimum concentrations in early winter. Lyngby and Brix (1982) attributed the variations to seasonal plant growth dynamics. Clearly, seasonal aspects of the composition of the plant material must be accounted for in any interpretation of past and future studies. This is especially pertinent for the roots and rhizomes which may store elements and carbohydrates during periods of reduced growth.

Confounding the analysis of seasonal variation in tissue composition are distinctive variations in proximate

Table 3. Representative summary of several aspects of the chemical composition of _Zostera marina_.

Component and plant part	Method of reporting	Estimate	Source of information
I. Organic matter content			
A. Leaves			
1. Living	% of dry weight	79.3, 80-90, 89-88	1, 7, 14, 16
2. Dead	% of dry weight	67.4, 70-80	1, 7
3. Detrital	% of dry weight	54.9, 60-70	1
B. Roots			
1. Living	% of dry weight	67.0	2
C. Rhizomes			
1. Living	% of dry weight	76.0	2
D. Roots and rhizomes combined	% of dry weight	60-83	14
II. Caloric content			
A. Leaves	calories/ash free g	4125	3
B. Rhizomes	calories/ash free g	3967	3
III. Protein			
A. Leaves	% of dry weight	10.62, 10.6, 19.04	4, 7, 16
B. Old, dead leaves	% of dry weight	4-5	7
C. Rhizomes	% of dry weight	6.14	4
IV. Crude fiber			
A. Leaves	% of dry weight	16.6, 18.4	16, 9
B. Rhizomes	% of dry weight	59.9, 13.3	4, 9
	% of dry weight	50.4	--
C. Roots	% of dry weight	41.7, 11.6	2, 9
V. Composites of crude fiber in leaves			
A. Hemicellulose	% of total organic weight	23.2	5
B. Cellulose	% of total organic weight	22.1	5
C. Lignin	% of total organic weight	7.3	5
VI. Carbohydrates in leaves			
A. Leaves			
1. Carbohydrates other than crude fiber	% of dry weight	5.6	4
2. Total nonstructural	% of total organic weight	3.0	5
3. Fructose	% extracted dry weight	2.6	6
Myo-inositol	% extracted dry weight	1.7	6
Sucrose	% extracted dry weight	18.4	6

(continued)

Table 3. (continued) Table 3. (concluded)

Component and plant part	Method of reporting	Estimate	Source of information
B. Rhizomes	% of dry weight in winter	33	7
1. Lipids			
a. Leaves	% of dry weight	1.6, 1.29	16, 7
b. Rhizomes	% of dry weight	0.91	7
VII. Carbon (organic)			
A. Leaves			
1. Living	% of dry weight	29, 38, 36.4, 43.8	1, 7, 8, 2
2. Dead	% of dry weight	22, 36	1, 7
3. Detrital	% of dry weight	19, 27.3	1, 8
B. Roots	% of dry weight	26, 41.2	9, 2
C. Rhizomes	% of dry weight	34, 43.4	9, 2
D. Roots and rhizomes	% of dry weight	30.6	8
VIII. Nitrogen			
A. Leaves			
1. Living	% of dry weight	1.85, 4.5, 1.8, 3.0, 2.59	1, 7, 8, 16, 9
2. Dead	% of dry weight	1.18, 2.6	1, 7
3. Detrital	% of dry weight	1.13, 1.7	1, 7
B. Roots	% of dry weight	1.4, 2.76	10, 9
C. Rhizomes	% of dry weight	1.4, 2.87	10, 9
IX. Phosphorus			
A. Leaves	% of dry weight	0.33-0.45, 0.386, 0.286	20, 4, 16
B. Whole plant	% of dry weight	0.4, 0.3-0.5	11, 12
X. Amino compounds			
A. Leaves			
1. Living	mg/g ash free dry weight	102.81	1
2. Dead	mg/g ash free dry weight	87.78	1
3. Detritus	mg/g ash free dry weight	123.40	1
XI. Trace elements			
A. Leaves			
1. Manganese	µg/g dry weight	154, 43, 140	13, 4, 15
2. Iron	µg/g dry weight	1240, 34, 810	13, 4, 15
3. Copper	µg/g dry weight	7.9, 1-40, 6	13, 14, 15

(continued)

Component and plant part	Method of reporting	Estimate	Source of information
4. Zinc	µg/g dry weight	70, 40-150, 2.7, 63	13, 14, 4, 15
5. Cadmium	µg/g dry weight	0.1-1.4	14
6. Lead	µg/g dry weight	1-23	14
7. Calcium	µg/g dry weight	453	4
8. Magnesium	µg/g dry weight	677	4
9. Potassium	µg/g dry weight	222	4
B. Roots and rhizomes			
1. Cadmium	µg/g dry weight	0.01-0.6	14
2. Copper	µg/g dry weight	2-20, 7.5	14, 16
3. Lead	µg/g dry	0.5-25	14
4. Zinc	µg/g dry weight	20-80	14
5. Manganese	µg/g dry weight	52, 1825	15, 16
6. Iron	µg/g dry weight	5900, 245	15, 16
7. Copper	µg/g dry weight	5	15
8. Zinc	µg/g dry weight	37	15
9. Magnesium	µg/g dry weight	738	16
10. Calcium	µg/g dry weight	2001	16
11. Sodium	µg/g dry weight	1959	16
12. Potassium	µg/g dry weight	2264	16
13. Molybdenum	µg/g dry weight	3.1	16
14. Boron	µg/g dry weight	309.7	16
15. Silicon	µg/g dry weight	84	16
16. Florine	µg/g dry weight	3.6	16
17. Bromine	µg/g dry weight	9.5	16
18. Iodine	µg/g dry weight	203	16
19. Chlorine	µg/g dry weight	4366	16
20. Sulfur	µg/g dry weight	730	16

1. Thayer et al. (1977)
2. Kenworthy (unpublished)
3. McRoy (1966)
4. Burkholder and Doheny (1968)
5. Godshalk and Wetzel (1978B)
6. Drew (1980)
7. Harrison and Mann (1975b)
8. Wetzel (1982)
9. Seki and Yokohama (1978)
10. Josselyn and Mathieson (1980)
11. Penhale (1977)
12. McRoy and Barsdate (1970)
13. Wolfe et al. (1976)
14. Lyngby and Brix (1982)
15. Drifmeyer et al. (1980)
16. Candussio (1960); as cited in Burkholder and Doheny 1968.

composition between ages of plant material. These differences are of special interest for eelgrass since at any given time materials of several different ages and in various stages of senescence are present on a plant. Decomposition of the plant material is accompanied by the leaching of soluble organic matter (See Chapters 3, 4, 5) and colonization by microorganisms (See Chapters 4,5). Consequently, aged material may have proportionately different quantities of an element or compound, depending on the stage of decay or the associated community of epiphytes.

2.5 BIOMASS

The range of values for the biomass of eelgrass leaves, roots, and rhizomes is quite large (Table 4). This is not surprising since eelgrass growth is influenced by several environmental parameters, as well as by recurring seasonal cycles of light and temperature. The wide ranges are also due, in part, to differences in sampling methods, sampling locations, and objectives of the individual studies. An example of the extent of biomass variability within a single estuarine system (lower Chesapeake Bay) is illustrated in Table 5 (Orth and Moore 1982a). Maximum and minimum values recur annually within a month or two, but the absolute biomass of plant material may vary by a factor of two or more. Generally in most surveys larger variability occurred with leaf standing crop than with roots and rhizomes. Leaves are subjected to physical exposure and have faster turnover rates than roots and rhizomes. During the periods of thermal stress, summer in the southern range and winter in the northern range, the plants assume a characteristic growth form. The leaves are much shorter and narrower and the standing crop is lower (Kenworthy 1981; Kentula 1983).

A large part of the recurring annual variation of the leaf standing crop can also be attributed to the synergistic effects of sexual and asexual reproduction and seasonal changes in plant morphology. Typically, an increase in shoot density occurs during the spring growing season followed closely by sexual reproduction. During this productive period

newly-produced shoots grow longer and wider and rapidly growing flowering stalks with maturing fruits add considerable biomass to the standing stock. As flowers die and are sloughed off at the termination of the reproductive cycle,

Table 4. Representative values for the standing crop, belowground biomass, total biomass, and productivity of _Zostera marina_.

Location	Component (total, leaves or roots and rhizomes)	Biomass g Dw m^{-2}	Productivity g C m^{-2} d^{-1}
Alaska	Leaves	25 - 1,000[b]	3.3 - 8.0[a]
	Roots and rhizomes	10 - 1,600[b]	
Puget Sound, Washington	Leaves	90 - 540[c]	
Humboldt Bay, California	Leaves	12 - 420[d]	
Japan	Leaves	4 - 192[e]	0.3 - 1.8[e]
Japan	Leaves	90 - 192[f]	
	Rhizomes	9 - 58[f]	
	Roots	1.6 - 18[f]	
Denmark	Leaves	58 - 216[g]	1.72[g]
	Rhizomes	99 - 217[g]	0.45[g]
Denmark	Leaves	272 - 960[h]	
France	Leaves	92 - 260[i]	1.06[i]
	Roots	50[e]	
	Rhizomes	49 - 244[i]	0.5[i]
North Carolina	Leaves	36 - 122[j]	0.59 - 1.23
North Carolina	Leaves	12 - 106[k]	0.9 - 1.04[k]
	Roots and rhizomes	45 - 285[k]	0.15 - 0.28[k]
North Carolina	Leaves	1 - 200[l]	
Virginia	Leaves	8 - 212[m]	
Virginia	Leaves	9 - 412[n]	
	Roots and rhizomes	6 - 206[n]	0.96[o]
	Total plant		
Long Island, New York	Rhizomes	360 - 960[p]	
Oyster Bay, New York	Leaves	134 - 2040[q]	
Rhode Island	Leaves	10 - 175[r]	
	Roots and rhizomes	5 - 50[r]	
Rhode Island	Leaves	10 - 436[s]	
	Roots and rhizomes	5 - 475[s]	
Great Bay, New Hampshire	Leaves	50 - 1000[t]	

a. Zieman and Wetzel (1980)
b. McRoy (1970)
c. Phillips (1974b)
d. Keller (1963)
e. Mukai et al. (1979)
   Aioi et al. (1981)
f. Aioi (1980)
g. Sand-Jensen (1975)
h. Petersen (1918)
i. Jacobs (1979)
j. Penhale (1977)
k. Kenworthy (unpublished)
l. Thayer et al. (1975a)
m. Marsh (1973)
n. Orth and Moore (1982a)
o. Wetzel (1982)
p. Riner (1976)
q. Burkholder and Doheny (1968)
r. Thorne-Miller et al. (1983)
s. Short (1975)
t. Riggs and Fralick (1975)

biomass is lost rapidly. It is replaced slowly as asexual reproduction declines, as parts of the plant die, and as the higher respiration rates reduce net production.

Despite the variation, there appears to be greater biomass in the center and northern range of eelgrass distribution. Throughout most of its range, leaf biomass exhibits an annual unimodal cycle, with a peak in mid- to late summer and a minimum in mid-winter. At the southern limit, leaf biomass appears to be bimodal (Kenworthy 1981; Orth and Moore 1982; Penhale and Wetzel 1983), with a first and maximal peak between March and early June in North Carolina, and between April and June in Virginia. This maximum is followed by a sharp decline between July and September, followed by a fall regrowth period.

Roots and rhizomes also exhibit seasonal fluctuations in biomass (Figure 21) (Sand-Jensen 1975; Jacobs 1979; Kenworthy 1981; Orth and Moore 1982a; Kentula 1983; Thorne-Miller et al. 1983; Robertson and Mann 1984; Kenworthy and Thayer manuscript in prep.). Rooting depth analyses show that more than 90% of the belowground biomass is located in the upper 10 cm of the sediment (Wetzel 1982). The turnover rate of root and rhizome biomass is much slower than that of leaves, and since so much organic matter is concentrated in the upper few centimeters of vegetated sediments, the rhizosphere of these plants has a measurable influence on the physical, chemical, and biological characteristics of the sediment.

An additional feature of plant abundance at the southern limit of its range is the co-occurrence of eelgrass with two other species, H. wrightii and R. maritima. In mixed beds the other species contribute a substantial portion to the

Table 5. Maximum and minimum values for shoot and root-rhizome standing crop for all sites (months in parentheses are when the value was recorded). Some sites were not sampled for the entire year. (Data from Orth and Moore 1982a.)

Sites	Shoot standing crop (g/m²)		Root-rhizome standing crop (g/m²)	
	Max.	Min.	Max.	Min.
Browns Bay				
1978		23(Oct)		6(Oct)
1979	161(July)	9(Sep) 11(Mar)	155(July)	15(Sep) 8(Mar)
1980	173(June)	48(Mar)	206(June)	48(Mar)
Guinea Marsh Offshore				
1978	158(Aug)	57(Oct)	105(June)	10(Oct)
1979	336(June)	70(Nov) 34(Mar)	130(June,July)	42(Nov) 10(Mar)
1980	397(July)	33(Mar)	155(June)	88(Feb)
Guinea Marsh Inshore				
1979	291(June)	9(Oct)	61(June)	3(Nov)
1980	412(July)	2(Jan)	121(July)	1(Jan)
Vaucluse Shores Zostera				
1978		28 (Sep)		12(Dec)
1979	161(July)	12(Mar)	130(Dec)	61(Sep) 6(Mar)
1980	230(July)	54(Mar)	121(Apr)	103(Feb)
Vaucluse Shores Mixed				
1979	131(July)	37(May)	112(July)	20(May)
1980	161(July)	52(Jan)	130(Feb)	52(Jan)

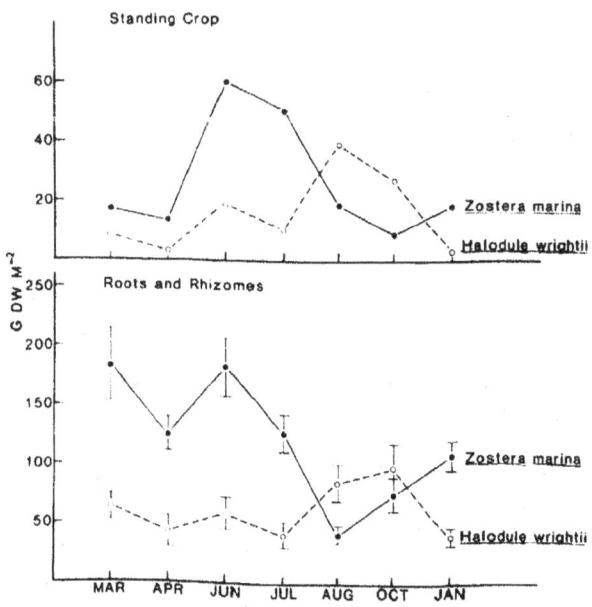

Figure 21. Seasonal cycle of leaf standing crop and root plus rhizome biomass in mixed beds of Zostera marina and Halodule wrightii near Beaufort, North Carolina. Bars in the root and rhizome graph indicate ± one standard error. (From Kenworthy and Thayer manuscript in prep.)

35

total plant biomass. Eelgrass and shoalgrass in mixed beds near Beaufort, North Carolina (Kenworthy 1981) (Figure 21), each reach a maximum biomass at different times of the year. Each species grows best during a time of year when water temperatures correspond to the ranges typical of the center of each species' distribution (Chapter 1): eelgrass grows best in spring and fall while Halodule grows best in summer. Where the plants occur in mixed beds there is much less overall seasonal variation in abundance, since they replace one another during a typical seasonal cycle.

There are extensive subtidal beds of eelgrass and widgeon grass in lower Chesapeake Bay, Virginia, which exhibit a seasonal pattern of biomass that is similar to the mixed eelgrass-shoalgrass meadows in North Carolina. Widgeon grass replaces eelgrass in early summer and appears to be more tolerant of a combination of relatively higher light intensity and high temperature. Ruppia thrives in the upper subtidal and lower intertidal beds, while eelgrass dominates the lower subtidal (Orth and Moore 1982a; Wetzel and Penhale 1983).

Macroalgae are a frequent component of the plant biomass in eelgrass meadows (Conover 1964; Thorne-Miller et al. 1983). Throne-Miller et al. (1983) reported that algal biomass made up 13% to 46% of the total submerged macrophyte biomass in Rhode Island coastal lagoons. McRoy (1970) estimated that 14% of the total plant biomass in Izembek Lagoon, Alaska, could be attributed to macroalgae. Dillon (1971) estimated that macroalgae constituted 10% of the total plant biomass in a North Carolina estuary.

In the Rhode Island lagoons the macroalgae were usually unattached and entangled among the rooted seagrasses. The algae were dominated by species of chlorophyta and rhodophyta and reached a maximum biomass of 1,200 and 835 g dry wt m^{-2}, respectively, in the densest mats (Thorne-Miller et al. 1983).

Epiphytes growing on the surfaces of the leaves, which include both micro- and macroalgae, reportedly constitute about 25% of the leaf biomass (Penhale 1977;

Kentula 1983). Because the epiphytes require the leaf surfaces for attachment the seasonal and annual biomass of epiphytes corresponds closely to the cycle of leaf biomass.

2.6 PRODUCTION

Seagrasses produce large quantities of organic matter (McRoy and McMillan 1977; Zieman and Wetzel 1980), and estimates of daily production for eelgrass meadows rank them among the most productive of marine plant ecosystems. Very high estimates of daily net leaf production are reported for Alaskan meadows (Table 4). In general the estimates of leaf net production for beds along the Atlantic coast of the United States and for Europe are on the order of 300-500 g C $m^{-2}yr^{-1}$. The values have a striking consistency even though they were derived by independent investigators using at least three different techniques. Values for net leaf production range between 0.3 and 1.8 g C m^{-2} d^{-1}, and average about 1 g C m^{-2} d^{-1}, which would yield an average annual leaf production of 300-400 g C m^{-2} yr^{-1}. Short-term productivities under optimum conditions may exceed these estimates. For example, Dennison and Alberte (1982) reported a range of 0.8-2.0 g C m^{-2} d^{-1} for shallow and deep water eelgrass during August near Woods Hole, Massachusetts, that coincide with a water temperature which probably is near optimum for eelgrass production at the latitude of Woods Hole.

Recently, investigators have simultaneously estimated the leaf and below-ground production of eelgrass in situ using a leaf-marking technique, dimensional analysis and estimates of the time interval between the emergence of two successive leaves on a shoot[1] (Sand-Jensen 1975; Jacobs 1979; Kenworthy 1981; Kentula 1983; Robertson and Mann 1984; D.G. Patriquin, Dalhousie Univ., Halifax, Nova Scotia; pers. comm.). Estimates of average daily root and rhizome production range from 0.15 and 0.5 g C m^{-2} d^{-1} and

[1]The time interval between the emergence of two successive leaves is referred to as the plastochrone interval (PI) (Tomlinson 1974; Patriquin 1973; Jacobs 1979).

36

yield approximately 50-182 g C m^{-2} yr^{-1}. Rhizomes account for most of the belowground production (Kenworthy 1981; Kenworthy and Thayer, in press). As is the case with leaves, under optimum conditions root and rhizome production can be quite high. During a study in April and May, Kentula (1983) estimated daily belowground production of 1.5 g C m^{-2}d^{-1}. The belowground production was nearly equivalent to leaf production during the same time period. On an annual basis, however, belowground production is between 15% and 43% of aboveground leaf production (Robertson and Mann 1984).

Primary production corresponds to the annual cycle of seasonal insolation and, to a lesser degree, temperature (Sand-Jensen 1975; Jacobs 1979; Thorne-Miller et al. 1983) (Figure 18). However, temperature becomes more influential at the extreme ends of the plant's geographic range. For example, leaf emergence rates in a semi-enclosed embayment near Beaufort, North Carolina, increased during severe heat stress in July and August (Figure 22). Throughout the remainder of the year, plastochrone intervals are similar in both habitats. Most notable is that on the open water

shoal, where water temperatures remain at least 3°-5°C cooler, the PI is unaffected in July and August. Net production estimates correspond closely with the intervals (Kenworthy, unpublished). For example, during July, August, and September, daily net leaf production at the shoal station was 0.452 g C m^{-2}d^{-1}, but in the embayment production declined to 0.074 g C m^{-2} d^{-1}. In northern latitudes leaf emergence ranged between 14 and 19.3 days (Sand-Jensen 1975; Jacobs 1979) but were fastest in May (PI=13) and declined to a minimum in December (PI=28), corresponding to the seasonal minimums and maximums of insolation and temperature of these latitudes (Jacobs 1979). A similar seasonal pattern has reported for Netarts Bay, Oregon (Kentula 1983). These PI values also corresponded to maximum and minimum seasonal production rates by the eelgrass (Jacobs 1979). The PI may be useful as a relative index of production and perhaps even as an indicator of stress in eelgrass communities. The PI is a promising method but must be used cautiously until we understand the environmental parameters controlling it.

Production by epiphytic algae and bacteria attached to the surface of the leaves has also been estimated. Penhale (1977) reported that epiphytic assemblages on eelgrass leaves produced an average of 0.2 g C m^{-2} d^{-1}. A much larger production, 0.3 - 4.9 g C m^{-2} d^{-1} was reported for Netarts Bay, Oregon (Kentula 1983). Since epiphytic biomass coincides with eelgrass leaf biomass, maximum epiphyte production occurs when leaf biomass reaches its peak biomass and not necessarily during peak leaf production.

Epiphytic bacterial production is tightly coupled to eelgrass production. Kirchman et al. (1984) demonstrated that bacteria obtain carbon directly from dissolved organic carbon leached from the actively photosynthesizing leaves. Bacterial doubling times were estimated to 8 days. The bacteria utilized virtually all the DOC released by the plants and exhibited a maximum production of 0.4 μg C hr^{-1} cm^{-2} of leaf surface. The maximum biomass and productivity occurred at the senescing tips of the leaves.

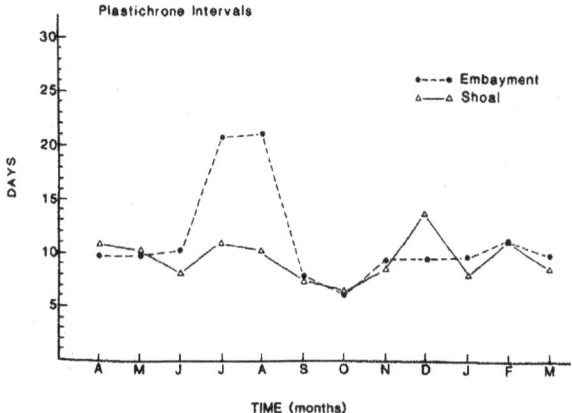

Figure 22. Monthly estimates of the plastochrone interval for eelgrass grown in an embayment and in an open-water shoal near Beaufort, North Carolina.

CHAPTER 3
THE EELGRASS MEADOW

Individual species of seagrasses, as well as communities of several species, form recognizable biological and physical entities which frequently are termed meadows. In common with many terrestrial systems, the seagrass meadow is defined by a visible boundary grading from unvegetated to vegetated substrate. Meadows vary in size from small isolated patches of plants less than a meter in diameter to a continuous distribution of grass many square kilometers in area (Figure 23). Within the meadows the plants may display a large variation in density.

Community development in marine systems, as opposed to development in terrestrial systems, must deal with a fluid medium approximately 60 times more viscous than air (Vogel 1981). The relative force per unit change in velocity of seawater, compared to that of air, has a much greater potential for drastically restructuring the community. One of the few plant genera that can exist under these conditions are the seagrasses, which can colonize extensive subtidal acreage across their range. Local distributions are controlled largely by geomorphology of the local basins, ambient light, and hydrodynamic conditions. The processes of eelgrass ecosystem development appear to be driven to a point where an equilibrium is reached between the structure of the meadow and dynamics of local current flow.

The meadow has multidimensional structure (Figure 24). The leaves extend upward into the water column, and since there are many age classes of leaves and shoots occurring together, the canopy is multilayered. The leaves are flat, strap-like appendages, while the lower part of the shoot is cylindrical. Currents and waves reshape the canopy with every change of the tide or passage of a wave. Small macrophytes attached to the shoots modify the overall appearance and physical characteristics of the leaves.

 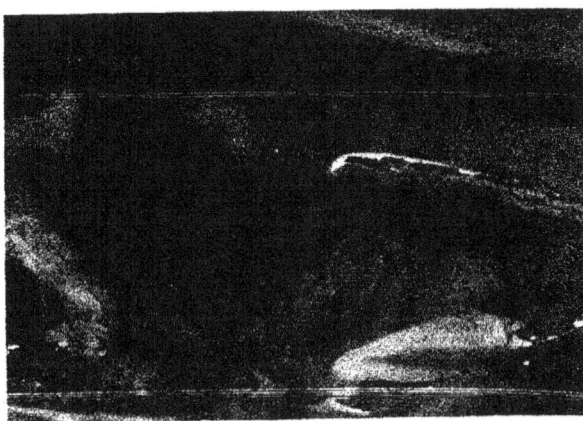

Figure 23. Aerial photographs illustrating various sizes and forms of eelgrass meadows typically found along the Atlantic coast of the United States.

38

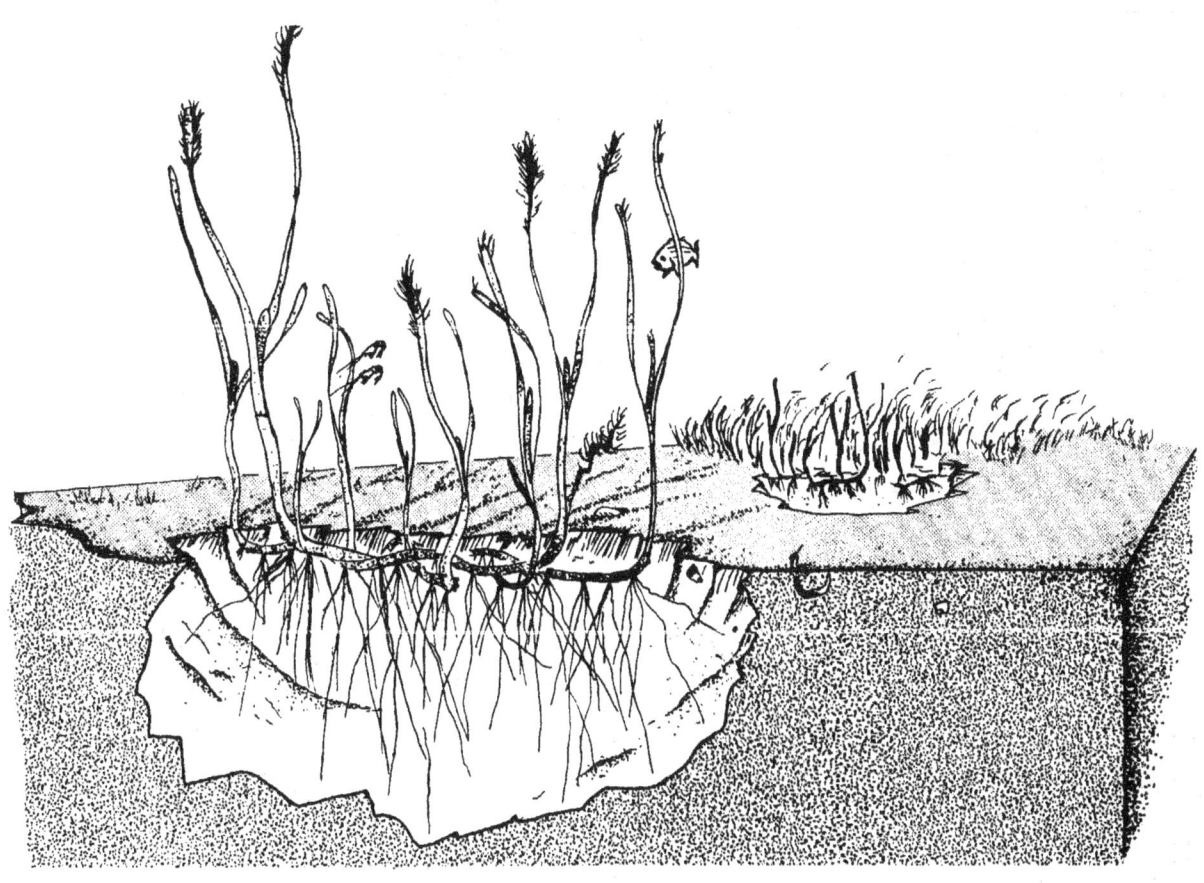

Figure 24. Three-dimensional illustration of an eelgrass meadow.

The meadow can appear as a dense, tangled web of leaves and epiphytes or a very organized assemblage of neatly spaced shoots. The variants between these two extremes of meadow form are enormous.

The dense, interwoven roots and rhizomes penetrating the substrate add a dimension to the meadow achieved by no other submergent marine plant (Figure 25). They form a mat of organic matter that secures the plant, stabilizes the bottom, and provides a unique and protected habitat for numerous organisms.

In this chapter we address the many aspects of structure, form, and processes that characterize an eelgrass meadow. To this end we will present and describe a conceptual model of the processes associated with its development and maintenance.

3.1 MEADOW SIZE AND FORM

Petersen (1918) was probably first to describe the role of eelgrass in stabilizing subtidal and intertidal habitats, and Wilson (1949) showed that loss of eelgrass through the "wasting disease" significantly affected shoreline slope and sediment composition. Ginsberg and Lowenstam (1958) incorporated tropical seagrasses into the concept of biotic modification of sedimentary processes, while other investigators (Molinier and Picard 1952; Swinchatt 1965; Scoffin 1970; Zieman 1972; Orth 1977; Christiansen et al. 1981; Fonseca et al. 1982b; Fonseca et al. 1983) described how temperate and tropical seagrasses, by reducing current flow, modified sediments and the growth pattern of the meadow itself. Kenworthy et al. (1982) described the seagrass-sediment interaction whereby the

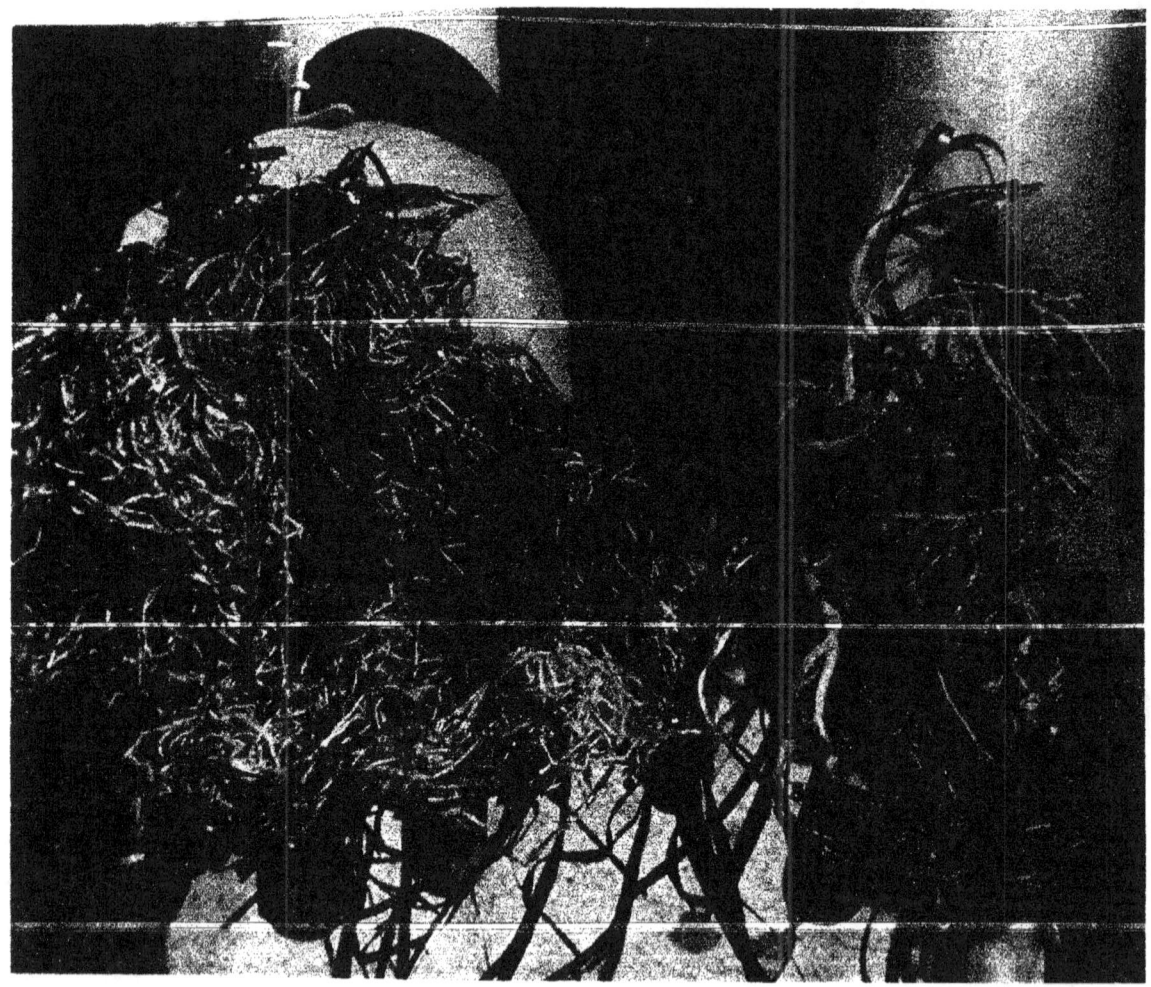

Figure 25. The root and rhizome mat of <u>Zostera marina</u> collected from open-water shoal environment (left) and a quiescent embayment (right) near Beaufort, North Carolina.

presence of eelgrass leads to a nutrient enrichment of the sediment. Patriquin (1975) described the dynamics of meadow erosion from wind-driven circulation which cause erosional scarps to migrate through tropical seagrass meadows (see parallel discussion for dune development by Harms 1969), whereas Wood et al. (1969) conceptually integrated the functional role of current velocity in affecting and sometimes controlling other biological, physical, and chemical processes. Water motion structures the shape and form of eelgrass meadows (and all other seagrass systems) through three physical phenomena: (1) tidal currents, (2) wind-generated waves, and (3) simultaneous interaction of currents and waves. These generally overlooked phenomena will be reviewed in order to understand how hydrodynamic regimes influence the structure and function of eelgrass meadows.

Current Flow

As tides move water over the estuarine floor, the velocity at any height above the bottom is influenced by the shape or roughness of the local benthic structures. Since an eelgrass meadow has a relatively uniform roughness in and of itself, it is difficult to assess its influence on current flow independently from the influence of the unconsolidated substrate, such as sand or mud which erodes and accretes in response to currents.

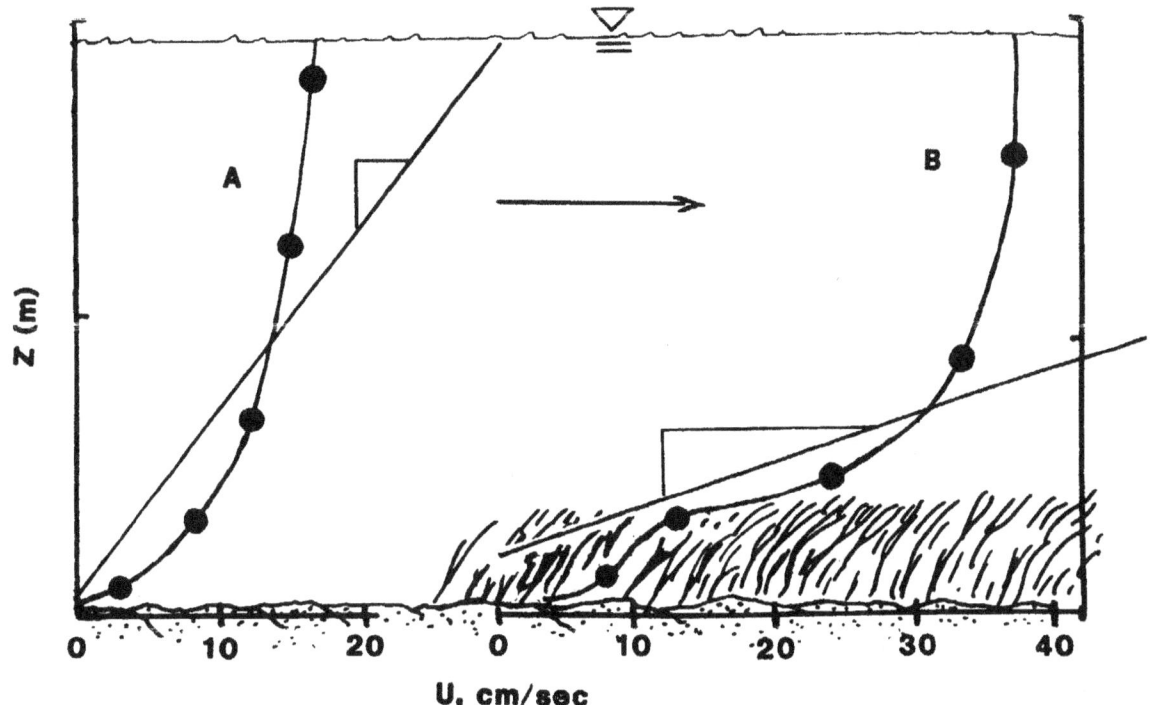

Figure 26. Velocity profiles are shown before (A) and after (B) entering an eelgrass meadow. Lines with dots, showing hypothetical velocity measurement locations above the bottom, represent the expected velocity (U, in cm/sec) versus depth (Z, in m). Straight lines are semi-log (ln) plots of those same profiles. Triangles on these lines represent slope and depict changes caused by the meadow. Arrow shows direction of flow.

One can describe the mechanics of current flow through a seagrass meadow by examining the vertical distribution of velocity (a velocity profile) above the bottom as water passes. Partly because the estuarine floor is rough and movable, the velocity profile is not constant. Velocity measurements at any height above the bottom should be averaged over a time substantially greater than the characteristic period of fluctuation. In turbulent conditions (which characterize flow through eelgrass meadows) the velocity profile is logarithmic (Figure 26a).

If we follow the flow of water into a meadow (Figure 26b), the eelgrass canopy functions to increase velocity over it and reduce velocity within it; momentum is conserved and some small amount of energy from the flow is probably lost as frictional heat to the grass itself. As a result of the current being slowed near the bottom and the presence of the

root-rhizome system, the sediment resists moving. The degree of stabilization that the canopy provides is indirectly measurable by transforming the logarithmic velocity profile into a semi-log plot (Figure 26a) yielding a straight line. The slope of the log-transformed profile (the straight line) is proportional to the shear velocity (U^*) which is a measure of the change in velocity per change in depth ($\frac{dU}{dz}$). In Figure 26a the intersection of this line with the ordinate roughly indicates the time-averaged location of the roughness height, i.e., the height above the bottom where velocity theoretically goes to zero. As this layer increases in thickness, the existing sediment surface is increasingly protected from erosion and suspended particles have a greater chance of being deposited.

The major mechanism accounting for this roughness height increase is the bending of the eelgrass canopy into a compact layer as current velocity

41

Figure 27. The effect of 0 (bottom) and 30 cm/sec (top) current flow on the canopy configuration of a natural eelgrass meadow transplanted into a flume.

increases (Fonseca et al. 1982b) (Figure 27). By deflecting flow over it, the canopy shields the bottom from the erosive forces of the current. For a more technical and analytical discussion of fluid flow, see Vogel (1981).

Waves

The other mechanically significant phenomenon affecting all seagrass meadows are water waves. For our purposes, waves can be classified as wind generated or vessel generated (boat traffic), the latter dominating in some sheltered areas. Of particular interest are waves of length, L (L = distance from crest to crest or trough to trough) that occur in water at a depth, d, such that the ratio d/L is less than one-half. These are termed shallow or transitional water waves. The significance of shallow-water waves is that more water movement is applied to the sediment (or eelgrass) surface. Waves with a d/L ratio > 1/2 do not transfer the movement as effectively (Figure 28). Specifically, as a trough passes and a crest approaches, a lift force is generated (Figure 28) that acts to suspend sediment into the water column when the ratio of force to particle size is sufficiently large. As waves pass through an eelgrass meadow, the eelgrass shoots wave in general synchrony with the passing crests and troughs. Some resistance of the shoots to flexing and inhibition of the forward velocity component of the wave by the relatively rough meadow combine to reduce the wave's kinetic energy and thus dampen it.

Seagrasses are as effective as emergent marsh plants in damping out waves if certain criteria are met. The most important criterion is that the grass canopy extend to the standing water surface (Figure 28). Under these conditions, both seagrasses and marsh plants effectively dampen out waves to 0 wave energy at approximately one meter into the meadow (Figure 29) (Wayne 1975; Knutson et al. 1982; Fonseca unpubl. data).

Unlike marsh plants such as _Spartina alterniflora_, eelgrass often grows at depths where the shoots reach up to occupy only a few percent of the water column. These deeper meadows, usually being sparser than their shallow water counterparts, have a varying but generally reduced effect on wave propagation. Eelgrass is relatively more pliant than _Spartina_, but an eelgrass meadow presents much more surface area to a wave per unit of canopy height. Eelgrass thus resists wave surge (and current flow) by being pliant and growing in a mutually sheltering structure, the meadow. A more detailed explanation of these phenomena are given in Wayne (1975).

Currents and Waves Together by Denice Y. Heller, University of Virginia

Waves and currents can occur together under infinite combinations of direction and magnitude. We shall only consider waves and currents moving in the same direction because this combination has the greatest potential for moving sediment and structuring eelgrass meadows. The interaction of waves and currents provides a unique physical condition due to differences in the boundary shear stresses they produce. A wave possessing near-bottom orbital velocities of a magnitude comparable to the velocity of the current flow will produce stresses on the sediment much larger than those of the current, due to its comparatively small boundary layer and large velocity gradient within that layer. Unfortunately, the results of the interaction cannot be described by combining the effects of each motion taken independently as shown in Figures 26 and 28. Instead, a nonlinear interaction between velocity and depth occurs, especially in the presence of the eelgrass canopy. The large shear stresses associated with the wave motion generate significant turbulence at the bed (Grant and Madsen 1979) and may even induce a net reduction of tidal current velocity.

The interaction of waves and currents enhance the opportunity for sediment

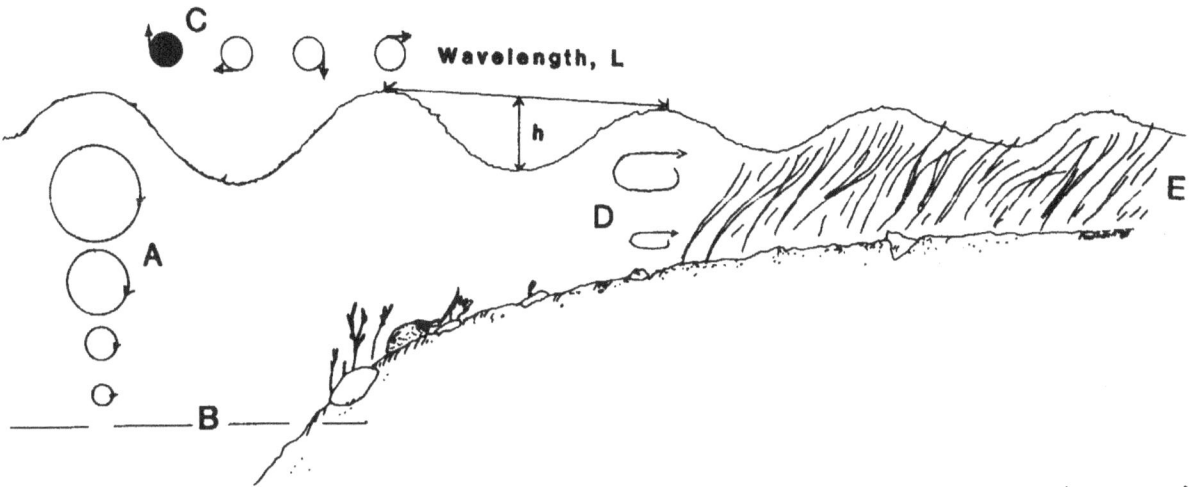

Figure 28. The damping of waves by the eelgrass canopy: (A) closed circles (orbitals) depict movement of water in the deepwater situation, (B) depth below which waves of this size do not transfer momentum, (C) velocity components corresponding to the portion of the wave train they are drawn over (the darkened circle indicates the area of lift force on the front of a wave as described in the text), (D) open orbitals depict net forward movement of water particles in the shallow area, (E) eelgrass meadow.

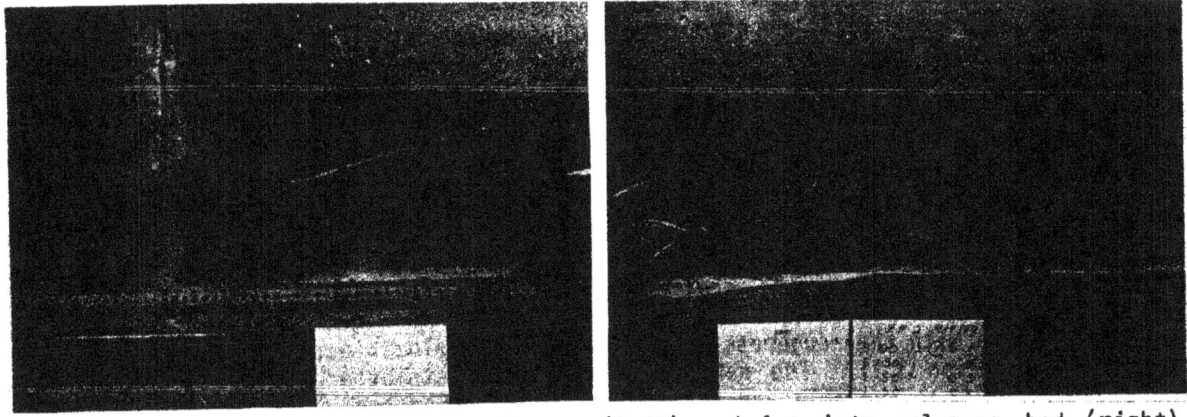

Figure 29. Wave before entering eelgrass (left) and 1 m into eelgrass bed (right).

transport in and around the meadow beyond that of either phenomenon considered separately. According to a model by Bagnold (1963), stress exerted by the wave motion is capable of suspending sediment, but is unable to transport it due to the closed orbitals. With the work of suspension done, the presence of even a weak current will cause a net transport of sediment in the direction of the current. This should prove true even within the eelgrass canopy. The frequent interaction of waves and currents makes the material flux in and out of eelgrass meadows a difficult phenomenon to predict.

3.2 SEDIMENTATION DYNAMICS

Many papers that have discussed the role of seagrass in slowing currents and promoting sedimentation (Wood et al. 1969; Marshall and Lukas 1970; Orth 1977; Kenworthy et al. 1982) clearly demonstrate the transition of sediment characteristics across the boundary of seagrass meadows. Sediments become better sorted (i.e., more equally represented across particle size classes) and are infused with more organic material the farther one travels into the meadow.

If one considers the important variables that determine the hydrodynamic setting of a meadow, it is obvious that not all eelgrass meadows have the same pattern of sedimentation dynamics. Important variables include water depth (affecting the d/L ratio), fetch, and proximity to inlets and channels (hence sediment source, tidal range, and current speed). Intuitively, an eelgrass meadow in shallow, open water will receive much more hydraulic scour over time than one in a sheltered cove. Fonseca et al. (1982b, 1983) have shown how currents are reduced and how the location of the meadow in the estuary results in diverse sedimentation patterns.

Sediment composition at any location in the estuary depends on the sediment sources and the interaction of the hydraulic regime with the roughness of the bottom (see Section 3.1). The nature of the sediment is more variable and depends to a large degree on whether the sources are organic or inorganic. Throughout the range of eelgrass on the east coast, the inorganic fraction is largely silicious. Particle sizes in the glaciated northern ranges often are large and meadows growing among cobble-sized sediments on the open coast are not uncommon. In protected areas, sediments may often be as high as 40% silt and clay (< 63 μ minimum diameter). Organic material in the meadow has more varied sources. Settlement of allocthonous material such as terrestrial leaves, marsh plants, drift algae, fauna, and detritus in eelgrass meadows is largely unquantified, but the mechanical potential of trapping senescent material is clear.

Autochthonous organic material has an even greater potential for retention in the meadow. Some specific organic inputs are dehiscing epiphytes, together or apart from the host eelgrass leaf, and senescent indigenous fauna and their fecal material. Each source varies in its response to waves and currents and thus, its distribution in the meadow is a function of its specific gravity, size, and shape. Sand-size grains, with a rounded shape and a specific gravity of 2.65 g/cc, are much more resistant to movement than fecal pellets of similar dimension and half the specific gravity (Fisher et al. 1979). Leaf particles with irregular shapes also appear to be particularly erodable (Fisher et al. 1979).

The senescence of roots and rhizomes, along with burrowing and tube-dwelling fauna, enrich the sediment with organic matter. Many of these sources are already incorporated in the sediment and are only indirectly affected by the ambient hydraulic regime.

Using the definition of current regime by Fonseca et al. (1983) (low current regime ≤ 50 cm/sec, medium > 50 to < 90 cm/sec, high > 90 cm/sec, maximum monthly surface velocity), let us examine sedimentary development under the extreme cases. The distribution of organic material predictably increases in meadows experiencing low, rather than high, current velocities; silt-clay was fairly evenly distributed in those low current meadows (Fonseca et al. 1983). Much of the organic input to the surface sediment is derived from seagrass leaves and from allochthonous material trapped by the seagrass canopy (Thayer et al. 1975b; Zieman 1975). In high current areas, especially those where tide changes produce strong flushing in opposite directions, leaves are redistributed or exported.

Silt and clay-sized particles generally have no predictable pattern of distribution within the low current meadows other than becoming more concentrated within the meadow. As the tide rises and the canopy becomes less effective in reducing current velocity, sediment settling at the meadow edge is lessened, and silt and clay-size particles appear to settle more evenly over the whole meadow. In high current areas the distribution of silt-clay particles is more closely correlated with the seagrass canopy and inversely related to U_* max.

In low current areas, distance into the meadow (X) and leaf area index (LAI) are positively correlated with surface organic matter concentration due to the effect both parameters have on reduction and maintenance of a reduced current velocity within the meadow. The deeper into the meadow, the less chance the organic material will be scoured away and the greater the potential for accumulation of autochthonous leaf material and allochthonous detrital material in the surface sediment.

There is an important distinction between eelgrass meadows which exist in different current regimes. All do not have the same functional roles in the nearshore ecosystem. High current areas are sources and low current areas are sinks for seagrass-derived detrital material. The influence of the canopy also changes through the year. As seasonal reductions in leaf area index occur, the canopy provides less protection of the sediment and seasonal erosion may thus occur. Further, the physical presence of the eelgrass canopy mediates sedimentary development and thus ambient elemental cycles.

3.3 ELEMENTAL CYCLES IN EELGRASS MEADOWS

Since eelgrass meadows are productive, reach large biomass, and are relatively long-lived components of coastal ecosystems, their role in the cycling of essential nutrients is important.

Our conceptual model of elemental cycling in an eelgrass meadow (Figure 30) has three essential attributes: (1) the functional components, particulate organic matter (POM), dissolved organic matter (DOM), and inorganic material, (2) the mechanisms for inputs and outputs of the components, and (3) the processes responsible for transforming components within and between the three principal reservoirs: water column, sediments, and biota. The chemical cycles come about through interactions between the supply of nutrients, the metabolism of plants, and heterotrophic utilization of organic and inorganic matter. The physicochemical properties of nutrient reservoirs and the ability of eelgrass to absorb elements from, as well as release them to, either the water column or the sediments, establishes a very complicated biogeochemical cycle.

Functional Components and Sources

Organic matter in both dissolved and particulate form is the principal source of all nutrient elements as well as the primary source of energy for heterotrophic consumers involved in the majority of transformations occurring within a seagrass meadow. POM is derived from primary and secondary production originating either outside the meadow (allochthonous) or within the meadow (autochthonous). Examples of allochthonous sources include larger animals, such as fish or invertebrates that move in and out of the meadow, animal feces, plankton, macroalgae, and dead organic matter (organic detritus) that are

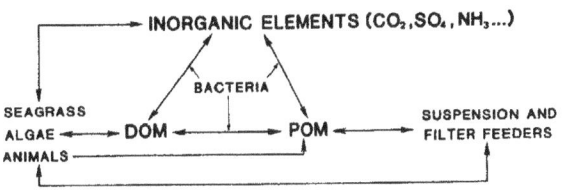

Figure 30. Simplified conceptual diagram of the cycling of elements in an eelgrass meadow. (See text for discussion.)

45

transported into the meadow either by tides or wind-driven currents. The principal autochthonous sources are the primary production of macrophytes, their associated epiphytes, phytoplankton, and the secondary production of the resident heterotrophs. A detailed description of components and of the biological interactions between and among the functional groups of animals is found in Chapter 4.

Although organic matter is derived from several sources, the seagrasses are principal components in all aspects of cycling. Where they exist, seagrass production may nearly exceed the primary production of all other autotrophs together (Thayer et al. 1975a). Eelgrass alone constitutes a very large, seasonally-recurring pool of nutrients, and the canopy reduces water motion, damps wave energy, and, together with the roots and rhizomes, stabilizes the sediment, directing the inputs and to some degree controlling the output of materials.

Numerous sources make dissolved organics a large pool of organic material in the water column reservoir and the quantity of DOM often exceeds POM in coastal marine water by a factor of 2 to 100 (Parsons 1963; Sharp 1973). By-products of plant and animal metabolism and the decay of dead organic matter are some of the major sources of DOM. Both phytoplankton and macrophytes, including eelgrass, release DOM while living (Penhale and Smith 1977; Wood and Hayasaka 1981), and release it in especially large quantities during senescence and decay of the organic detritus (Godshalk and Wetzel 1978b). As much as 30% or more of the biological production in marine systems may be channeled through the DOM pool (Fenchel and Blackburn 1979).

The chemical composition of the DOM includes a spectrum of organic compounds ranging from very small or simple molecules, such as sugars and amino acids, to complex and refractory compounds, such as humic acids (Khailov and Finenko 1970). Dissolved organic matter leached from seagrasses is a substrate for bacterial growth (Robertson et al. 1982; Kenworthy and Thayer, in press), and is utilized almost exclusively by microorganisms and possibly to a minor degree by specially

adapted invertebrates and some unicellular eukaryotes (Fenchel and Blackburn 1979).

External sources of inorganic elements are ubiquitous. Inputs occur as dissolved ions or particulate matter transported by water flow, matter deposited directly onto the water surface from the atmosphere, or, in the case of gaseous forms, diffusion between reservoirs. Where there is sufficient turbulence, inorganic materials are continually deposited and resuspended and readily transported between the sediment and water column.

Biological activity within each reservoir is responsible for the majority of transformations of organic and inorganic matter. The rates of these transformations fluctuate in response to changing temperatures and the qualitative properties of the components. During mineralization processes, mediated principally by microorganisms and involving the solubilization of organic matter and the release of dissolved inorganic ions (e.g. NH_4, CO_2, SO_4, NO_3), elements may be temporarily retained within the microorganisms or immobilized for an extended period of time within the longer-lived biota and dead organic matter. Inorganic elements in gaseous forms are continually being consumed and produced by the biotic reservoir.

Since each of the three major reservoirs has substantially different physical and chemical properties, the reactants, products, and pools in the elemental cycles are distinguishable between the reservoirs. To facilitate our discussion, we will address the nutrient cycles within each reservoir and, where appropriate, their interactions between reservoirs.

Sediment-Nutrient Cycle

Seagrass meadows are depositional environments, except where fluid energy is high. Organic matter and fine-textured sediments tend to be retained where they were produced or deposited. Consequently, the quantity of total organic matter in meadow sediments normally is larger than in unvegetated substrates (Figure 31) (Marshall and Lukas 1970; Wood et al.

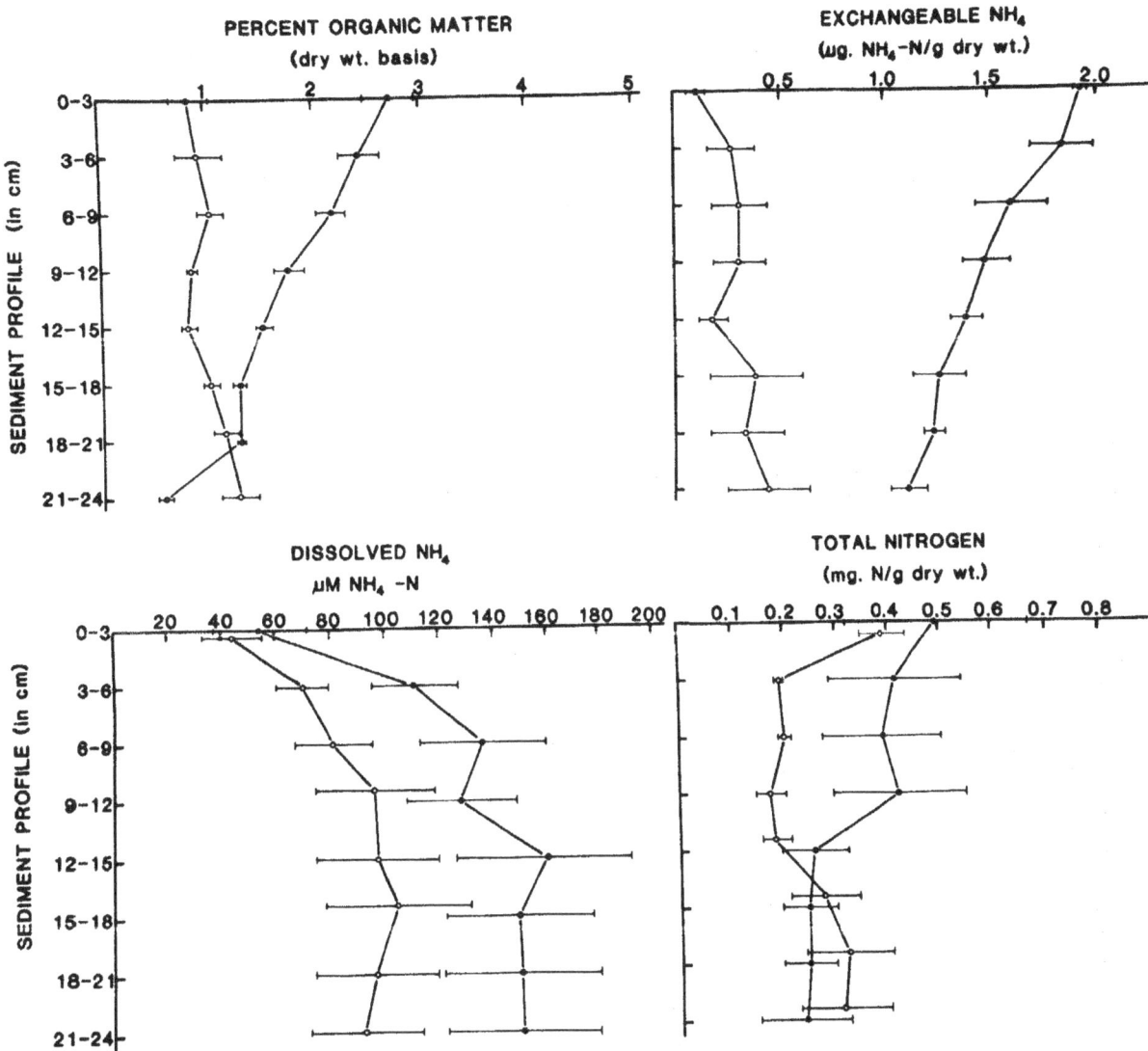

Figure 31. Sediment profiles for organic matter and three nitrogen cycle intermediates in vegetated (●——●) and unvegetated (O——O) sediments. (From Kenworthy et al. 1982.)

1969; Thayer et al. 1975a; Orth 1977; Kenworthy et al. 1982; Fonseca et al. 1983).

Production and deposition of large quantities of organic matter and fine-grained sediments accompanied by high rates of metabolism and insufficient supplies of oxygen cause vegetated sediments to be anoxic. Except for a few millimeters at the flocculent sediment-water interface and in oxidized microzones, anaerobic processes dominate the chemistry of eelgrass bed sediments (Klug 1980). Typically, redox profiles in

sediment cores taken in eelgrass meadows show an abrupt transition from oxidizing to reducing conditions beneath the flocculent sediment-water interface (Figure 32) (Kenworthy 1981).

Anaerobic metabolism involves tightly coupled interactions between a heterogeneous group of facultative and obligatory anaerobic microorganisms capable of converting complex organic macromolecules (e.g., proteins, lipids, and carbohydrates) to soluble, low molecular weight fermentation products (e.g., volatile fatty acids, alcohols,

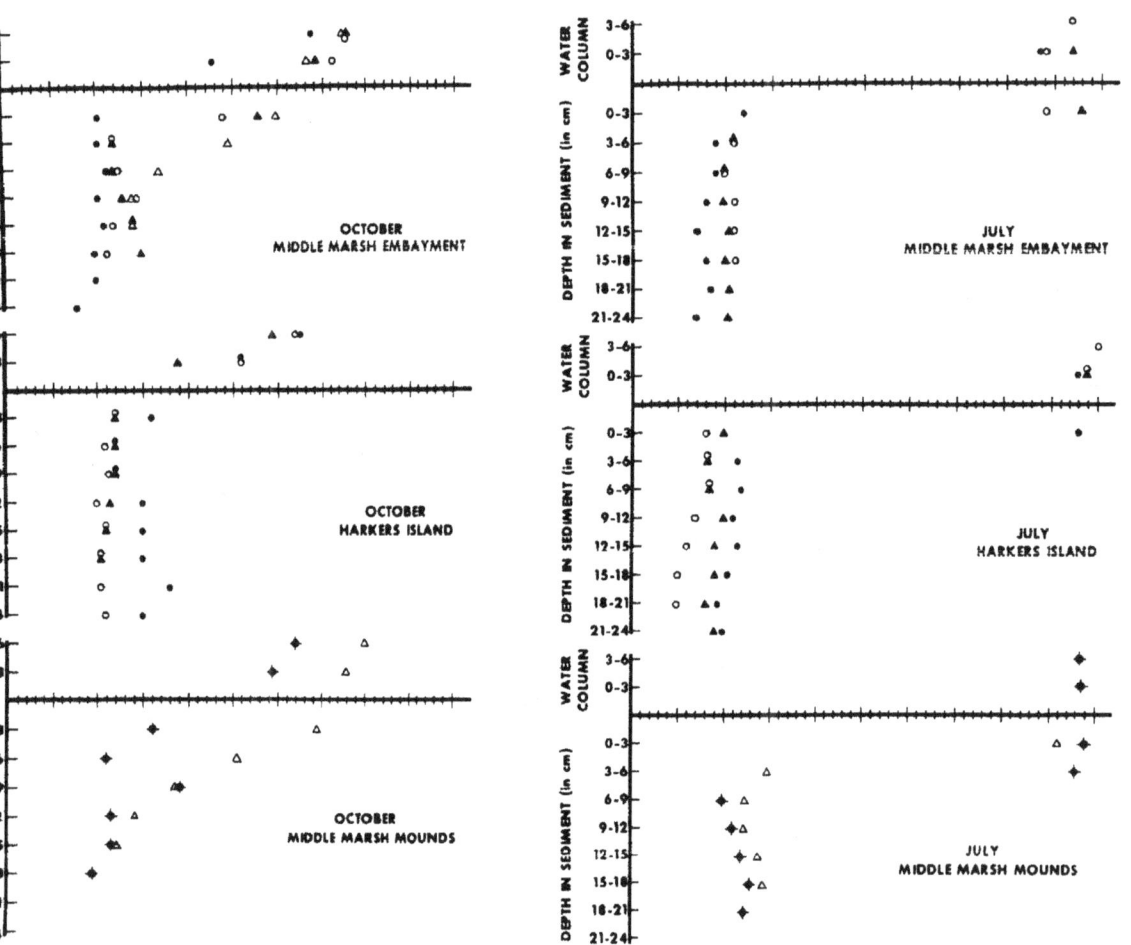

Figure 32. Estimates for Eh in several sediment profiles and in the water column vegetated with eelgrass. (Redrawn from Kenworthy 1981.)

H_2S, CO_2, H_2), which serve as substrates for other microorganisms. The latter group of organisms, specialized by their ability to use sulfate, nitrate, and carbon dioxide as terminal electron acceptors, are able to metabolize these fermentation products and function in the absence of molecular oxygen.

More specifically, complex organic molecules are metabolized principally by sulfate reducers (Figure 33) (Fenchel and Riedl 1970; Jorgensen and Fenchel 1974; Klug 1980). In a model laboratory system where eelgrass leaves were the sole carbon source, Jorgensen and Fenchel (1974) demonstrated that more than 50% of the

carbon was oxidized by sulfate reducers. They demonstrated that a constant input of organic matter was required to insure that reoxidation was prevented. Because sulfate is so abundant in seawater and in situ organic matter inputs to eelgrass beds are quite large, it appears that this particular model system is an accurate representation of organic matter cycling eelgrass bed sediments.

Classically, carbon turnover in anaerobic conditions has been considered inefficient, but it was shown that the transfer of electrons between substrates and terminal electron acceptors in these coupled systems is very efficient (Hungate

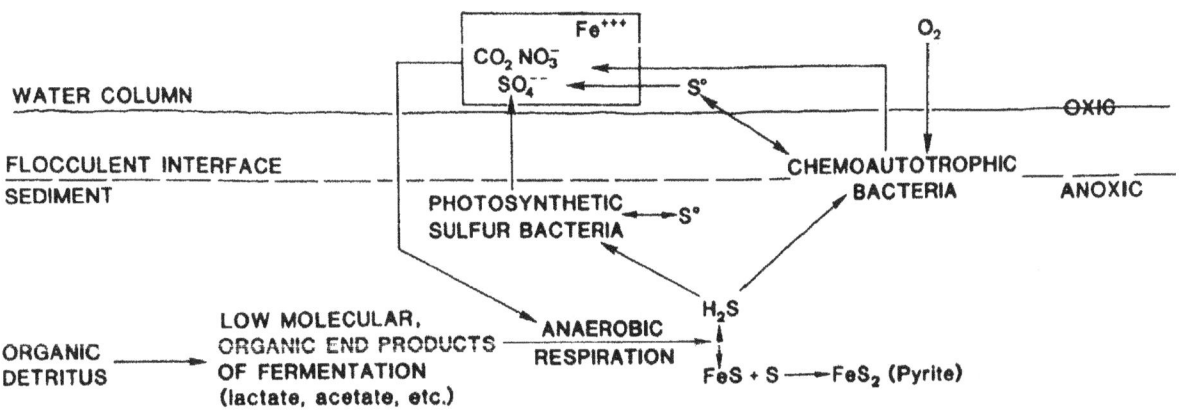

Figure 33. Conceptual diagram of the sulfur cycle in eelgrass meadows.

1966). Evidently, one mechanism for assuring high rates of productivity by seagrass is the efficient recycling of carbon and other essential elements by anaerobic and facultative bacteria.

An additional consequence of sulfate reduction is production of dissolved sulfides (H_2S or HS), which react with trace elements to form metal-sulfide complexes. The reduced sulfur that is not complexed with metals diffuses into oxygenated sediment microzones or into the water column where it may be oxidized to SO_4. Ferrous iron is especially reactive with the reduced sulfur, forming FeS_2 (pyrite) that precipitates and accumulates in anoxic sediments. The consequences of pyrite formation are twofold: (1) some of the iron that may have been combined with phosphates reacts and precipitates with elemental sulfur, freeing phosphate ions; and (2) the precipitation of reduced forms of sulfur which are toxic to many organisms relieves some of their poisonous effects. Generally, the sulfur cycle appears to be an open system with a constant flux of sulfur mediated by biogeochemical oxidation and reduction reactions (Jorgensen and Fenchel 1974).

In anoxic sediments and interstitial waters, organic nitrogen compounds are remineralized to the most reduced forms of inorganic nitrogen, ammonia, or ammonium (Figure 34). The pH of eelgrass sediments indicates that the likely form of the inorganic species is ammonium (Kenworthy et al. 1982). Compared to concentrations in unvegetated substrates, ammonium concentrations are usually higher in vegetated sediments (Figure 31) (Kenworthy et al. 1982), but may be dramatically reduced by short-term and extremely rapid assimilation by plants and microorganisms (Short 1981; Iizumi et al. 1982). Redox conditions should prevent oxidation of any substantial quantities of ammonium to nitrate. Nitrate does diffuse into the flocculent surficial sediments from the water column and some ammonium may oxidize in aerated microzones around the roots (Iizumi et al. 1980) and excavations of animals (Aller 1978). The extent to which nitrate is available remains to be determined. Cycling associated with reactions involving nitrate have been detected in sediment of an eelgrass bed (Koike and Hattori 1978), and losses of available nitrogen by denitrification may be an important process in coastal waters (Nixon 1981).

In addition to decomposition of organic matter (Iizumi et al. 1982), important sources of inorganic nitrogen in eelgrass bed sediments are derived from excretions of the biota and by fixation of dissolved molecular nitrogen gas. Since molecular nitrogen is such a large nutrient pool, yet cannot be directly utilized by the plants, processes that make it available are vital to seagrass ecosystems. Nitrogen fixation has been detected in anaerobic, intact sediments of the rhizosphere of Zostera (Patriquin and Knowles 1972; Capone 1982) as well as aerobically on the surfaces of roots and rhizomes (Capone and Budin 1982; Smith and

49

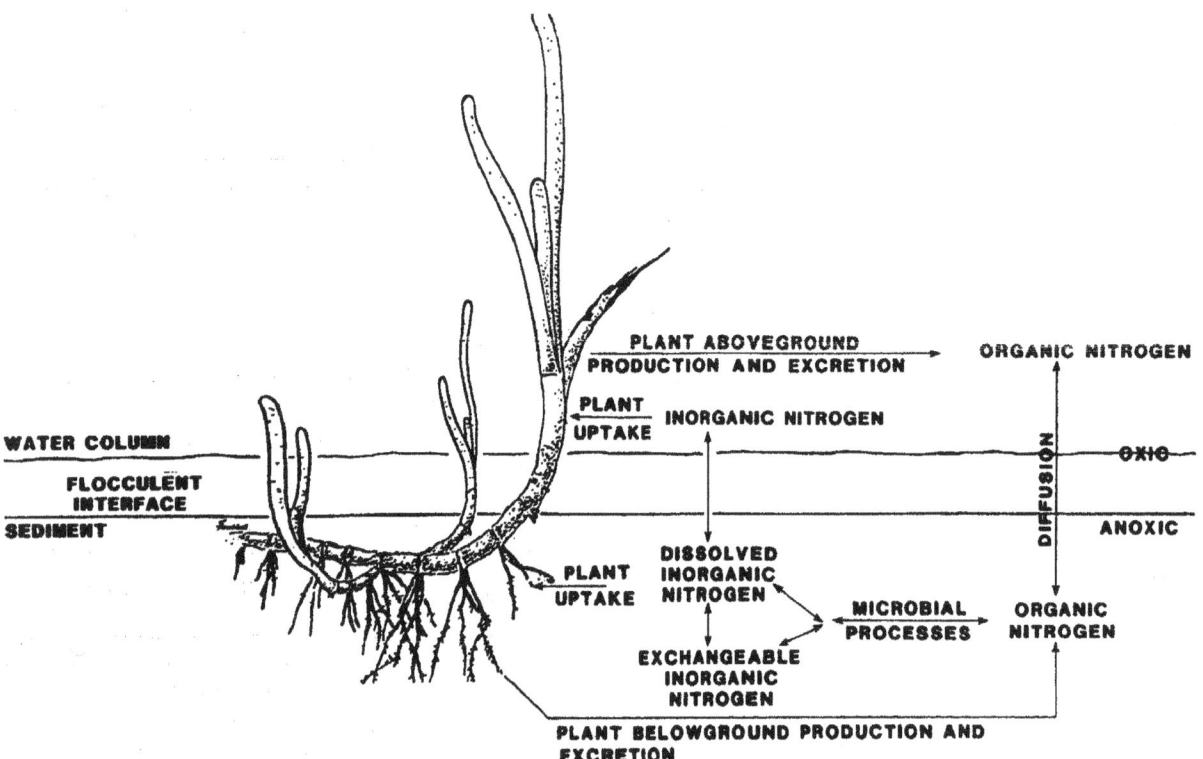

Figure 34. Conceptual diagram of the nitrogen cycle in eelgrass meadows.

Hayasaka 1982). Capone (1982) estimated that nitrogen fixation by intact rhizosphere sediments may supply up to 20% of nitrogen required by the plants in a temperate estuary in Long Island, New York. Inputs by this process may prove to be even larger than currently expected when rates of fixation associated with the roots and rhizomes are estimated with reasonable confidence (Capone and Budin 1982). The detection of aerobic, microaerophilic, and anaerobic nitrogen fixation processes (Smith and Hayasaka 1982; Capone 1982; Capone and Budin 1982) suggests that a diverse assemblage of microorganisms are associated with nitrogen inputs to the rhizosphere of eelgrass.

Inorganic ions, especially ammonium, are either adsorbed onto surfaces of organic matter or sediment particles (Rosenfield 1979a), diffuse along horizontal or vertical concentration gradients (Dietz 1982), or are assimilated by eelgrass plants and microorganisms (Iizumi et al. 1982). Rosenfield (1979a)

estimated that adsorbed or exchangeable ammonium may be twice as high as free ammonium in sediments. In eelgrass beds the combination of large quantities of organic matter and fine-textured sediments results in relatively high concentrations of exchangeable ammonium (Figure 31) (Kenworthy et al. 1982; Short 1981; Rosenfield 1979a). This exchangeable pool is capable of replacing reserves of dissolved ammonium that are depleted through uptake or diffusion.

Regeneration, consumption, and reversible adsorption-desorption processes that tend to recycle nitrogen internally within the sediment are offset by a combination of strictly physicochemical and biological processes that cause losses of nitrogen from the sediment. These losses of regenerated nitrogen across the sediment-water interface can be accounted for, in part, by diffusion, advection, and biological transformations occurring primarily at the interface of the sediment and water column (Dietz 1982).

50

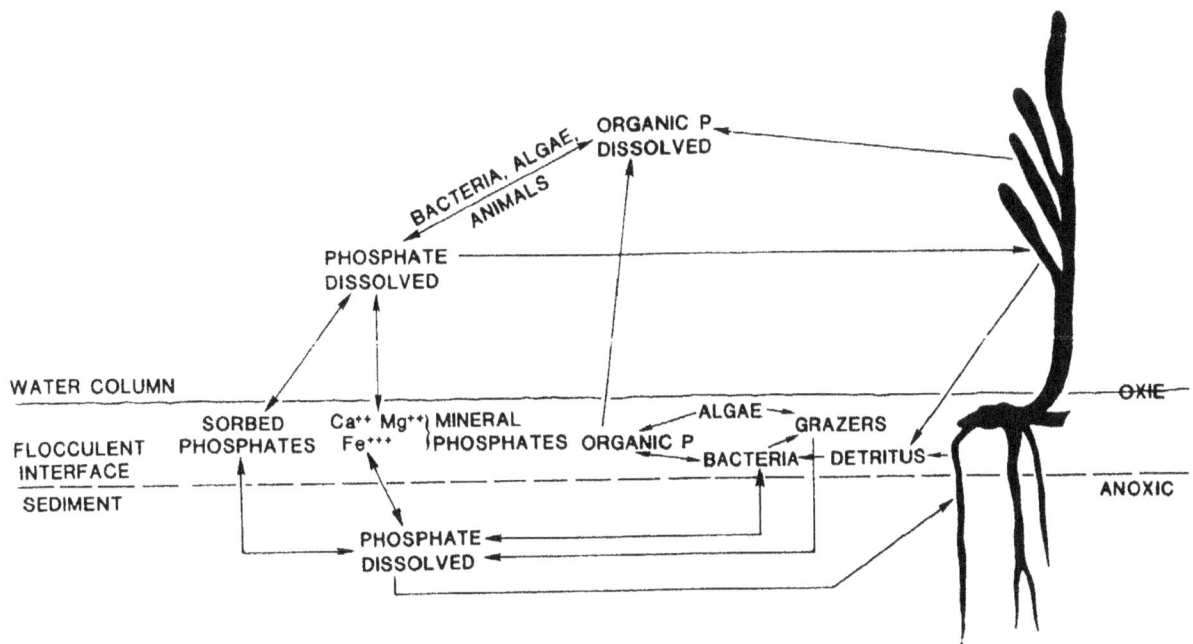

Figure 35. Conceptual diagram of the phosphorus cycle in eelgrass meadows.

Sediment profiles of total nitrogen (Figure 31) indicate that nitrogen declines with depth and that nitrogen cycle intermediates (e.g., NH$_4$) are quite large (Kenworthy et al. 1982). Rates of ammonium regeneration in eelgrass bed sediments are high relative to those in coastal sediments in general (Billen 1978; Blackburn 1979; Iizumi et al. 1982). If sediment accretion and burial rates were sufficiently rapid, particulate organic nitrogen, and especially dissolved organic nitrogen (Rosenfield 1979b), could become unavailable for recycling. Some of the buried nitrogen is retained in humic macromolecules, which are chemically refractory and are long-term sinks for nitrogen (Nissenbaum et al. 1972; Rice 1982). Evidence suggests however that even though organic inputs are quite large, effective recycling mechanisms operate within eelgrass meadows.

Phosphorus, unlike carbon, nitrogen or sulfur, has no gaseous form (Figure 35), and is derived as orthophosphate from weathering of phosphate minerals, solubilization of metallic and adsorbed phosphates (Stumm and Morgan 1970), and excretions of bacteria (Cosgrove 1977), zooplankton and other marine animals

(Johannes 1964; Kuenzler 1961). These same sources also release soluble organic phosphorus in excretions and leachates released during autolysis of dead cells.

Phosphorus concentrations are measurably greater in vegetated than in unvegetated sediments (McRoy et al. 1972). From a geochemical standpoint, the strong tendency of phosphates to be adsorbed to clays and positively charged cations makes sediments important in the overall cycling of this element. As mentioned earlier, an important reaction occurs in anaerobic sediments containing sulfide where pyrite is reduced and orthophosphate is released. If the sediment becomes anaerobic to the surface, a condition that may frequently occur in an eelgrass bed, the dissolved orthophosphate is mobilized in the sediments and released to the overlying water. During periods of low productivity, decreased organic inputs, or physical disturbances (e.g., during winter turbulent conditions), an aerobic surface layer develops, and the release of orthophosphate is limited primarily by its tendency to precipitate with ferric iron.

Aerobic, phosphate-solubilizing bacteria also play an important role in the sediment phosphorus cycle (Cosgrove 1977). Craven and Hayasaka (1982) isolated an aerobic rhizosphere bacterium associated with eelgrass roots that was capable of solubilizing calcium phosphate. Since hydroxyapatite, a form of calcium phosphate, is a large component of the sediment phosphorus pool, its solubilization by bacteria may be an important source of available phosphorus for both plants and micro-organisms.

Sediments are large reservoirs of metallic elements in estuaries (Wolfe et al. 1973). Substantial rates of sedimentation together with anaerobic conditions suggest that eelgrass beds may act as sinks for many trace metals (Wolfe et al. 1976). Most metals should exist in an insoluble form at the typical Eh and pH of the sediment, while others such as iron and manganese may occur in excessive concentrations (Pulich 1982 a,b). Most of the metals probably are immobilized as insoluble sulfides (Burrell and Schubel 1977). However, since eelgrass is capable of releasing oxygen from the roots (Iizumi et al. 1980), there may be an oxygenated microzone that would actually promote the mobilization of some metals and the co-precipitation of others as hydroxides in the immediate area of the root (Burrell and Schubel 1977).

Pulich (1982 a,b) suggested that the growth of H. wrightii on previously unvegetated sediment increases sulfide production which subsequently precipitates with excess soluble iron. A depletion of excess soluble iron reduces luxury uptake of iron, thereby relieving the potential for an imbalance in the iron to manganese ratio in the plants. The extent to which this process functions in an eelgrass bed is not known, but we expect that they are similar due to typical redox conditions in seagrass bed sediments.

A number of transformations involving the oxidation and reduction of trace elements are mediated by bacteria, either directly by uptake or release of elements, or indirectly by their influence on Eh and pH. The best understood example of this is pyrite oxidation and involves the sulfur cycle discussed earlier. This can occur abiologically, but is greatly accelerated by the activity of Thiobacilli.

Recent work by Smith et al. (1982) demonstrates that there is a heterogeneous community of bacteria associated with eelgrass sediments. Isolates of rhizoplane bacteria were more sensitive to high concentrations of trace metals than were rhizosphere bacteria. Smith et al. (1982) argued that microzones of extremely high concentrations of trace elements make necessary some mechanism for the protection of bacteria against heavy metals. Smith et al. (1979) observed that eelgrass rhizoplane bacteria were imbedded in an amorphous mucoid substance (mucigel) on the root surface. Mucigel is likely to consist of organic by-products of the plant as well as extracellular capsular material produced by the microorganisms. Material of similar origin has been implicated in the protection of specific bacterial isolates. Additionally, many bacteria and higher plants, including eelgrass (Wood 1953), are known to produce organic reducing substances which may chelate metals.

The knowledge of trace metal cycles in eelgrass bed sediments is limited. It will become obvious in our discussion of the biotic reservoir that far more is known about biological fluxes than the geochemical aspects.

Water Column

Usually eelgrass beds occur in shallow, well-mixed, and well-aerated water. Except where they are found in enclosed embayments and where nighttime low tides occur in conjunction with high summer temperatures (Nixon and Oviatt 1972), oxygen is abundant and elemental cycling in the water column is dominated by aerobic respiration. The water column receives organic matter that is produced in situ, is advected in with water flow, or is resuspended from the sediments.

Phytoplankton assimilate large quantities of inorganic elements and release DOM. Since phytoplankton turnover rapidly, there is relatively brief storage of elements in this form of POM. Rapid phytoplankton growth, characterized by seasonal plankton blooms, can reduce dissolved inorganic nutrients in the water column to barely detectable levels. Zooplankton consume part of the phytoplankton and release DOM and inorganic nutrients. Larger vertebrates and numerous other invertebrates consume the smaller plankton while also regenerating nutrients and DOM. Migrating animals, especially fishes, shrimp, and crabs, transport large quantities of nutrients in and out of eelgrass meadows (see Chapters 4 and 5).

Autolysis of dead macrophyte cells releases nutrients to the water as inorganic matter or DOM, which are metabolized along with the remaining POM by bacteria and fungi (Linley et al. 1981; Robertson et al. 1982). Bacteria are especially important in decomposing and converting the various forms of matter into particulate aggregates that can be utilized by suspension and filter-feeding organisms (Linley et al. 1981; Robertson et al. 1982).

More refractory sources of POM and DOM are derived from material such as vascular plants and macroalgae retained in the grass bed. These materials are transformed slowly and in some cases take months or years to turn over. As a consequence, much of the larger POM is either transported out of the meadow or is deposited onto the sediment-water interface, where it is difficult to determine if the majority of it is cycled in the water or in the sediment.

Smaller particles of POM (Kirchman and Mitchell 1982), colloidal material (Siglio et al. 1982), and DOM are all utilized by bacteria in the water column. Recently, Robertson et al. (1982) demonstrated that bacteria rapidly converted DOC that was leached from dead leaves of two seagrass species into aggregates of POM. The leached DOC represented 12% to 20% of the total plant carbon. This source of DOM, which is probably continuously produced throughout the growth cycle of the plant, may be extremely large. In and around intertidal grass beds, which are periodically exposed and resubmerged, the DOM release probably is pulsed and occurs during periods of exposure and resubmergence (Penhale and Smith 1977).

Since rates of autotrophic production are quite high (Chapter 2), there is a large demand for inorganic macronutrients.

In an eelgrass bed in Alaska (Iizumi et al. 1982) the assimilation to regeneration ratio for ammonium of 6.2 suggested that additional supplies of ammonium must come from sources outside the bed or from rapid regeneration in the sediments in order to sustain the observed elemental concentrations and primary productivity in the water column.

The cycling of trace elements within the water column of eelgrass beds is not well known. Many trace elements are associated with living and dead POM, and the concentrations of dissolved metals are very low (Wolfe et al. 1973; Wolfe et al. 1976; Drifmeyer et al. 1980). Nonetheless, turnover rates of trace metals could be such that their availability is substantial.

Biota

Since the biota form such a large and functional part of each reservoir, we unavoidably discussed many essential attributes of this component already. To recapitulate, we have identified their major contributions: autotrophs (phyto-plankton, macroalgae, and seagrass), unicellular heterotrophs (primarily bacteria), and multicellular heterotrophs (invertebrates, fish, and birds).

In terms of abundance, the seagrasses dominate autotrophs to a large degree and act as effective conduits between the sediments and water column, while phytoplankton and macroalgae recycle elements at an apparently faster rate and do not achieve as large a standing crop. Roots and leaves absorb elements such as carbon, nitrogen, and phosphorus, and a functional vascular system translocates them throughout the plant (McRoy and Barsdate 1970; Penhale and Thayer 1980; Thursby and Harlin 1982). Non-conservative, or luxuriant, uptake of inorganic phosphorus as orthophosphate by eelgrass roots has been reported (McRoy and Barsdate 1970; McRoy et al. 1972). In these studies, orthophosphate absorbed by the roots was excreted into the water column by the leaves, suggesting that Zostera is a major biological intermediate in the estuarine phosphorus cycle. Penhale and Thayer (1980), however, found

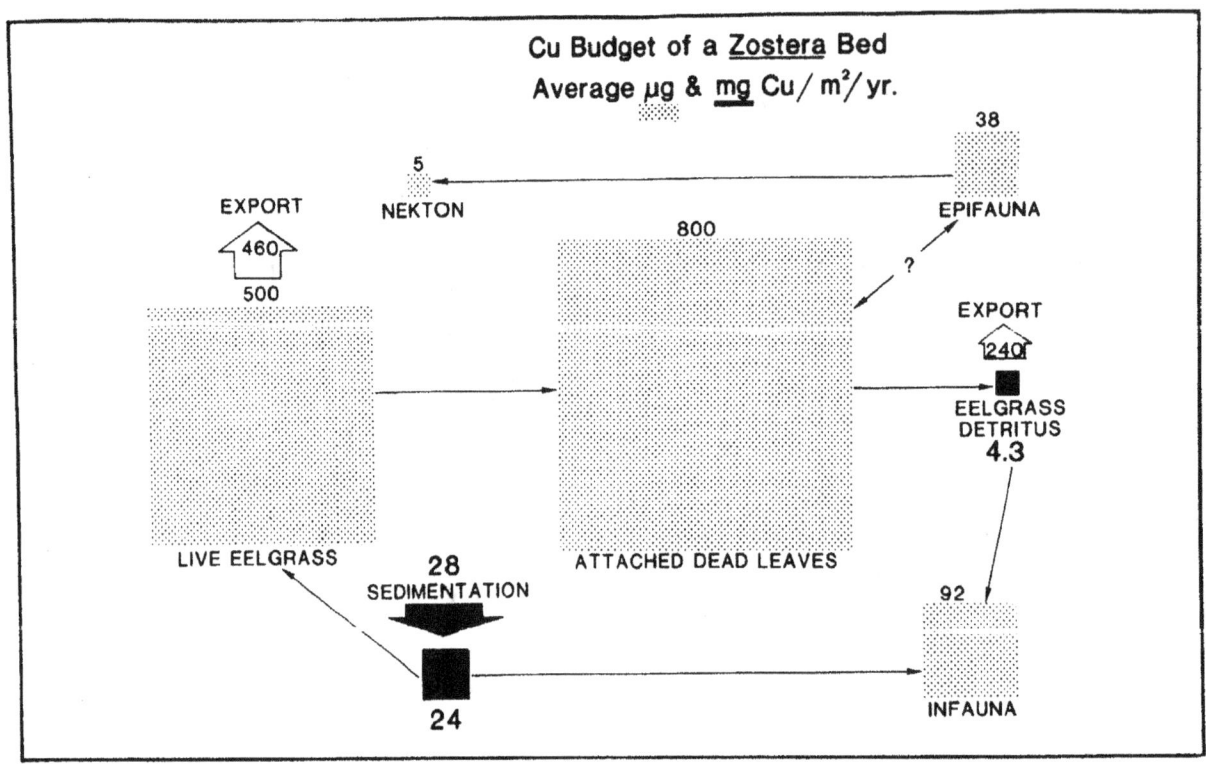

Figure 36. Estimates of the total amount of copper in the biotic and abiotic reservoirs of an eelgrass meadow. (From Drifmeyer et al. 1980.)

little release of phosphorus. More than likely, the direction of the flux will depend on the relative concentration gradients between the mediums (Penhale and Thayer 1980), and the plants probably are more conservative with respect to most of the elements.

Micronutrients, such as zinc, cadmium, lead, copper, and manganese are also absorbed by both the roots and leaves (Brinkhuis et al. 1980; Drifmeyer et al. 1980; Lyngby and Brix 1982; Lyngby et al. 1982), but the amount of metal translocated is insignificant compared to the estimated movement of C, N, and P.

In the water column, DOM produced by a variety of sources is transformed almost exclusively by bacteria, which consume and produce inorganic elements, DOM, and detrital aggregates. Typically, turnover time is rapid, although some particles are transferred up the food chain to larger organisms (see Chapter 4), which retain more elements for longer periods.

Consequently, some nutrients are exported by the larger organisms.

By far, Zostera is the largest reservoir of all elements (Figure 36), due to its high rate of organic productivity, its longevity, and the large biomass of both living and dead POM. A substantial flux of elements occurs during senescence and decomposition of the seagrasses (Drifmeyer et al. 1980). Leaf turnover rates, on the order of 4-10 crops per year, constitute the largest flux in this particular pool. When the productivity of the attached epiphytes on the leaves is considered, the flux is even greater. Since there is relatively little direct herbivory (less than 10% of the net production), the nutrients in the plant tissue are recycled through some very complex biophysical processes (see 4.11). Some of the plant material and, consequently, the nutrients contained within the material are exported to adjacent coastal systems (Steven Bach, WAPORA, Inc., Norcross, Georgia, and G.W. Thayer, unpubl.).

3.4 A SCENARIO OF EELGRASS MEADOW DEVELOPMENT

We have tried to conceptualize how short-term and long-term interactions of waves, currents, tides, light, temperature, salinity, and nutrients influence the form and function of eelgrass meadows. Since the number of combinations of environmental factors would only serve to confuse the larger picture, we have begun to develop a simplified conceptual model. The drawback is that one cannot always determine if a factor, or a combination of factors, influences the development of a meadow or if the meadow in its development, modifies or influences the factors. Both scenarios are probably important but have different developmental (time) histories. In any event, we use a scenario that demonstrates how all factors can interact. The patterns that we discuss appear to hold not only for meadows on the east coast of the United States, but for other coasts and other seagrass species as well.

The rate at which eelgrass covers the bottom is a function of several factors, including: (1) how quickly shoots are added and lost to the population, (2) how long during the year they are added or lost, and (3) the initial density and spacing of the shoots. The first two factors are mediated directly by a number of environmental conditions, especially light, temperature, and available nutrients (Chapter 2), and indirectly by hydrodynamic conditions. Factors that control shoot spacing are not clearly understood, but meadows existing under high current and wave regimes are more densely packed. High current areas also have much more root standing crop (Kenworthy et al. 1982). The density of the root-rhizome system also is proportional to the frequency of branching and frequency of leaf emergence from the meristem (Chapter 2). At the same time, high current areas have characteristically lower sediment organic matter and nutrient concentrations than low current substrate areas (Kenworthy et al. 1982) (Chapter 2). Percentages of silt-clay and organic matter, as well as exchangeable NH_4, dissolved NH_4, and total nitrogen, may increase along a temporal-spatial gradient of meadow development (Kenworthy et al. 1982).

Eelgrass may develop more root biomass and greater surface area when nutrient concentrations are low in order to extract sufficient nutrients to meet metabolic requirements (Short 1981, 1983a,b). It is probably more than mere coincidence that an extensive root system that resists sediment erosion develops in high-current areas, since eelgrass that has been transplanted from low to high current areas, and vice versa, will grow a root system characteristic of its new habitat (Kenworthy, pers. observ.). Higher root biomass also provides organic matter directly to the sediment matrix, and is especially important in the early stages of meadow development and in high current areas where scouring limits the input of organic material to the sediment.

External environmental factors, as well as genetic factors, also influence the structure of individual plants and, hence, the form and structure of meadows. If light, temperature, nutrients, and salinity are not limiting, hydrodynamic factors will control the physical form and ecological functions of a meadow as it develops. Water depth and turbidity, either alone or in combination, reduce available light energy to the plants (Chapter 2) and thus determine the lower depth limit of the meadow. Tides influence energy availability to the plant by changing the distance through which the light must pass (depth). The upper depth limit may be determined by the length of time an area is exposed at low tide (Chapter 1). The meadow edge where current flow is rapidly restructured is a transition zone for sediment transport. Fonseca et al. (1982b) demonstrated that for every cm/sec of current velocity the flow intrudes 1.25 cm into most eelgrass meadows before a reduction in velocity is measurable. The distance from the edge where maximum reduction in velocity occurs is determined by the ratio of 2.07 (cm/sec velocity). Over time, sediments that have settled can be trapped by the plant's root-rhizome system. Sediment particles in eelgrass meadows are generally from sources outside of the meadow whereas in tropical seagrass meadows they are from sources within the meadow (Burrell and

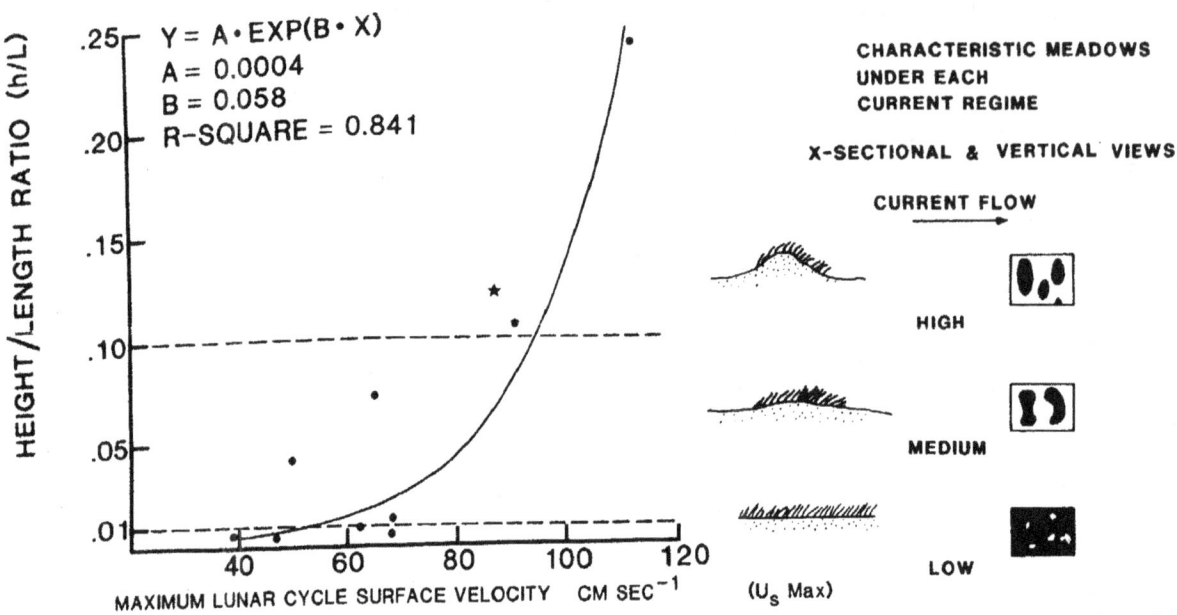

Figure 37. The height/length ratio of several eelgrass meadows (dots) and one _Thalassia testudinum_ meadow (star) (Scoffin 1970) regressed on current velocity. Cross-sectional and vertical view diagrams of the degree of mounding and coverage patterns, respectively, are on the right. Horizontal lines describe useful numerical height/length limits for high (> 0.1), medium (0.01-0.1), and low (0-0.01) current regimes. (From Fonseca et al. 1983.)

Schubel 1977). Some eelgrass meadows exist under a gradient of current regimes, and are no more than mounded patches a meter or two across (Figures 37, 40 a,b). These patch meadows were described by den Hartog (1971) as the "leopard-skin" distribution, and are contrasted with the broad, low-relief flats more characteristic of meadows (Figure 37, 20) (Kenworthy et al. 1982).

The environmental disturbance provided by waves and currents is fairly constant over time for a given meadow; the degree of disturbance diminishes as energy is lost from waves and currents across a meadow. _Zostera_, according to den Hartog (1971), is restricted to habitats where sediment erosion and deposition are in equilibrium, since he suggests the species cannot grow vertically. We have observed, however, a strong vertical growth response of eelgrass under transplanting conditions (Figure 60). Flume studies (Fonseca, pers. observ.) demonstrate that seagrasses in general accumulate sediments rapidly and under many natural conditions their survival depends on the ability to grow vertically, the vertical upper limit being the frequency and duration of exposure to the air. Because rhizome growth is slow (approx. 0.5 - 1.0 mm day^{-1}, Fonseca unpubl. data), eelgrass probably does not respond well to rapid sedimentation, but it seems able to respond to sediment deposition caused by its own presence. Eelgrass and seagrass meadows in general develop to a point where they are in hydrodynamic equilibrium with several factors: (1) sediment stabilization by the root-rhizome system, (2) boundary layer development within the canopy, (3) velocity increase caused by mounding, and (4) ambient flow regime (Figure 38).

In the classical terms of Odum (1969), eelgrass meadows are generally monospecific and the "pioneer" as well as the "climax" species. An equilibrium results that produces a range of meadow forms that are correlated with current regime (Fonseca et al. 1983; Kenworthy et al. 1982) and to some degree with wave energy. Each meadow can be characterized by the ratio of its height (h) over its down-current length (L). The h/L ratios are correlated with the ambient current

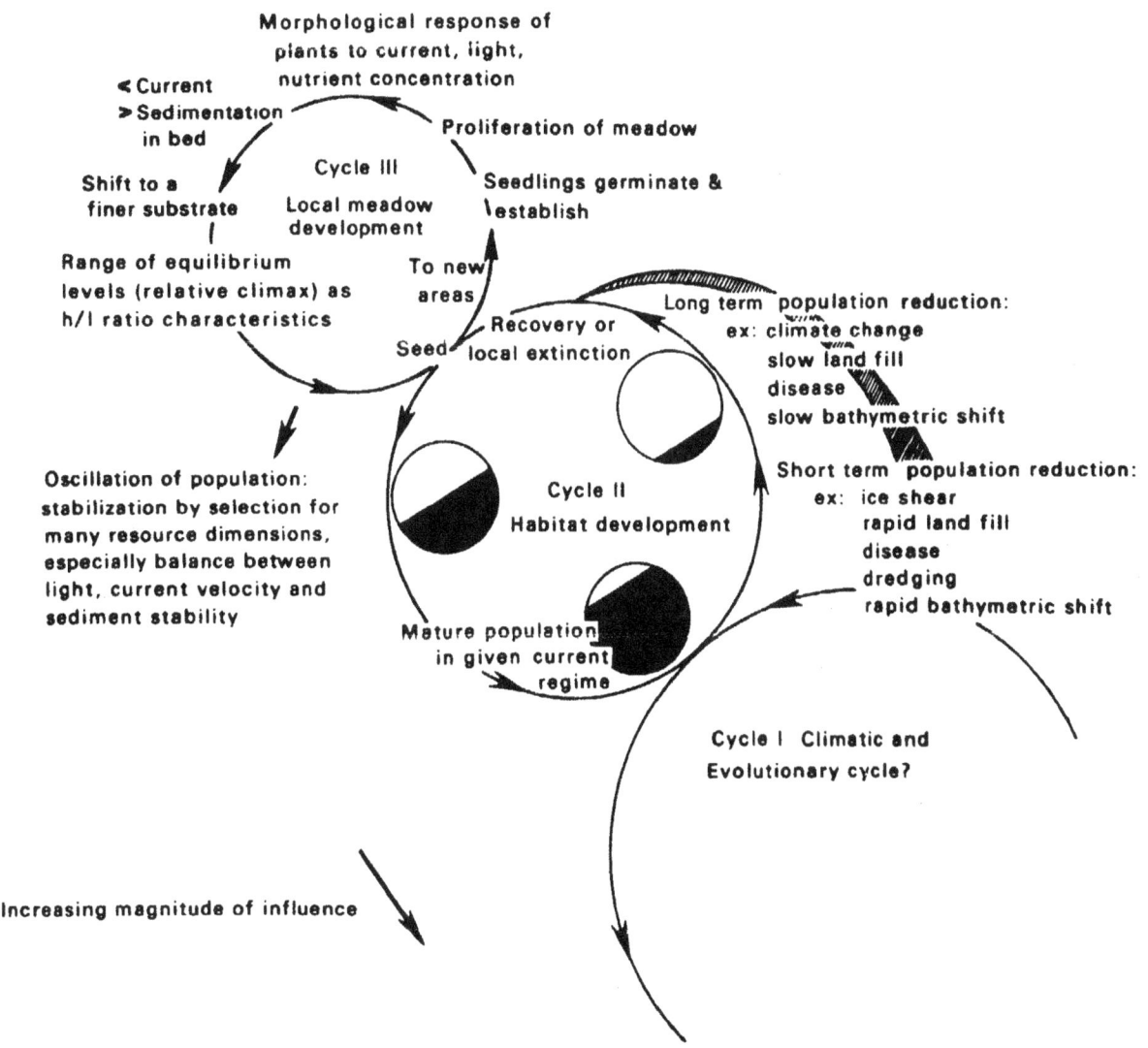

Figure 38. Theoretical influence of current velocity in the development of an eelgrass meadow. Each circle designates different time scales. (From Fonseca et al. 1983.)

regime (Figure 37). Each h/L class represents patterns of meadow development that have characteristic current reduction patterns and sedimentary development and that denote several relative climaxes or polyclimaxes of the system. As long as the hydrodynamic conditions are maintained, meadow development and configuration will exhibit the responses shown in Figure 37 and 38.

High current and low current meadows usually are associated with open water and sheltered areas, respectively. Exceptions to this are tidal and man-made channels. Open water meadows, which are very susceptible to wave-induced scour, often export a large portion of their foliar production, although they do so less frequently in clearer and deeper areas, especially in the New England coastal lagoons and fjord-like coastal habitats. Here, where the grasses exist at depths below the influence of all but large storm waves, more autochthonous detritus may accumulate. Another critical factor for meadow development is sediment depth above a consolidated (bedrock) layer, which must be of sufficient thickness to support the root systems (Zieman 1975; Burrell and Schubel 1977). We have observed eelgrass growing on virtually all unconsolidated sediments, including cobble beaches. Since geomorphology and ambient wave and current characteristics structure the physical form of the eelgrass meadow and control the rate at which elemental cycling within the meadow may occur, local geomorphology is an overriding factor in meadow development, directly correlated with the input of organic material to the sediments.

Kenworthy et al. (1982) measured dissolved nitrogen, exchangeable NH_4, and total nitrogen, in sediments of three eelgrass beds in North Carolina. A spatial gradient analysis approximating a temporal sequence of grass bed development, consisting of small colonizing patch stations at the outer edges of the bed and mid-bed stations, demonstrated a consistent trend for each nitrogen parameter. The concentrations of nutrients were lowest in unvegetated stations, intermediate at patch and at edges, and largest in the mid-bed regions, where stations represented the most advanced stage of development and eelgrass cover. These findings were consistent with Odum's hypothesis (1969) that the most developed stage of this ecosystem has a greater capacity to trap and retain nutrients for internal recycling.

In this same study the authors reported that at high energy sites, grass beds consisted of small isolated patches of grass and that there was very little difference in the sediment properties between the vegetated and adjoining unvegetated bottom. The small hummocks were suggested to be semi-permanent features existing in a temporary equilibrium with the physical forces.

To verify these observations, we have transplanted eelgrass into a range of energy types and studied its development (Fonseca et al. 1979; Kenworthy et al. 1980; Fonseca et al. 1982a). Predictably, the low-energy sites developed low h/L ratios and a broad, continuous cover, while the high-energy sites developed a discontinuous series of small raised and moderately dense patches (Figure 39) within two growing seasons.

Waves have substantial effect in shallow open-water meadows during different tidal stages and may be in part responsible for the resulting meadow configurations. At low tide, where waves refract over the patch and come in phase over the center of the meadow, a wave often exceeds its critical height and breaks and plunges into the meadow. This forms a characteristic scour patch whose focus moves over the meadow at a rate that depends on wind direction, wave height, and tidal stage (Figure 40 a). Another factor contributing to the development of scour patches may be the demise of the root-rhizome system following the centrifugal or radial growth of eelgrass (Setchell 1929). As eelgrass branches and grows from a point of origin (e.g., a seed), the rhizome system that is left behind to decompose forms a zone in the center of a mounded meadow of senescing material that has less sediment-binding integrity. Waves plunging in this elevated zone only exacerbate the disruption of the dying rhizome and accelerate sediment erosion. Bioturbation of crabs, rays, and some gastropods also

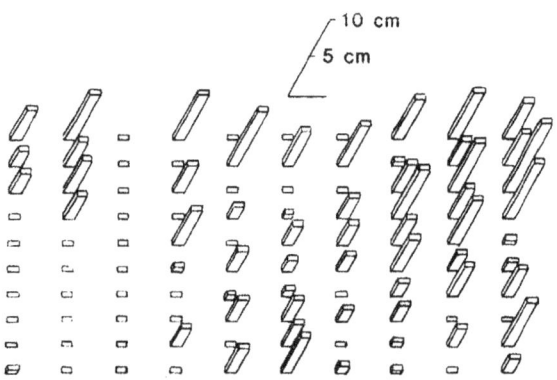

Figure 39. Computer simulation of mounding in a 200-day-old eelgrass transplant in a high current North Carolina shoal in Back Sound, Carteret County. The grid is 9 x 9 m with each vertical block showing a 10X vertical exaggeration on the sand trapped by each planting. Roughly 0.90 m^3 sand was added and maintained in this 81 m^2 plot by the transplanted eelgrass.

58

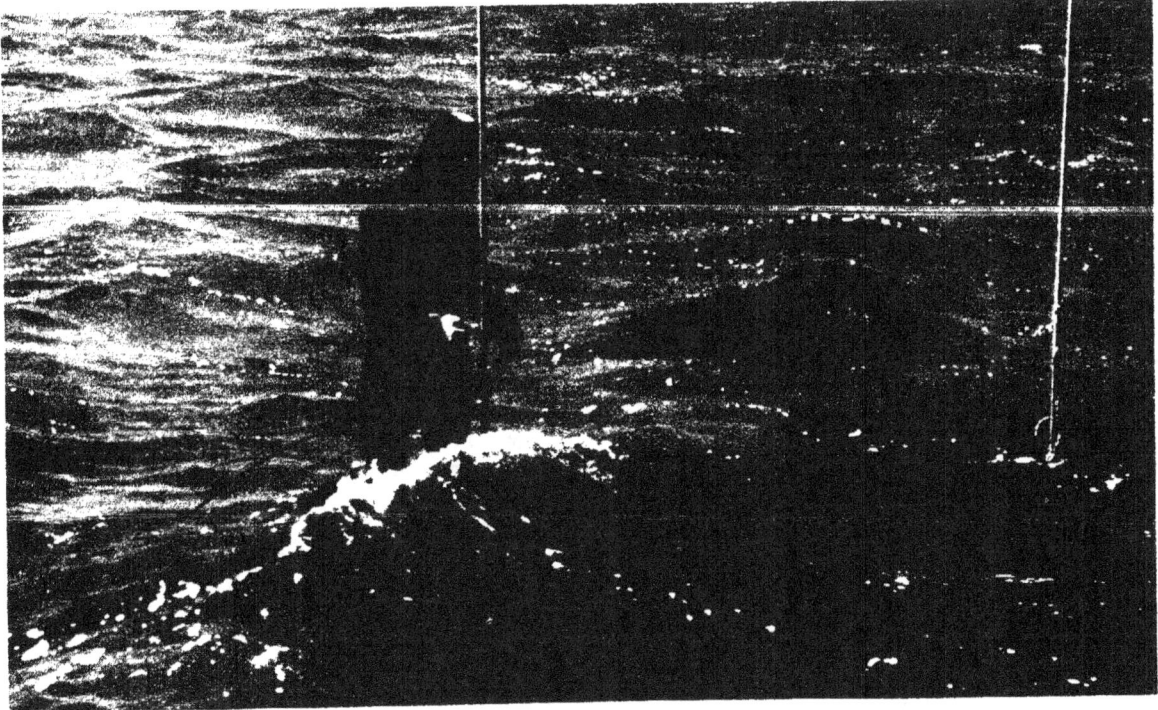

Figure 40. (a) Wavelets refracting around a typically isolated eelgrass patch with scour area (1-m wide) on a high current shoal at low tide. The waves come in phase and break as they refract around the patch. Wave breaking is suspected to be an important mechanical phenomenon in the maintenance of these meadows as isolated patches. (b) Similar patch at midtide. The patch has little effect on the waves and is thoroughly scoured by their passing.

may create erosional faces that exacerbate meadow disruption; such activity could add to maintaining patchiness in moderate and high current areas. But at high tides, larger waves entering these shallow areas (Figure 40 b) are affected less by the patchy meadows. An overall stronger surge and lift force is experienced over the whole meadow.

We hypothesize that these relative climaxes (meadow forms under hydrodynamic regimes; polyclimaxes) provide varying potentials for utilization by other flora and fauna. Fauna must have specific adaptations to exist and thrive in meadows of fast currents or high waves; low-energy sites are likely to be more accessible and faunal composition may differ as a result of reduced current stress (see Chapter 4). Although faunal development in the strictest sense has not been thoroughly analyzed, we can draw some inferences from a few selected studies. Thayer et al. (1975a) surveyed the structure and fauna of a recently developed eelgrass bed near Beaufort, North Carolina, that had not become a permanent feature of the embayment until 1968. The bed covered approximately 30% of the embayment in 1969 and 1970 and had increased to 55% by 1973. The species composition of the infauna and epifauna was quite different from that of an adjacent unvegetated estuary, and more importantly, the density and biomass of invertebrates were greater in the grass bed. In just a few years the eelgrass bed had developed to the point that it could be distinguished from areas where grass was absent. Although in most studies the relative age of grass beds are unknown, there does seem to be consistent support for the argument that faunal abundance in eelgrass beds is substantially greater.

The rate at which animals recolonize a transplanted eelgrass meadow is another indicator of the potential of or development of the faunal community. Homziak et al. (1982) reported that macrofaunal density and number of species increased nonlinearly with increasing eelgrass shoot density in a developing transplanted meadow (Figure 64). Faunal densities were significantly higher in vegetated than in unvegetated treatments. Development of the faunal community was closely coupled to the development of the plants. Homziak et al. (1982) studied approximately one growing season, and nearly 60% of the eelgrass net production (estimated by comparison to adjacent, undisturbed meadows) was recovered (Thayer et al. in press b). The asymptotic response of the infaunal density suggests that they may have approached the carrying capacity at the highest shoot densities (~ 300 shoots/m^2). In a recent study at a site adjacent to Homziak's, Stuart (1982) found that epifaunal communities recovering from disturbance reached abundances which were equivalent to undisturbed controls in just 90-100 days. The disturbance was slight, however, compared to the large meadow in which it was located.

Development of Two-Species Communities

Our scenario of meadow development would be incomplete if we were to ignore those circumstances where two grasses may coexist. We alluded to the Zostera-Halodule beds in North Carolina and the Zostera-Ruppia beds in the Chesapeake Bay. There are remarkable similarities in the patterns of growth in both systems. In both systems, Zostera achieved the highest biomass in spring and early summer. During the summer, however, plant biomass in the mixed beds is higher than in monospecific beds because additional biomass was contributed by either one of the other species (Figure 21). In the colder months, only Zostera was dominant. We speculate that faunal development in the mixed beds may express different characteristics. For example, associated faunal communities adapted to different thermal regimes may find food or shelter in a mixed bed throughout the year, while these opportunities may be limited during the declining periods in a monospecific bed. Likewise, predator-prey interactions are possibly more complex in the mixed beds. During certain seasons, cover declines in the monospecific bed and predators may gain access to benthic food sources, while in the mixed bed, constant cover and rhizome mat integrity could protect certain prey (Peterson 1982).

We have little data to support the above speculations. We can only suggest

60

that future studies be directed to these matters. In that way essential information may be provided as to the role of eelgrass and mixed grass communities in maintaining the valuable secondary productivity of estuaries.

CHAPTER 4
THE EELGRASS COMMUNITY: BIOLOGICAL
COMPONENTS AND FUNCTIONAL RELATIONS

4.1 GENERAL CONSIDERATIONS

The eelgrass meadow is a discrete ecosystem composed of biological components interacting with the physicochemical environment in a manner leading to defined trophic structure, biological diversity, and material cycles. Aspects of the interaction of the plant with the physicochemical environment and material cycles were discussed in previous chapters. This chapter deals with biological components of eelgrass ecosystems, both in terms of structure (or composition) and function. Functional aspects also are included since processes described in Chapters 2 and 3 determine the relationships between and among components of the system. Whereas the species of plants and animals associated with the eelgrass system may change, both temporally and spatially, processes generally are the same, varying primarily in magnitude.

Wood et al. (1969) described seven basic functional roles of tropical seagrass ecosystems, which also apply to temperate seagrass systems (Thayer et al. 1975b). Although the description was based primarily on observations and intuition, research over the past 14 years has not altered significantly but has strengthened the basic concepts it embodied. Although each aspect has been discussed to varying degrees already, we list them here because they serve as an abbreviated summary and as guideposts to the remainder of this profile.

The elements as they pertain to eelgrass include: (1) eelgrass has a high rate of leaf growth (Chapter 2); (2) leaves support large numbers of epiphytic organisms, which are grazed extensively and may be of comparable biomass to the leaves themselves (Chapter 4); (3) leaves produce large quantities of organic material which decomposes within the meadow or is transported to adjacent systems (Chapters 3, 5); (4) few organisms graze directly on the living eelgrass blade, and the detritus formed from leaves supports a complex food chain (Chapters 3, 4); (5) shoots, by retarding or slowing currents, enhance sediment stability and increase the accumulation of organic and inorganic material (Chapters 3, 4); (6) roots, by binding sediments, reduce erosion and preserve sediment microflora (Chapters 3, 4, 5); and (7) plants and detritus production influence nutrient cycling between sediments and overlying waters (Chapter 3).

To these functions should be added three others that were not specifically addressed in the original scheme: (8) decomposition of roots and rhizomes provides a significant and long-term source of nutrients for sediment microheterotrophs (Chapters 3, 4); (9) roots and leaves provide horizontal and vertical complexity which, coupled with abundant and varied food resources, leads to densities of sessile and mobile fauna generally exceeding those in unvegetated habitats (Chapter 4); (10) movement of water and fauna transports living and dead organic matter (particulate and dissolved) out of eelgrass meadows to adjacent systems (Chapters 4, 5).

4.2 VERTICAL STRUCTURE

The physical structure of the seagrass

system is dominated by the plant cover, which consists of leaves and the belowground network of roots and rhizomes. This ecosystem, with its dense leaf canopy, shallow root-rhizome complex, and locally and geographically variable substrate (i.e., particle size distribution), offers habitat for a wide variety of micro- and macroflora and fauna. The diversity of organisms and overall abundance of both species and individuals are higher in eelgrass meadows than in adjacent unvegetated areas (Orth 1973; Thayer et al. 1975a; Summerson and Peterson 1984).

Kikuchi (1966, 1980) and Kikuchi and Peres (1977) proposed a functionally related classification for the flora and fauna of Japanese eelgrass meadows that has been applied to both temperate and tropical meadows. In this classification, described below, the biotic components are divided into several subunits on the basis of microhabitat structure and mode of existence of the organisms. In the first category are epiphytic organisms that grow (sensu Harlin 1980) on eelgrass blades, including micro- and macroalgae and micro- and meiofauna that are associated with these organisms; sessile fauna attached to the leaves; mobile fauna crawling on the leaves; and swimming fauna which rest on the leaves. In the second category are biota that attach to the blade stem and rhizomes. A third group includes the highly mobile fauna that swim within and over the leaf canopy: decapod crustaceans and fishes that may be either diurnal or seasonal transients or permanent residents. The fourth category includes epibenthic and infaunal invertebrates which dwell on or within the sediments. Many of these species may display nocturnal vertical migration patterns between the sediment and leaves (Kikuchi 1980). Rather than being endemic to the eelgrass habitat, they appear to be an extension of the benthic community that dwells on adjacent unvegetated substrates (Orth 1973; Thayer et al. 1975a; Summerson 1980).

Eelgrass leaves, together with the epiphytic community, form the basis of several heterogeneous trophic pathways. In simplest terms (developed in more detail in Section 4.10) the pathways among the four functional groupings of Kikuchi (1980) are displayed by fauna that (1) feed directly on eelgrass blades; (2) graze primarily on epiphytes; (3) graze both on leaves and the epiphytic community; (4) obtain energy and nutrients from decaying material (detritus) within the meadow; and (5) feed, to varying degrees, on epiphytes, detritus, and animals within the meadow. Many are opportunistic species and others display ontogenetic diet shifts.

The functional categories and trophic pathway groups, all closely linked to eelgrass, exhibit shifts in abundance in response to changes in eelgrass density as well as to seasonal changes in environmental parameters. Thus, within any one meadow there is considerable temporal variation in associated plant and fauna composition and abundance, aspects which have received a great deal of attention (e.g., Orth 1973; Thayer et al. 1975a; Summerson 1980; Stuart 1982).

4.3 HORIZONTAL STRUCTURE

Coupled with vertical and temporal aspects of community variability is a dimension that is less well documented--horizontal gradients in structure. Kenworthy et al. (1982) demonstrated that silt-clay, organic matter, and nitrogen pools consistently were lowest outside eelgrass meadows near Beaufort, North Carolina, and increased in magnitude toward the center of the meadows. Shoot density and standing crop of leaves and of root-rhizomes increased from the edge to the inside. These aspects of eelgrass ecosystems should be reflected in the faunal communities along the edge-to-center gradient, but there are few data to support this hypothesis. Whether in response to chemical conditions, food resources, or protection from predators (all of which are influenced by the hydraulic regime across the meadow), there is evidence that diversity and abundance of infauna and mobile animals are greater within eelgrass meadows than in adjacent unvegetated areas (Thayer et al. 1975a; Orth and Boesch 1979; Summerson 1980). In one of the few studies that focused on horizontal gradients in fauna in eelgrass beds, Orth (1977) demonstrated an increase in both density and diversity from the edge to the center (Figure 41). He related this change to the sediment-stabilizing function of the eelgrass.

Superimposed over vertical and horizontal gradients are hydrodynamic regimes that may account for the gradient itself in some areas. Differences in meadow forms (see Figure 37), sedimentary development, and fluid energy in these different regimes influence the adaptive strategies used by both plants and animals to cope with diverse hydraulic conditions. We hypothesize from our field observations that high-current meadows, in contrast to low-current meadows, would have (1) fewer detritivores, (2) a greater percentage of total faunal species residing in the sediment, (3) fewer epifauna and seasonally fewer epiphytes, and (4) obvious morphological differences between one meadow type versus another.

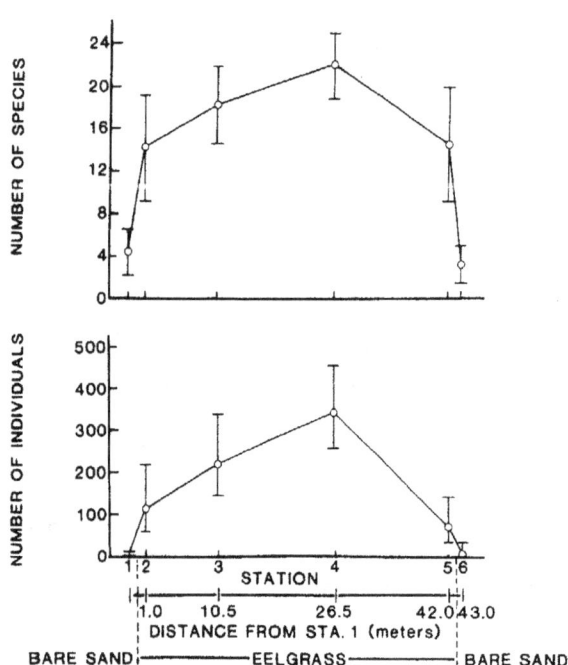

Figure 41. Mean number of species and individuals of invertebrates per core (0.07 m^2) for six stations located along a transect across an eelgrass meadow at Sandy Point in the Chesapeake Bay. Vertical bars are 95% confidence intervals. (From Orth 1977.)

High-current meadows should have epibenthic fauna that are more massive, better developed for clinging, or hydrodynamically streamlined (such as are many stream insects). The leading edge of the meadow, because it intercepts the initial wave and current energy, should exhibit a different epiphytic and faunal assemblage than the more quiescent internal portion. We believe, therefore, that all eelgrass meadows or all portions of a single meadow will not provide equivalent habitat utilization potential.

There have been no studies designed to compare faunal development among eelgrass beds classified by current and/or wave regime. O'Gower and Wacasey (1967) presented some information describing faunal differences between tropical seagrass meadows, and more recent research has emphasized the influence of water motion on the distribution of small marine fauna (Wildish and Kristmanson 1979; Warwick and Uncles 1980; Grant 1981; Jumars et al. 1981). We propose that quantitative comparisons of fauna between seagrass meadows of known hydrodynamic conditions would enhance our understanding of the role of fluid energy in structuring both meadow form and faunal distribution. Stratification of future sampling sites by current regime probably would reduce some of the inexplicable variation seen in eelgrass faunal studies.

4.4 EPIPHYTIC COMMUNITY

The epiphytic components of the eelgrass community are those organisms that grow on the leaves of the plant and that may or may not derive nutrition from the plant itself (Kikuchi and Peres 1977; Harlin 1980). This is an extremely diverse assemblage, comprising bacteria, microalgae, macroalgae, and fauna ranging in size from micro- to macroforms. Distribution and abundance of this component are influenced by the physical substrate, access to the photic zone, nutrient exchange with the plant source or detrital matter within the community, and organic carbon source (Harlin 1975). As noted earlier, the current regime of the area also influences distribution and abundance. The total biomass of epiphytes (Figure 42) can exceed that of the eelgrass leaf itself, and its density can reduce leaf productivity significantly (Sand-Jensen 1977), even though the algal component may contribute significantly to the primary production of the system (Penhale 1977).

Macroalgae

Based on extensive review of the literature, Harlin (1980) compiled a list of 354 macroalgae epiphytic on seagrasses, 120 of which are epiphytic on eelgrass leaves (Appendix A). In a series of collections near Beaufort, North Carolina, Brauner (1973, 1975) recorded 79 species of macroalgae belonging to four taxonomic divisions: 11 Cyanophyta, 12 Chlorophyta, 26 Phaeophyta, and 30 Rhodophyta. Of the Chlorophytes, only Enteromorpha prolifera was present throughout the year. Blue-green algae were uncommon; when present, they were most frequently associated with moribund leaves. Three species of brown algae (Acinetospora pusilla, Myrionema obiculare, and Pseudostictyosiphon onusta) and six species of red algae (Goniotrichum alsidii, Fosliella farinosa, Heteroderma lejolisii, Dermatolithon pustulatum, Champia parvula, and Polysiphonia flaccidissima) were found throughout the year. In the Kouchibouguac area of New Brunswick, Canada, Patriquin and Butler (1976) reported that Polysiphonia subtilissima (red alga) and blue-green algae are common epiphytes on eelgrass leaves.

Abundance and taxonomic composition of the macroalgal epiphytes vary seasonally in response to both temperature and surface area available for attachment. Penhale (1976, 1977) reported that near Beaufort, North Carolina, biomass of epiphytes represented 17%-52% of the total dry weight of eelgrass blades; maximum

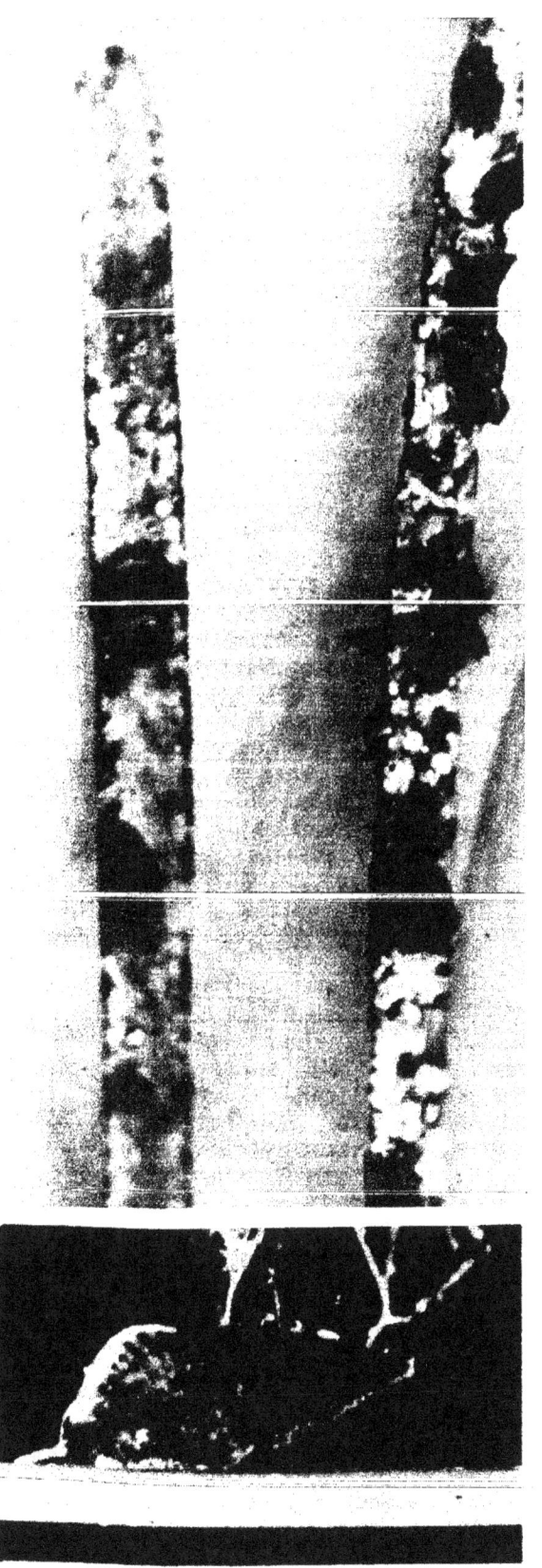

Figure 42. (A) Epiphytized blades of eelgrass showing numerous gastropods, Bittium varium. (B) Enlargement of B. varium on a blade of Halodule. Photograph (B) by P.A. Carbonara, Harbor Branch Foundation, Fort Pierce, Florida.

percentages occurred during spring and late summer and minimum percentages during mid-summer (Figure 43). Since half of the red algae in this area become established in spring (Brauner 1975), these algae may have accounted for the spring peak in epiphytic biomass observed by Penhale (Figure 43). Brauner noted that green and blue-green algae were the prevalent taxonomic groups in summer and fall, whereas Penhale (1977) indicated that three species of calcareous red algae accounted for the peak in biomass she observed. Both investigators observed decreases during winter, and Brauner stated that nearly half of the species terminated growth at this time.

Eelgrass meadows characteristically are also habitats for benthic macroalgae that are not attached to the plant and that are seasonally ephemeral because of periodic scouring by wind and waves associated with storm events. These generally foliose drift algae add to the

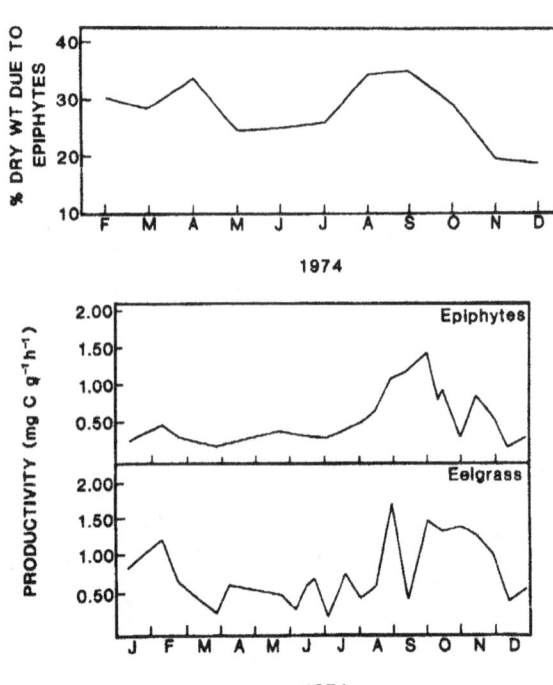

Figure 43. Dry weight biomass of epiphytes as a percent of total leaf plus epiphyte biomass (top) and productivity of both epiphytes and eelgrass (bottom) near Beaufort, North Carolina. (From Penhale 1977.)

habitat complexity, frequently harboring large numbers of faunal organisms (Nelson 1979b). Common algae are _Chaetomorpha brachygona_, _Codium decorticatum_, _Ulva lactuca_, _Dictyota dichotoma_, _Sargassum filipendula_, _Gracilaria verrucosa_, _Hypnea musiformis_, _Laurencia poitei_, and _Agardhiella tenera_ (Dillon 1971; Stuart, unpubl. data). In the Beaufort area, _G. verrucosa_ and _S. filipendula_ predominate. Together, these algae generally contribute little to the yearly mean aboveground biomass (2%-4%; Stuart, unpubl. data) and are most prevalent during winter when eelgrass is in low abundance.

Microalgae, Fungi, and Bacteria

Harlin (1980) compiled a list of 152 species of microalgae epiphytic on seagrasses, of which 91 have been reported on eelgrass leaves (Appendix B). There is disagreement regarding the uniqueness of this group and whether the microalgae are dependent on the eelgrass blade for attachment and/or nutrition. Kita and Harada (1962), for example, indicate that near Seto, Japan, the species of phytoplankton in the water column and the microalgae on eelgrass form separate and distinct entities with little overlap. Dodd (1965), on the other hand, listed 20 genera of diatoms on eelgrass blades in Great South Bay, Long Island, only four of which were not found in associated plankton samples: _Eunotia_, _Thalassiothrix_, _Actinoptychus_, and _Plagiogramma_. Brown (1962) and Main and McIntire (1974) also suggested, on the basis of leaf and sediment analyses, that the microalgal community on eelgrass is not dissimilar to that on sediments or in the overlying water column.

Based on the experimental work of Harlin (1973), McRoy and Goering (1974), Wetzel and Penhale (1979), Penhale and Thayer (1980), and Kirchman et al. (1984) there is little doubt that once epiphytes are attached there is a direct coupling between the plant and the epiphyte in terms of carbon, nitrogen, and phosphorus transfer. Whether this transfer is through inorganic or dissolved organic fractions is not known. Thayer et al. (1978), using stable carbon isotope analysis, estimated that 50% of the carbon present in the epiphytic community on eelgrass may be derived from uptake of dissolved carbon released by the leaf.

Microalgal epiphytes exhibit vertical stratification on eelgrass leaves and a sequential pattern of colonization. The distal portion of the blade may contain the highest concentration of epiphytes (Brown 1962). Dodd (1966) found the following diatom densities (no./m^2) on the upper, middle, and lower third of leaves, respectively, in two areas in Great South Bay: 315 x 10^3, 203 x 10^3, and 35 x 10^3 in one area, and 116 x 10^3, 50 x 10^3, and 27 x 10^3 in a second area. A similar vertical density gradient was reported in Canada by Harrison (1982b), who also found the older portion of a leaf was more heavily colonized than younger leaves. This vertical gradient may reflect that (1) the upper portion of the blade simply has been accessible for colonization the longest, or (2) microalgae respond to chemical changes as a leaf or portion of a leaf ages. The process of leaf colonization apparently occurs almost immediately as the new leaves emerge from the substrate (Brown 1962; Sieburth and Thomas 1973), although Hargraves (1965, as cited in Sieburth and Thomas 1973) did not report this to be the case in his study. Sieburth and Thomas (1973, p. 49) reported the following temporal sequence for colonization in Rhode Island: "[The pennate diatom] Cocconeis scutellum forms virtually a unialgal mat which apparently accumulates broken frustules, as well as diatoms, to form a crust....During the later stage of crust formation, other pennate diatoms, including Navicula, Pleurosigma, Amphora, and Nitzschia species join C. scutellum as members of the epiflora. The crust appears to approach the thickness of the supporting blade."

In their scanning electron microscopic study of the epiphytic community on eelgrass leaves, Sieburth and Thomas (1973) noted that the epiphytic crust also supports bacteria (they reported one form) as well as fungal mycelia and sporangia. Surprisingly few studies of the abundance and composition of fungi and bacteria on eelgrass leaves have been carried out. Newell (1982) reported six genera of fungi on green and brown leaves

of eelgrass in Chesapeake Bay: Sigmoidea sp., Dendryphiella salina, Cladosporium sp., Acremonium sp., Varicosporina ramulosa, and Lulworthia sp. Although there was little difference in the frequency of occurrence of species on green and brown leaves (submerged or in the wrackline), sterile mycelium dominated decaying leaves within eelgrass beds, while Sigmoidea and Dendryphiella predominated in leaves decaying in the wrackline on shore. Newell concluded that few fungi were associated with eelgrass, contributing much less than 0.5% of the leaf biomass. Bacteria attached to green leaves appear to fall within a narrow range, 1-2 x 10^5 cells mm^{-2} (Harrison and Harrison 1980; Newell 1982), although densities at Woods Hole, Massachusetts, were reported by Kirchman et al. (1980) to be 10^7 cells cm^{-2}. The former values are equivalent to about 10^6 cells per gram of dry leaf. Kirchman et al. (1984) reported that bacterial abundance and production increased significantly from the base to the tip of Zostera leaves and exhibited large variation between leaves. Newell (1982) further noted that as leaves aged from green to detached brown states, standing stocks of epiphytic bacteria increased two to three fold, and estimated that bacteria may contribute only 0.04% - 0.11% of the biomass of the living eelgrass blade.

Faunal Epiphytes

A diverse and complex assemblage of animals, about which little was known until the work of Nagle (1968), is closely associated with seagrass blades. It includes protozoans, nematodes, polychaetes, oligochaetes, hydroids, bryozoans, sponges, molluscs, decapods, and barnacles; often included in faunal lists are some fishes which are adapted to clinging on grass blades (Ledoyer 1962). Zieman (1982), in a survey of the tropical seagrass community of Florida Bay, stated that the diversity and abundance of faunal epiphytes is evidence of the ability of seagrasses to provide a substrate for attachment. Few of the faunal species appear to be obligate epiphytes, since they often can be found associated with macroalgae in the meadow, on shells, pilings and rocks, and on or in the substrate. Eelgrass, however, occurs in areas frequently devoid of other surfaces for attachment and, therefore, can form a significant area of attachment.

The complexity of the epiphytic fauna is further evidenced by the four subdivisions described by Kikuchi and Peres (1977) and Kikuchi (1980). One subunit consists of microfauna and meiofauna that dwell within the "felt-like" coating of micro- and small macroalagae: ciliates, flagellates, foraminiferans, nematodes, polychaetes, rotifers, tardigrades, copepods, and ostracods. The second subcommunity type is the sessile fauna: hydrozoans, actinians, bryozoans, tube-building polychaetes, and compound ascidians. The third includes gastropods, polychaetes, turbellarians, nemerteans, crustaceans, and some echinoderms that are free to move over the blades. Swimming animals which rest on the leaves -- mysids, hydromedusae, small squids, and special fishes -- are included in the fourth category.

Since Nagle's (1968) publication, there has been increasing awareness of the importance of epiphytic fauna, particularly as food for fishery organisms. Harlin (1980), surveying the epiphytic literature between 1962 and 1977, listed 177 faunal species that are associated with seagrass blades, 124 of which have been reported on eelgrass (Appendix C). Few studies, however, have focused on micro- and meiofauna. Although most studies have emphasized juvenile and adult macrofauna, the scientific community still does not agree as to whether certain species are, in fact, epifauna on the grass blades or benthic fauna associated with eelgrass meadows; we recognize that they may be both at different times. These general disagreements stem from the fact that many species have diel activity patterns and move between sediments and grass blades. Hence, the time of sampling (day versus night) and the sampling technique (grab or core versus solely selection of plant leaves) dictate categorization of the fauna.

Unlike microalgae, which tend to increase in density from the leaf base to the tip, faunal epiphytes display a variety of distributional trends: those that decrease in abundance up the stem; those which increase in abundance up the stem; and those which vary with the density of plant epiphytes. Nagle (1968) showed that Crepidula, Littorina, Corophium acherusicum, Corophium acutum, and some mites, polychaetes, and nematodes tended to be more abundant at the base of the stem. Samples of the adjacent sediment showed these species also were abundant there. Nagle concluded that these epiphytic fauna are a spill-over from normal benthic populations. He also found that some snails, caprellid amphipods, copepods, turbellarians, and bryozoans increased in density up the stem, while several species (e.g., Bittium, Cymadusa, Microdeutopus) were most dense on areas of the leaves with dense epiphytes. These distributions appear to be related either to currents or to feeding activities of the fauna. Robertson and Mann (1982) showed that there also are age-specific vertical gradients. Whereas adult Littorina neglecta were predominant near the leaf tip, newly-recruited 0+ age L. neglecta in Nova Scotia were most dense near the leaf base.

Similar distributions have been observed for sessile invertebrates on the west coast. Dykhouse (1976) found that the dominant sessile species on eelgrass in Humboldt Bay were Hippothoa hyalina (Bryozoa), Obelia longissima (Hydrozoa), Botrylloides sp. (Ascidiacea), and Diplosoma macdonaldi (Ascidiacea). H. hyalina was most prevalent near the base of the leaves and O. longissima was prevalent near the tip; the other two species were distributed randomly along the blade.

In a 14-month study of the fauna on eelgrass leaves near Chesapeake Bay, Marsh (1973) found high affinity indices among the samples taken, suggesting a fairly homogenous fauna at the sites he sampled. Most of the numerically dominant species were present throughout the year, with peak abundances during summer when grass was abundant, and minimum numbers during winter when eelgrass was sparse. During periods of low eelgrass density, many species apparently move onto/into the bottom sediments. Thayer et al. (1975a) observed a similar trend in one meadow in North Carolina with maximum numbers from March-July and minimum numbers during late fall and winter. There was a significant correlation observed between the decline in numbers in late summer through fall and an increase in fish biomass that suggested that predators also play a role in controlling these epifaunal abundances. Patterns of abundance, however, are not always consistent, for Nelson (1979a) reported maximum numbers of amphipods during winter (September-March) and low abundances throughout the summer near Beaufort (April-August), whereas Stuart (1982) found no significant differences in amphipod densities between winter and summer. Seasonality of epiphytic fauna, in addition to being influenced by available surface area for attachment and by predator interactions, also is influenced by spawning and recruitment, an aspect discussed by Nagle (1968). The baffling of waves and currents may allow for increased settlement of epi- as well as infaunal invertebrates (Orth 1977; Fonseca et al. 1983). The abundance per se of a species may be a function of its life history characteristics and have little to do with the dynamics of eelgrass.

Gastropods and amphipods dominated the seagrass fauna in studies in the York River (Marsh 1973) and near Beaufort (Stuart 1982) representing 43% and 18% of the numbers in the York River and 62% and 28% of the numbers near Beaufort. Bittium varium, Paracerceis caudata, Crepidula convexa, Ampithoe longimana, and Erichsonella attenuata accounted for almost 60% of the species in the York River (Marsh 1973), and B. varium, Cymadusa compta, A. longimana, Mitrella lunata, and Melita appendiculata accounted for almost 80% of species near Beaufort. Stauffer (1937) also reported Bittium and Mitrella common on eelgrass near Woods Hole prior to "wasting disease", but rare after it. Although many species of amphipods are epiphytic on eelgrass, frequently building tubes on the blades, Nelson (1979a) reported that infaunal amphipods were ~1.3 times more abundant than epifaunal tube-building forms and ~4 times more abundant than non-building epifaunal amphipods. Stuart (1982), however, found that these ratios may vary

greatly between eelgrass beds and suggested that differences may be a function of sediment particle size and organic content. Of course, current regimes also may play an important role.

Fauna on eelgrass blades can attain large numerical abundances. Marsh (1973) reported total densities of up to 400-500 organisms per gram dry weight of eelgrass leaves from the York River, which he extrapolated as being equivalent to 20-24 x 10^3 organisms m^{-2}. In a study of eelgrass, widgeon grass, and mixed grass beds in Chesapeake Bay, Orth and Boesch (1979) reported densities of about 80-8,000 animals per gram of grass, with the greatest density on eelgrass blades in October 1978 and June 1979 and on widgeon grass in April 1979 (~8,000 per gram). Maximum densities near Beaufort reported by Thayer et al. (1975a) were considerably smaller, 1,800 organisms m^{-2}, while Stuart (1982; unpubl. data) found maximum numbers in the same general area of ~21,000 m^{-2}. For individual species, Bittium varium (Figure 42) alone can attain densities of 200 individuals/gram of eelgrass in the Chesapeake Bay (Marsh 1973), and Littorina neglecta adults can reach a density of 20 individuals 100 cm^{-2} of leaf surface area (Robertson and Mann 1982). The maximum number of colonies (per meter of blade) of the bryozoan Hippothoa hyalina and hydrozoan Obelia longissima hydrocauli have been reported to be ~21 and 200, respectively (Dykhouse 1976).

4.5 BENTHIC AND EPIBENTHIC FAUNA
by H. Hoffman Stuart, North Carolina State University

Because of the extensive distribution of eelgrass along the east coast of the United States, and the wide variation in temperature and other factors over this area, benthic and epibenthic fauna associated with eelgrass can be categorized by three geographical zones. Cape Cod and Cape Hatteras are points that divide the coast into three different climatic, physiographic, and hydrographic regions. Sixty to 80% of the taxa north of Cape Cod also are found in northern Europe, but only 7% or 8% of the species found south of Cape Cod are shared with

Europe (Gosner 1971). Thirty percent of the decapods found south of Cape Hatteras are not found north of it (Williams 1965). Thus, benthic fauna in eelgrass beds at different latitudes may vary greatly in species composition (Table 6). Different species of the same genus, however, may occur at different latitudes. Most of these species seem to be epifaunal such as the gastropod genera Bittium and Anachis, the isopod Erichsonella, and the shrimp Hippolyte. Others are more clearly infaunal such as the bivalve Tellina, the polychaete Nereis, and the amphipod Corophium.

The distribution of species may be a function of interactions as well as physicochemical conditions both latitudinally and within a geographic area. Changes in species interactions may come about because some species are limited in their distribution. For example, distribution of the crab Carcinus maenas, a predator of the clam Mya arenaria (Glude 1954), may change in response to climatic cycles, and hence influence abundance of the clam. Many other species, such as the snapping shrimp Alpheus, also are limited in their distribution; the significance of the contribution of these species to community structure is unknown but may be important. Distribution of fish also may influence the community composition of invertebrates. For example, pinfish, Lagodon rhomboides, the most common fish in Beaufort eelgrass beds (Adams 1976a,b), are rare in grass beds in Chesapeake Bay and further north.

Within the same estuary, physicochemical conditions other than climatic changes associated with latitude also influence the distribution of fauna. Salinity, type of substratum (mud, sand, gravel, etc.), and energy from waves and currents have a strong influence on local distribution of animals. Disturbances such as storms, ice scouring, temperature extremes, temporary anoxic conditions, or other events can change community species composition by physically removing or by killing large numbers of one or more species.

The definition of animal habitats must be regarded as flexible since many animals may move in and out of beds or may change their microhabitat within beds, spending part of their time on the grass and part in or on the sediment. For example, bay scallops, Argopecten irradians, attach to eelgrass as juveniles, but later drop to the sediment surface (Thayer and Stuart 1974). The gastropod, Littorina neglecta, in Nova Scotia, moves to the sediment during December through mid-March and thereby avoids becoming frozen in the ice. Bittium and other snails may spend more time on leaves during the egg-laying season (Rasmussen 1973). In tropical grass beds in Florida the shrimp, Penaeus, is more common in night collections than during the day (Greening and Livingston 1982), but this may be a function of collection method and daylight burrowing behavior of these shrimp.

If species associated with eelgrass occur over a latitudinal range within the tolerance limits of the species, it is in part because the resources provided by the grass are similar within this gradient. The plant is important to the fauna and flora in many ways (Kikuchi and Peres 1977; Thayer et al. 1978). It influences the community indirectly by stabilizing sediments, calming waters, lowering turbidity, and recycling nutrients. Eelgrass is directly utilized by flora and fauna as a substrate for epiphytic micro- and macroalgae and sessile and resting animals. Animals also find shelter from predators and protection from sunlight at low tide. Heck and Thoman (1981) and Nelson (1979b) demonstrated that eelgrass shoots interferred with predator effectiveness in grazing on epifauna and epibenthos, but both studies demonstrated that a threshhold density of seagrass was required. Peterson (1982) demonstrated that the root-rhizome complex of Halodule interferes with predation of clams (Mercenaria mercenaria) by whelks (Busycon). The dog clam, Chione cancellata, however, did not receive the same degree of predator protection, presumably because it is a shallow-sediment dweller.

Epibenthic and infaunal invertebrates, as well as fauna on the grass blades, provide diverse food resources for resident and migratory predators, yet there is little experimental evidence to

70

Table 6. Partial list of epibenthic and benthic fauna reported from eelgrass meadows of the east coast of North America; (E) = primarily epibenthic; N = primarily north of Chesapeake Bay; S = primarily south of Chesapeake Bay.

CNIDARIA

    Ceriantheopsis americanus

GASTROPODS

Acteocina canaliculata	S
Anachis avara	
Bittium sp.	(E)
Crepidula sp.	(E)
Ilyanassa obsoleta	N
Lacuna vincta	N
Littorina littorea	N
Mitrella lunata	
Nassarius vibex	
Pyrgocythara plicosa	S

BIVALVES

Abra aequalis	
Argopecten irradians	
Atrina rigida	S
Chione cancellata	S
Cumingia tellinoides	N
Chione grus	S
Ensis directus	
Laevicardium mortoni	
Lyonsia hyalina	
Macoma tenta	
Mercenaria mercenaria	
Musculus lateralis	S
Mya arenaria	N
Mytilus edulis	N
Solemya velum	
Tagelus divisus	
Tellina sp.	

POLYCHAETES

Diopatra cuprea	S
Marphysa sanguinea	
Melinna maculata	(E)
Nereis falsa	
Nereis succinea	
Nereis virens	N
Notomastus hemipodus	S
Platynereis dumerilii	
Polydora ligni	
Prionospio heterobranchia	
Sthenelais boa	
Streblospio benedicti	

AMPHIPOD CRUSTACEANS

Ampelisca abdita	
Ampelisca vadorum	
Ampithoe longimana	(E)
Corophium acherusicum	
Corophium insidiosum	
Corophium bonelli	
Cymadusa compta	(E)
Gammarus mucronatus	(E)
Listriella barnardi	(E)
Lysianopsis alba	
Melita appendiculata	(E), S
Trichophoxus epistomus	S

ISOPOD CRUSTACEANS

Cyathura sp.	
Edotea triloba	
Erichsonella sp.	(E)
Idotea baltica	N
Paracerceis caudata	(E)

TANAID CRUSTACEANS

Leptochelia savigni	(E)

CUMACEAN CRUSTACEANS
    Oxyurostylis smithi

DECAPOD CRUSTACEANS
  Shrimp:

Alpheus sp.	S
Crangon septemspinosa	
Hippolyte sp.	(E)
Palaemonetes vulgaris	(E)
Penaeus sp.	

  Crabs:

Carcinus maenas	N
Callinectes sapidus	
Menippe mercenaria	S
Neopanope sayi	
Pagurus longicarpus	
Panopeus herbstii	S
Upogebia affinis	

OTHER ARTHROPODS
    Limulus polyphemus

ECHINODERMS

Ophioderma brevispinum	S
Sclerodactyla briareus	

indicate that predators regulate benthic prey abundances within these systems. Numerous field studies have shown that bivalves, polychaetes, amphipods, and crabs are consumed by fishes utilizing eelgrass beds (e.g., Thayer et al. 1975a; Adams 1976b; Orth and Boesch 1979; Merriner and Boehlert 1979; Summerson 1980; Thayer et al. 1980b; Lascara 1981). Predator exclusion experiments for the most part, however, have not demonstrated differences in total number of species or individuals inside cages relative to outside (Orth 1977; Nelson 1979b; Summerson 1980; Peterson 1982; Stuart 1982). Results of predator exclusion studies must be considered cautiously, because prior to about 1979 most studies lacked cage controls to estimate cage artifacts and they generally lacked replication (Stuart 1982).

In studies lacking cage controls, amphipod density within cages generally increased (Young and Young 1977; Nelson 1981). Nelson (1979b) and Stoner (1980) invoked the paradigm of predator control when seasonal increases in predators coincided with declines in amphipod abundance. Stuart (1982), however, was unable to demonstrate any significant difference between seasonal amphipod densities (P > 0.05) in eelgrass beds near Nelson's (1979b) study area two years later. The differences between the two studies simply may reflect year-to-year differences in either predators, prey, or both. Even though Choat and Kingett (1982) observed a decline in amphipod abundance that coincided with an increase in abundance of a sparid fish associated with macroalgae, they were unable to demonstrate an increase in amphipod density when predators were experimentally excluded.

Little information is available on the meiofauna and microfauna present in eelgrass meadows except for the work of Tietjen (1969). He found an average (per m^2) of 2×10^6 nematodes, 2×10^5 harpacticoid copepods, 6×10^4 ostracods, 4×10^4 polychaetes, 3×10^4 juvenile and larval bivalves, and 8×10^3 amphipods in sediments in eelgrass beds on Connecticut and Rhode Island. These densities were similar to those found in adjacent unvegetated areas, except densities of

harpacticoid copepods and polychaetes were 75% and 49% higher in grass beds, respectively.

4.6 ZOOPLANKTON by Jefferson T. Turner, Southeastern Massachusetts University

There have been few comparisons of the zooplankton in waters overlying seagrass beds and in those over unvegetated areas. Meyer (1982) sampled surface zooplankton over Ruppia maritima and Zostera marina beds and over unvegetated sandy substrates in the eastern Chesapeake Bay. Samples were collected at high tide, and most (81) were taken at night. However, 12 samples were taken in daylight for day-night comparisons.

Meyer found no significant differences between vegetated stations relative to unvegetated in zooplankton biomass over the 13-month period. Numbers and biomass levels were, however, one to two orders of magnitude higher at night than during the day. Some zooplankters, such as medusae and ctenophores, were more abundant over grass beds, where Meyer suggested they were concentrated by grass blades. Also, demersal plankton (benthic organisms that enter the plankton at night) such as amphipods, isopods, harpacticoid copepods, cumaceans, tanaids, mysids, and adult polychaetes, were more abundant over grass beds at night. Other than gelatinous and demersal plankton, however, the species composition of grass bed plankton resembled that over sandy substrate or in open waters of the lower Chesapeake Bay, and abundance was similar.

Meyer suggested that demersal plankton are important forage items for pelagic-feeding planktivorous fishes which reside in grass beds at night. During the day these same organisms appear to be important food for diurnal benthic-feeding fishes. Since many planktivorous fishes appear to use grass beds as refuges, Meyer suggested that if nondemersal, open-water zooplankton are concentrated in grass beds on flood tides, they might provide elevated intermittent food sources for grass bed fishes.

Part of the reason for elevated zooplankton abundance in seagrass beds may relate to swarming behavior of the zooplankters themselves. In situ observations using SCUBA techniques have revealed that the copepods Acartia spinata and Oithona nana swarm in grass beds in the Florida Keys (Emery 1968). These swarms maintained their positions against wave surge and water currents, and if dispersed, would quickly reform. Using hand-held bottles for collection of copepods from swarms, Emery found densities of 110,000 copepods/m^3. Hamner and Carleton (1979) also used SCUBA to observe copepod swarms over seagrass beds in Palau, and over coral reefs in Palau and Australia. Numerous monospecific swarms of the copepods Oithona oculata and Acartia bispinosa were observed, and Hamner and Carleton found copepod densities in swarms to be even higher than those reported by Emery (1968). As many as $0.5-1.5 \times 10^6$ copepods m^{-3} were recorded for swarms over grass beds and coral reefs. Hamner and Carleton suggested that protection against predators was a likely advantage of swarming.

The most comprehensive examination of the relationship of zooplankton to seagrass beds to appear thus far is that of Fulton (1982). In this study, the zooplankton of a Zostera marina bed near Beaufort, North Carolina, was compared over several years with that of nearby unvegetated estuarine channels. Fulton also used both field and laboratory experimental techniques to examine the roles of the eelgrass bed as both a refuge from predation for zooplankton, and as a source of abundant food for predators.

Fulton found that the copepod assemblage of the grass bed was dominated by epibenthic littoral species (Pseudodiaptomus coronatus, Ridgewayia sp., Hemicyclops americanus, Cyclopina sp., and benthic harpacticoids). These copepods were at least an order of magnitude more abundant in the grass bed than in an adjacent unvegetated channel. Most of the epibenthic copepods were aggregated near the bottom of the grass bed during the day and became planktonic mainly at night. Also, the epibenthic copepods were a minor component of the zooplankton in channels where more pelagic copepods such as Oithona colcarva, Acartia

tonsa, Paracalanus crassirostris, and in winter, Centropages hamatus dominated. Although there were seasonal, diel, and taxon-specific variations, the abundances of Acartia tonsa and other pelagic copepods were usually an order of magnitude lower in the grass bed than in the channel. Fulton also compared the abundances of zooplankton predators (postlarval fish and decapod shrimps) in the grass bed and the channel. These predators were usually aggregated in the grass bed, particularly from spring through fall. Abundances of all zooplankton (except for epibenthic species that were always abundant in grass beds) were lower in grass beds in summer. Also, in late winter, the decline in abundance of Centropages subadults, the dominant nonlittoral copepod in the grass bed, coincided with an influx of large numbers of late-stage fish larvae (e.g., Leiostomus xanthurus). Together, these observations suggested that fish predation on pelagic copepods in grass beds was intense, but that epibenthic copepods might find the grass bed to be a refuge from predation.

Both gut content and experimental laboratory feeding studies supported the hypothesis that the midsummer decline in pelagic zooplankton abundance in the grass was due to daytime planktivory by silversides (Menidia menidia). In addition, larval spot (L. xanthurus) showed a clear preference, both in gut content examinations and in predation experiments, for Centropages subadults over similarly-sized Acartia tonsa. The virtual absence of predation by fish on Pseudodiaptomus coronatus in feeding experiments and the rare occurrence of this copepod in the guts of field-collected fish supported the hypothesis that this copepod used the grass bed as a refuge. Planktivorous silversides were observed by Fulton (1982) to feed in midwater in aquaria, but not off aquarium sides and bottoms. Since P. coronatus aggregated near the bottoms of aquaria in the day, but other highly predated pelagic copepod species did not, the pelagics rather than P. coronatus were selectively eaten by silversides. Conversely, pinfish (Lagodon rhomboides), which did feed near sides and

73

bottoms of glass aquaria, ate substantial amounts of P. coronatus. However, when substrate of similar dark coloration to that in the grass beds was placed in aquarium bottoms, the darkly pigmented P. coronatus became more cryptic and suffered lower predation from pinfish. Based on these laboratory studies, Fulton concluded that eelgrass beds can serve as refuges against predation for certain epibenthic zooplankton species such as P. coronatus. The epibenthic habitat of P. coronatus protects it from predation by midwater planktivores such as silversides, and its cryptic coloration retards predation by epibenthic planktivores such as pinfish. Conversely, nonepibenthic pelagic zooplankters appear to experience substantial predation in grass beds, relative to unvegetated areas, because the grass beds expose them to higher abundances of planktivores without offering any refuge from predation. By inference, it appears that grass beds are areas of elevated food concentration for planktivores, and perhaps that is one explanation for their great abundance there.

4.7 NEKTON

Eelgrass meadows have long been considered nursery or feeding areas for a wide variety of nektonic species, many of which are of direct commercial or recreational value (Table 7), or which are important as food for other fish and for birds. To be of significance as a nursery, a habitat must provide protection from predators, a substrate for attachment of sessile stages, and/or a plentiful food

Table 7. Partial list of representative species of commercially and recreationally important species collected from temperate seagrass beds. Life history stages (A = adult, J = juvenile, L = larvae, E = eggs), if reported, are shown. Modified from Thayer et al. (1979).

Common name	Scientific name	Life stage
Spotted seatrout	Cynoscion nebulosus	J
Mullet	Mugil cephalus	J
Spot	Leiostomus xanthurus	A,J
Pinfish	Lagodon rhomboides	A,J
Pigfish	Orthopristis chrysoptera	J
Gag grouper	Mycteroperca microlepis	J
Sheepshead	Archosargus probatocephalus	A,J
Holbrooks porgy	Diplodus holbrooki	J
Halfbreak	Hyporhamphus unifasciatus	J
Pacific herring	Clupea harengus pallasi	E
English sole	Parophrys retulus	J
Striped sea perch	Embiotoca lateralis	J
Thread herring	Opisthonema oglinum	J
Permit (pompano)	Trachinotus falcatus	J
White grunt	Haemulon plumieri	J
Silver perch	Bairdiella chryosura	J,A
Mojarra	Gerres cinereus	J
Bluefish	Pomatomus saltatrix	A,J
Tautog	Tautoga unitis	J,E
Summer flounder	Paralichthys dentatus	A,J
Southern flounder	Paralichthys lethostigma	A,J
Menhaden	Brevoortia tyrannus	A,J,L
Brown shrimp	Penaeus aztecus	A,J
Pink shrimp	Penaeus duorarum	A,J
Blue crab	Callinectes sapidus	A

supply (Thayer et al. 1979). Seagrass habitats fulfill all of these criteria and, as a consequence, there has been considerable effort to describe both their composition and functional relations to nekton. Based largely on research in southern Japan (Kikuchi 1961, 1962, 1966), Kikuchi (1980) subdivided the nekton into four major categories: (1) permanent residents, (2) seasonal residents (further subdivided into juvenile and subadults, and spawning season residents), (3) transients, and (4) casual species. The nekton display diel, tidal, and seasonal movements, and thus, are an important factor in the coupling of the eelgrass system to adjacent aquatic habitats (see Section 4.10 and Chapter 5).

Prior to research of Briggs and O'Conner (1971) in Great South Bay, New York, there had been few published accounts of nekton communities in eelgrass meadows along the Atlantic coast of North America. Since this publication, however, there have been numerous attempts to describe their structure and function. Research has centered largely in two geographic areas: Chesapeake Bay area (Merriner and Boehlert 1979; Orth and Heck 1980; Heck and Orth 1980a,b; Lascara 1981; Weinstein and Brooks 1983) and North Carolina (Thayer et al. 1975a; Adams 1976a,b; Nelson 1979 a,b; Summerson 1980; Summerson and Peterson 1984). These studies and others in temperate areas (Kikuchi 1966; Robertson 1980) show, in general, that the nekton component is a dense and diverse assemblage of animals compared to 'the fish community of unvegetated habitats and that it displays diel, tidal, and seasonal fluctuations in abundance and composition. Heck and Orth (1980a) speculated that the abundance and diversity of fish species should increase in accordance with eelgrass bed structural complexity until feeding efficiency is reduced by interference with grass blades or until other unfavorable conditions occur, at which point densities should decrease. Seasonal fluctuations in abundance and biomass appear to be in response to both water temperature and eelgrass density. Whereas Adams (1976a) suggested that temperature was the main factor influencing the biomass of fishes, Orth and Heck (1980) stated that within the normal environmental activity range of

the fishes using these habitats, abundance and composition were more correlated with eelgrass density than with water temperature.

Few studies have been directed specifically at decapods as a component of the nekton. Between September 1976 and December 1977, Heck and Orth (1980a) took monthly trawls in monospecific eelgrass and in mixed eelgrass-widgeon grass meadows in the lower Chesapeake Bay, and found a high degree of similarity in the decapod fauna. Six species dominated the fauna, representing 98% of the total numbers: Palaemonetes vulgaris (68% of the total), P. pugio, P. intermedius, Crangon septemspinosa, Callinectes sapidus, and Penaeus aztecus. With the exception of C. septemspinosa, these species also were important components of eelgrass meadows of North Carolina (Stuart 1975, 1982; Thayer et al. 1975a; Summerson 1980) and of tropical seagrass meadows (Zieman 1982). Differences do exist between meadows in Chesapeake Bay and North Carolina and subtropical systems, however. For example, caridean shrimps (Hippolyte, Tozeuma, Thor, and Periclimenes) are numerous in North Carolina and Florida seagrass areas, but are rare in Chesapeake Bay.

Like many temperate species, decapods generally attain maximum numbers in late spring-midsummer. Maximum abundances tend to be earlier near the southern limit of eelgrass range (Thayer et al. 1975a) and progressively later northward (Heck and Orth 1980a). Recruitment of young appears to be responsible, in part, for seasonal increases; and predation or migration to deeper waters at times of extremely warm water temperatures (frequently characteristic of shallow eelgrass meadows) appear to be responsible for declining numbers in early summer (North Carolina: Thayer et al. 1975a; Adams 1976a) or late summer (Chesapeake Bay: Heck and Orth 1980a). Decapod crustaceans also are more abundant in night samples than in day samples, possibly a function of diel migration patterns or because many species may burrow into sediments during the day. These crustaceans are considerably more abundant in grass meadows than in adjacent unvegetated habitats. An example of these differences and densities that can be attained is shown in Table 8 a,b. Fishes common to eelgrass meadows display diel, tidal, and seasonal patterns of abundance and species composition. Fish densities frequently exceed those in adjacent unvegetated areas of similar depth. Because fish are highly mobile they are difficult to label as resident or nonresident species. Unlike tropical and subtropical environments, temperate eelgrass meadows experience a greater tidal range and frequently are exposed during spring low tides. This not only stresses the seagrass plants (see Chapter 2), but also reduces, or eliminates temporarily, the fish component of the system. Therefore, few species have been

Table 8a. Decapods collected in a mixed eelgrass-widgeon grass meadow (six 2-min tows) and in an adjacent unvegetated area (three 5-min tows) in the lower Chesapeake Bay. (Taken from Heck and Orth 1980a, Table 2.)

Species	February Veg.	February Unveg.	March Veg.	March Unveg.	April Veg.	April Unveg.	June Veg.	June Unveg.	July Veg.	July Unveg.	September Veg.	September Unveg.	October Veg.	October Unveg.	December Veg.	December Unveg.
Callinectes sapidus	25	--	5	1	5	4	14	--	319	40	33	3	55	1	--	--
Palaemonetes vulgaris	35	--	16	3	785	10	10,660	3	53	--	7	--	24	--	--	--
Palaemonetes pugio	37	--	4	2	31	--	167	--	--	--	--	--	2	--	2	2
Palaemonetes intermedius	-	--	--	--	4	--	12	--	2	--	--	--	--	1	--	--
Crangon septemspinosa	5	--	4	13	26	4	365	--	3	1	29	--	39	9	5	1
Hippolyte pleuracanthus	2	--	--	--	--	--	--	--	--	--	--	--	--	--	--	--
Penaeus aztecus	-	--	--	--	--	--	--	--	--	--	7	--	27	--	--	--
Alpheus heterochaelis	1	--	--	--	--	--	--	--	--	--	--	--	--	--	3	--
Pagurus longicarpus	2	--	10	1	46	--	12	1	1	--	3	--	41	1	--	1
Neopanope sayi	9	--	12	2	8	--	25	7	16	1	12	--	1	--	--	--
Libinia dubia	4	--	--	--	--	--	--	--	--	--	8	3	9	--	--	--
Total	120	0	51	22	905	18	11,255	11	394	42	99	6	198	12	10	4

Table 8b. Day-night collections of decapods in mixed eelgrass-widgeon grass and in an adjacent unvegetated area in the lower Chesapeake Bay. (Taken from Heck and Orth 1980a, Table 3.)

Species	July 29 Day Veg.	July 29 Day Unveg.	July 29 Night Veg.	July 29 Night Unveg.	Oct. 10 Day Veg.	Oct. 10 Day Unveg.	Oct. 10 Night Veg.	Oct. 10 Night Unveg.
Callinectes sapidus	319	40	53	3	54	7	256	23
Palaemonetes vulgaris	53	--	1,484	--	5	3	87	1
Palaemonetes pugio	--	--	2	--	--	--	1	--
Palaemonetes intermedius	2	--	--	--	--	--	--	--
Crangon septemspinosa	3	1	237	--	34	63	1,354	581
Penaeus aztecus aztecus	--	--	--	--	34	--	168	--
Pagurus longicarpus	1	--	5	--	8	9	5	5
Neopanope sayi	16	1	2	--	6	27	22	3
Libinia dubia	--	--	2	--	13	32	20	10
Hippolyte pleuracanthus	--	--	--	--	--	--	10	--
Leander tenuicornis	--	--	3	--	--	--	--	--
Ovalipes ocellatus	--	--	--	--	--	--	--	1
Portunus gibbesii	--	--	--	--	--	--	--	1
Tozeuma carolinense	--	--	--	--	--	--	1	--
Total	394	42	1,788	3	154	141	1,924	625

recorded as permanent residents of eelgrass meadows; most are considered seasonal residents.

Robertson (1980) defined permanent residents as those species that remain in a grass bed throughout the tidal cycle and, agreeing with Kikuchi (1980), pointed out that these normally are small species. We use the term residents to mean species common to and utilizing the grass beds as nursery areas or refuges over a protracted period (several months). Therefore, we do not make a distinction between Kikuchi's permanent and seasonal resident categories. There have been, however, several species collected in grass beds in North Carolina, Chesapeake Bay, and Long Island that, according to Robertson's definition, could be considered more or less permanent members: Syngnathus fuscus, S. floridae, Gobionellus boleosoma, Gobiosoma bosci, Hypsoblennius hentzi, and Chasmodes bosquianus.

Seasonal residents of eelgrass beds are a diverse and a large group, and many are also common inhabitants of other wetland and aquatic areas that constitute estuaries and the shallow coastal zone. As noted by Weinstein and Brooks (1983), many of the common species present in shallow water estuarine habitats, and frequently considered generalists with respect to habitat requirements, actually show a clear habitat preference and should not be labeled habitat generalists per se. Their preferences depend not only on season, but also on geographic locality. Sparids (e.g., porgies), sciaenids (e.g., drums), and engraulids (e.g., anchovies), appear to dominate the seasonal fish fauna of eelgrass beds along the Atlantic coast of North America, although gerreids (e.g., mojarras), atherinids (e.g., silversides), and lutjanids (e.g., snappers) also are prevalent. Lagodon rhomboides (pinfish), a sparid, dominates near Beaufort (Adams 1976a,b) and also is prevalent in subtropical Florida areas (Zieman 1982); Leiostomus xanthurus (spot), a sciaenid, dominates grass beds in the lower Chesapeake Bay (Orth and Heck 1980); and Menidia menidia (Atlantic silverside), an atherinid, dominates grass beds of Long Island Sound (Briggs and O'Conner 1971). Other species are also prevalent in different grass beds or in other years.

Frequently not considered true residents because of their pelagic and schooling behavior, Atlantic silversides do occur in relatively high numbers, particularly at night, and as a consequence, may have considerable impact on the planktonic component of the system (Merriner and Boehlert 1979).

Although these three species may, in fact, dominate fish communities in eelgrass beds, they also are characteristic of other habitats. Weinstein and Brooks (1983) published one of the first direct comparions between two representatives of each of two primary temperate nursery areas: seagrass beds (Zostera and Ruppia) and marsh creeks (upstream and downstream) in the lower Chesapeake Bay (Table 9). Using cluster analysis, they were able to distinguish seven species groupings: I, Anchoa mitchilli was evenly distributed among the four sample areas; II, Paralichthys dentatus and the blue crab, Callinectes sapidus, also were spread fairly evenly, distributed with a trend toward greater abundance in seagrass beds; III,

Table 9. Two-way coincidence table comparing station (Groups A and B) and species (Groups I-VII) associations at Vaucluse Shores, Virginia. Clustering by flexible sorting strategy = 0.25; similarity index C (Morisita 1959), all data untransformed. (From Weinstein and Brooks 1983, Table 2.)

Species	A		B	
	Zostera	Ruppia	Marsh upstream	Marsh downstream
I Anchoa mitchilli	139	104	183	69
II Paralichthys dentatus	71	78	5	62
Callinectes sapidus	1004	1409	661	1282
III Leiostomus xanthurus	3794	3270	11307	14354
Anguilla rostrata	3	6	7	36
Trinectes maculatus	2	6	16	48
IV Brevoortia tyrannus		3	390	38
Gobiosoma bosci	2		29	7
V Eucinostomus argenteus	12	8		
Urophycis regia	13	10		
Syngnathus fuscus	753	871		
Gobiesox strumosus	6	10		
Ophidion marginatum	36	46		
VI Tautoga onitis	13	7		
Bairdiella chrysoura	123	64	16	11
Apeltes quadracus	105	2		
VII Hypsoblennius hentz	19	53		
Opsanus tau	15	45		
Centropristis striata	8	33		
Chasmodes bosquianus	2	16		

Leiostomus xanthurus was the dominant species found in grass beds, but along with two other species (Anguilla rostrata and Trinectes maculatus) showed a preference for the marsh habitat; IV, both Brevoortia tyrannus and Gobiosoma bosci preferred the marsh habitat; and V-VII, all species preferred grass beds, being evenly dispersed between eelgrass and widgeon grass (Group V), prevalent in eelgrass (Group VI), or more abundant in widgeon grass (Group VII).

We collected 56 species of fish (seasonal residents, transients, and casual members) from three eelgrass beds, three Spartina marsh channels, and one intertidal sand flat near Beaufort, North Carolina, during 1978-80 (Table 10). A majority are common to eelgrass beds elsewhere in North Carolina, Chesapeake Bay, and Long Island Sound. Menidia menidia, Leiostomus xanthurus, and Mugil cephalus were abundant in each habitat. The relative abundance notation, however, may be misleading, since species dominance varied both spatially and temporally, and the three habitat types were dominated by entirely different species at different times during the 24-month collection period (all species were collected by gill net, fyke net, and seine). Bairdiella chrysoura, Mustelus canis, and L. xanthurus constituted >50% of the nekton numbers collected in eelgrass; M. menidia, L. xanthurus, and A. mitchilli >50% in the marsh channels; and L. xanthurus and F. majalis >50% in the intertidal flat (Table 11). L. xanthurus was the only dominant common to all three habitat types, and as was observed by Weinstein and Brooks (1983), was

Table 10. Relative abundance of fishes collected in 1978-80 from three habitat types in the Newport River (North Carolina) estuary-sound complex. ***=abundant, **=common, *=rare. (J) refers to small juveniles only.

Species name	Common name	Seagrass	Marsh channel	Intertidal flat
Menidia sp.	Silverside	***	***	***
Leiostomus xanthurus	Spot	***	***	***
Anchoa mitchilli	Bay anchovy	**	***	*
Anchoa hepsetus	Striped anchovy	*	**	*
Fundulus majalis	Striped killifish	-	***	***
Fundulus heteroclitus	Mummichog	-	***	***
Bairdiella chrysoura	Silver perch	***	***	*
Lagodon rhomboides	Pinfish	***	***	-
Paralichthys lethostigma	Southern flounder	**	**(J)	*
Paralichthys dentatus	Summer flounder	*	**	*
Mugil cephalus	Striped mullet	***	***	***
Brevoortia tyrannus	Atlantic menhaden	**	*	*
Micropogonias undulatus	Atlantic croaker	**	*	-
Membras martinica	Rough silverside	***	*	*
Monacanthus hispidus	Planehead filefish	**	*	**
Aluterus schoepfi	Orange filefish	*	-	*
Pomatomus saltatrix	Bluefish	**	*	-
Hyporhamphus unifasciatus	Halfbeak	**	*	-
Strongylura marina	Atlantic needlefish	*	*	*
Syngnathus fuscus	Northern pipefish	*	-	-
Menticirrhus americanus	Southern kingfish	*	*	-
Lutjanus griseus	Gray snapper	-	*	*
Peprilus triacanthus	Butterfish	*	*	-
Cynoscion nebulosus	Spotted trout	*	*	*

(continued)

Table 10. (concluded).

Species name	Common name	Seagrass	Marsh channel	Intertidal flat
Caranx hippos	Crevalle jack	-	*	**
Sphyraena barracuda	Great barracuda	*	*	*
Mycteroperca microlepis	Gag	*	*	-
Sphaeroides maculatus	Northern puffer	-	*	-
Chilomycterus schoepfi	Striped burrfish	-	*	-
Chloroscombrus chrysurus	Atlantic bumper	-	*	-
Cyprinodon variegatus	Sheepshead minnow	-	**	***
Chaetodipterus faber	Atlantic spadefish	-	*	*
Trachinotus carolinus	Florida pompano	-	*	***
Opsanus tau	Oyster toadfish	**	*	-
Orthopristis chrysoptera	Pigfish	**	**	-
Rissola marginata	Striped cusk-eel	-	*	-
Citharichthys spilopterus	Bay whiff	-	*	-
Eucinostomus gula	Silvery jenny	*	*	*
Hypsoblennius hentzi	Feather blenny	*	*	-
Chasmodes bosquianus	Striped blenny	-	*	-
Selene vomer	Lookdown	*	*	-
Fistularia tabacaria	Bluespotted cornetfish	-	*	-
Trinectes maculatus	Hogchoker	-	*	-
Sciaenops ocellatus	Red drum	*	*	-
Synodus foetens	Inshore lizardfish	-	*	-
Archosargus probatocephalus	Sheepshead	-	*	-
Mustelus canis	Smooth dogfish	***	*	-
Rhizoprionodon terraenovae	Atlantic sharpnose shark	*	-	-
Cynoscion regalis	Weakfish	*	-	-
Symphurus plagiusa	Blackcheek tonguefish	*	*	-
Prionotus evolans	Striped searobin	*	*	*
Prionotus scitulus	Leopard searobin	*	-	-
Stenotomus caprinus	Longspine porgy	*	-	-
Histrio histrio	Sargassum fish	-	-	*
Balistes capriscus	Gray triggerfish	-	-	*
Gobiosoma bosci	Naked goby	-	*	-

Table 11. Dominant fish species collected from three habitat types in the Newport River estuarine-sound complex during 1979-80. Percent of the total represented by each is shown.

Zostera marina habitat	Spartina marsh channel	Intertidal sandflat
Bairdiella chrysoura (21.8)	Menidia sp. (22.0)	Leiostomus xanthurus (35.2)
Mustelus canis (15.7)	Leiostomus xanthurus (21.2)	Fundulus majalis (30.0)
Leiostomus xanthurus (14.5)	Anchoa mitchilli (18.7)	Menidia sp. (11.0)
Menidia sp. (11.8)	Fundulus heteroclitus (17.2)	Cyprinodon variegatus (8.6)
Membras martinica (11.3)	Bairdiella chrysoura (8.6)	Trachinotus carolinus (8.3)
Lagodon rhomboides (9.9)	Mugil cephalus (8.6)	Mugil cephalus (8.3)
Micropogonias undulatus (3.3)		
Orthopristis chrysoptera (2.8)		

numerically more abundant in marsh channels. These data contrast with those of Adams' study (1976a), where fish were collected by drop net and the community was dominated by pinfish.

A large proportion of the seasonal residents of eelgrass meadows within the geographic scope of this profile spawn over the continental shelf and enter estuaries in winter as late-stage larvae or early juveniles, taking up residency until the following fall when they move offshore to renew the cycle. The cycle follows the general sequence of low abundance in winter, increased abundance during spring, and maximum abundance in summer-early fall (Figure 44). The initial increase in spring tends to occur later as one moves north. Because the spring increase results primarily from recruitment of early-stage juveniles (Adams 1976a; Orth and Heck 1980; Weinstein and Brooks 1983), the peak in fish biomass is displaced somewhat, with increasing biomass in late spring and maximum biomass in July and August (Figure

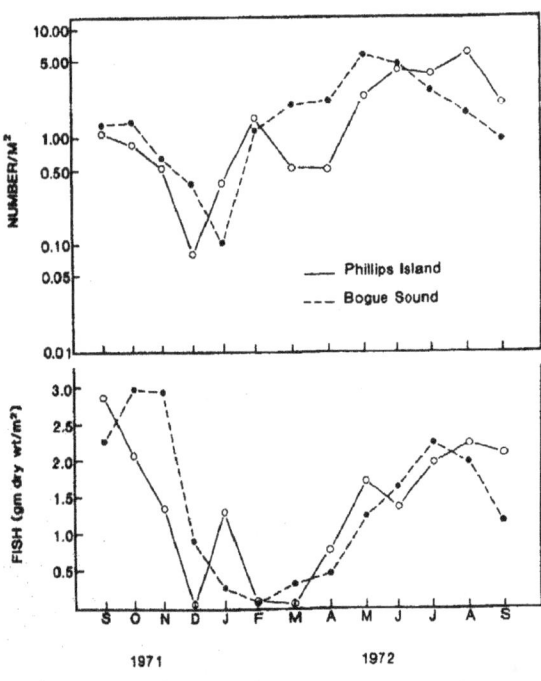

Figure 44. Temporal distribution of numeric abundance (upper) and biomass (lower) of fishes collected in two eelgrass beds near Beaufort, North Carolina. (Modified from Adams 1976a.)

44). Thayer et al. (1975a) and Adams (1976a) reported that near Beaufort, North Carolina, the fall peak in biomass seen in Figure 44 was the result of an influx of adult pinfish (L. rhomboides), whereas the summer biomass was composed of a combination of juvenile pinfish, pigfish (Orthopristis chrysoptera), and silver perch (Bairdiella chrysoura), which entered the meadows as larvae in early spring through early summer and grew at an exponential rate during this period.

Thus, the seasonal fish fauna in grass beds at any given time of year is composed of larvae, juveniles, and adults, and many of the species, although also found in adjacent systems, display fairly distinct preferences. By-and-large, the major life history stages are juveniles, which use these meadows as a refuge and for food resources.

Food habit studies leave little doubt that nekton feed within and remove considerable biomass and thus energy from eelgrass meadows (e.g. Thayer et al. 1975a; Adams 1976b; Merriner and Boehlert 1979; Orth and Boesch 1979; Lascara 1981). Five species of juvenile fish were collected day and night throughout the tidal cycle from three seagrass meadows near Beaufort, North Carolina (Thayer, unpubl.). Seventy-six percent of the fish leaving the beds on ebbing tide, as opposed to 46% entering the beds on flooding tide, had food in their guts. The total mass of food in the gut of fish leaving relative to that in fish entering was about 3:1. The nursery function of these meadows also is evidenced by the abundance and apparent growth (e.g., increase in mean size over time) of these juveniles (see Adams 1976a).

Few investigations of the fish fauna of eelgrass meadows have addressed large and/or schooling fishes. These fish generally are carnivores and, although they represent only a small proportion of the fish numbers or biomass, may be important in structuring both the nekton and benthic populations of seagrass beds. Species which can be included in the groupings of transient and casual community components include: bluefish (Pomatomus saltatrix), cownose ray Rhinoptera bonasus), bluntnose stingray (Dasyatis

80

sayi), sandbar shark (Carcharhinus plumbeus) = (C. milberti), smooth dogfish (Mustelus canis), Atlantic sharpnose shark (Rhizoprionodon terraenovae), weakfish (Cynoscion regalis), and spotted seatrout (Cynoscion nebulosus). Based on sampling within eelgrass and eelgrass-widgeon grass meadows with gill nets it can be concluded that C. plumbeus, C. regalis, and M. canis are slightly more abundant in grass meadows than in unvegetated areas and that they utilize the habitat regularly over a protracted period (Merriner and Boehlert 1979; Lascara 1981; Thayer unpubl. data). Sampling time (diel or seasonal) thus influences the species collected, and the technique used to collect organisms also influences one's decision regarding whether a species is a resident or not.

These large predators could be of considerable importance in structuring seagrass communities, since the majority appear to be highly selective feeders. Merriner and Boehlert (1979) collected 79 Carcharhinus plumbeus in eelgrass beds in the lower Chesapeake Bay. Fishes -- Brevoortia tyrannus, Leiostomus xanthurus, and Hypsoblennius hentzi -- dominated the gut contents. Fifteen percent of the sharks had fed exclusively on crabs, 31% on fish, and 54% on both fish and crabs. In the stomach contents of 208 Mustelus canis, ranging in size from 325 to 400 mm, collected from eelgrass beds near Beaufort, North Carolina (Thayer et al. 1980b), crabs (primarily portunids) constituted over 50% of the diet (Figure 45), and in almost every case stomachs were full.

Feeding activity of large carnivores may alter faunal structure directly by predation or indirectly by uprooting the seagrass or by altering the substrate. Orth (1975) reported significant changes not only in the density of the primary food (Mya arenaria) of the cownose rays (Rhinoptera bonasus), but also in the density of seagrass and other infauna following movement of the rays into the lower Chesapeake Bay. Cownose rays apparently dig into the bottom when they feed. Mya populations were reduced from original levels of 60-1000/m^2 to zero following cownose ray feeding, and virtually all of the eelgrass was uprooted

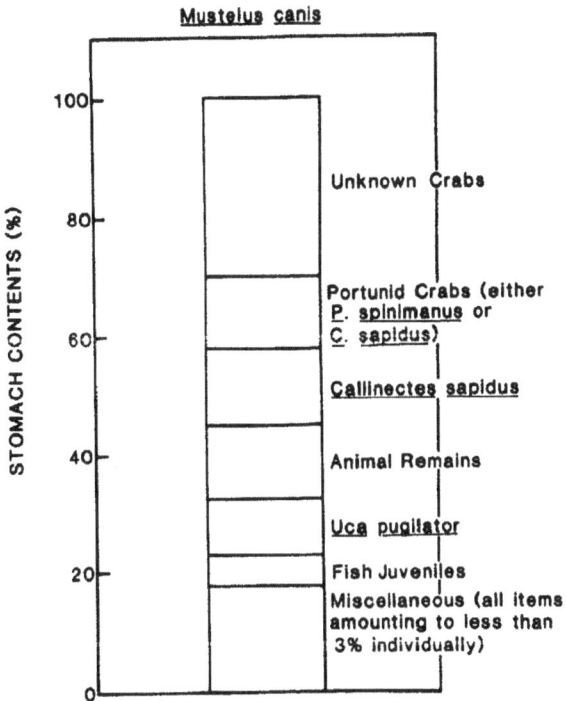

Figure 45. Stomach contents of Mustelus canis collected from eelgrass beds near Beaufort, North Carolina.

and removed from the feeding area. Sediments were altered and there was a reduction in other infauna too.

4.8 REPTILES AND MAMMALS

To our knowledge, the adult green turtle, Chelonia mydas, is the only reptile reported to utilize eelgrass beds; we have seen many diamondback terrapin passing through eelgrass beds near Beaufort on their way to lay eggs, however. Felger and Moser (1973) reported that C. mydas feeds on eelgrass on the west coast and is actively hunted by the Seri Indians of Sonora, Mexico; occasionally green turtles are seen in the estuaries of North Carolina (F. Schwartz, Institute of Marine Sciences, University of North Carolina, Morehead City, North Carolina; pers. comm.). Zieman (1982) described the occurrence of this species in tropical seagrass meadows, and Fenchel et al. (1979), Bjorndal (1980), and Thayer et al. (1982, in press a) discussed aspects of their feeding

81

ecology. Dugongs (Dugong dugon) also use eelgrass (Zostera capricorni) in Australia. Numerous other mammals, including minks, wolverines, otters, foxes, bears, and raccoons, occasionally feed on fauna in eelgrass meadows. The Seri Indians of Mexico and the Kwakiut Indians of British Columbia reportedly used the seeds and shoots of eelgrass as food. Of course, man, too, makes his presence known through fishery harvest.

4.9 BIRDS

Prodigious numbers of birds (Figure 46) can be observed feeding in eelgrass meadows at both low and high tide.

Although a list of 37 species of birds reported to feed on temperate seagrasses is presented in the next section of this chapter, there have been few published accounts on the use of eelgrass beds by birds (Thayer et al. in press a). The avian fauna reportedly associated with temperate seagrass meadows can be classified as waders, shore birds, aerial searchers, floating and diving water birds, and birds of prey (Table 12). The diets of these fauna span the trophic scale from direct herbivory on submerged aquatic plants to direct carnivores on invertebrates and fish, although a large proportion appear to be flexible omnivores displaying dietary shifts in accordance with food resource availability. Because

Figure 46. Birds feeding on an exposed eelgrass meadow near Beaufort, North Carolina.

82

of their seasonally large numbers and feeding habits, birds may affect standing crops and biomass of plants, invertebrates, and fishes within eelgrass meadows (Thayer et al. in press a).

Several studies suggest that there is a direct link between abundance or grazing process of birds that feed on eelgrass and density of the grass. These waterfowl include black and American brant geese, swans (Figure 47), and ducks. The saga of the brant is probably the most frequently cited example of a direct link between eelgrass and the abundance of avian fauna. McRoy (1966) established that black brant use the seagrass beds of Izembeck Lagoon, Alaska, as their principal feeding area during fall migrations, consuming ~4% of the standing crop of eelgrass during their stay. Cottam (1934) indicated that on the east coast, American brant, whose diet can approach 80% eelgrass, were severely reduced in numbers following the eelgrass "wasting disease". These birds switched to a diet dominated by widgeon grass and sea lettuce (Ulva sp.) following the decline of eelgrass. Other species of

Table 12. Seasonal occurrence of some representative birds observed in North Carolina eelgrass meadows.

Common name	Species name	Season
WADERS:		
Snowy egret	Egretta thula	Year-round
Little blue heron	Egretta caerulea	Summer
Tricolored (Louisiana) heron	Egretta tricolor	Year-round
Great blue heron	Ardea herodias	Year-round
SHORE BIRDS:		
Semipalmated sandpiper	Calidris pusilla	Transient
Western sandpiper	Calidris mauri	Winter
White-rumped sandpiper	Calidris fuscicollis	Transient
Sanderling	Calidris alba	Winter
AERIAL SEARCHERS:		
Forster's tern	Sterna forsteri	Fall-winter
Herring gull	Larus argentatus	Winter
Laughing gull	Larus atricilla	Year-round
Brown pelican	Pelecanus occidentalis	Year-round
FLOATING AND DIVING WATER BIRDS:		
Tundea (whistling) swan	Cygnus columbianus	Occasional winter
Canada goose	Branta canadensis	Winter
Brant	Branta bernicla	Winter
Redhead	Aythya americana	Winter
Lesser scaup	Aythya affinis	Winter
White-winged scoter	Melanitta fusca	Winter
Surf scoter	Melanitta perspicillata	Winter
BIRDS OF PREY:		
Osprey	Pandion halietus	Summer

Figure 47. Swans feeding in an eelgrass meadow in Rhode Island. Note the blades of grass in the beaks of the two swans on the left.

waterfowl in the United States likewise were affected (Chapter 1, Section 1.3). The increase in dark-bellied brant geese (Branta bernicla bernicla) in southern England since the 1950's has been related to the recovery of eelgrass as well as to other factors (Ogilvie and St. Joseph 1976).

Feeding by herbivorous birds can significantly alter seagrass density (Jacobs et al. 1981; Thayer et al. in press a; Cobb and Harlin, unpubl. data, University of Rhode Island). Jacobs et al. (1981) showed that grazing by geese and ducks in the Dutch Wadden Sea resulted in eelgrass (Z. noltii and Z. marina) meadows being converted from dense, homogeneous beds to heterogeneous stands with an almost total disappearance of the aboveground parts of the plant. Wilkins (1982) estimated that during winter 1978-79 the Canada goose (Branta canadensis) consumed about 21% of the standing crop of seagrasses in the shallow portion of the lower Chesapeake Bay. Dann (Penguin Reserve, Cowes, Victoria, Australia, pers. comm.) showed that black swans (Cygnus atratus) uprooted 94% and consumed 82% of the net annual production of Zostera muelleri in Rhyll Inlet in southern Victoria, Australia. As noted earlier for the cownose ray, removal of seagrass roots and blades by large

herbivores can significantly alter the fauna dependent upon the system (Thayer et al. in press a). Buffleheads, Bucephala albeola, consumed about 50% of the fall standing crop of gastropods and polychaetes in eelgrass beds in the lower Chesapeake Bay during 1979-80 (Wilkins 1982).

These large herbivores can significantly influence their primary food resources to the point where both the distribution and abundance of eelgrass and the herbivores are affected. Tubbs and Tubbs (1983) have shown that the present-day distribution of brant geese (B. bernicla bernicla), wigeon (Anas penelope), and teal (Anas crecca) in the Solent estuarine system on the central south coast of England is related, in part, to the abundance of eelgrass (Z. marina and Z. noltii). Both the brant and wigeon feed on leaves and rhizomes, and teal consume seeds. As the amount of eelgrass leaves decreased, there was a concomitant sharp decrease in numbers of birds feeding. Wigeon shift their feeding grounds to marsh areas, feeding on grassland. Teal move to marshes, feeding in pools of fresh and brackish water. Tubbs and Tubbs (1982) showed that the brant switch to a diet of green algae when eelgrass leaf cover decreases to less than 10%, and then to pasture grass and cereals when algal cover becomes sparse.

Present-day changes in temperate seagrass abundance in the United States, whether natural or man-induced, also can influence abundance and feeding patterns of the avian fauna. In a survey of literature on waterfowl of Chesapeake Bay, Stevenson and Confer (1978, p. 113) stated "The overall decline of Redheads and Whistling Swans suggest that the diminishing supply of a traditional food source of submerged macrophytes is a contributing factor ... Canada Geese, Mallards and Black Ducks have adapted to terrestrial feeding. Diving ducks such as Canvasbacks have adapted to a more animal diet. Apparently, a decrease of a traditionally desired food source such as SAV [submerged aquatic vegetation] results in several options for native and migratory waterfowl. They can either seek an alternative food source or compete for the diminishing food source. Either alternative could result in population reductions and locale changes."

4.10 TROPHIC RELATIONS

The pathways by which organic matter is processed and made available to consumers are intricate. Without exception, the entire trophic spectrum, i.e., herbivores, detritivores, omnivores, and carnivores, is represented within each structural category discussed previously. An example of the trophic relations within an eelgrass-epiphytic compartment is shown in Figure 48. This diagram is based on an original conceptual model for freshwater and macrophyte-epiphyte interactions by Allen (1971) and was modified by Stevenson and Confer (1978) for temperate seagrasses; the model shows not only the trophic pathways but also nutrient

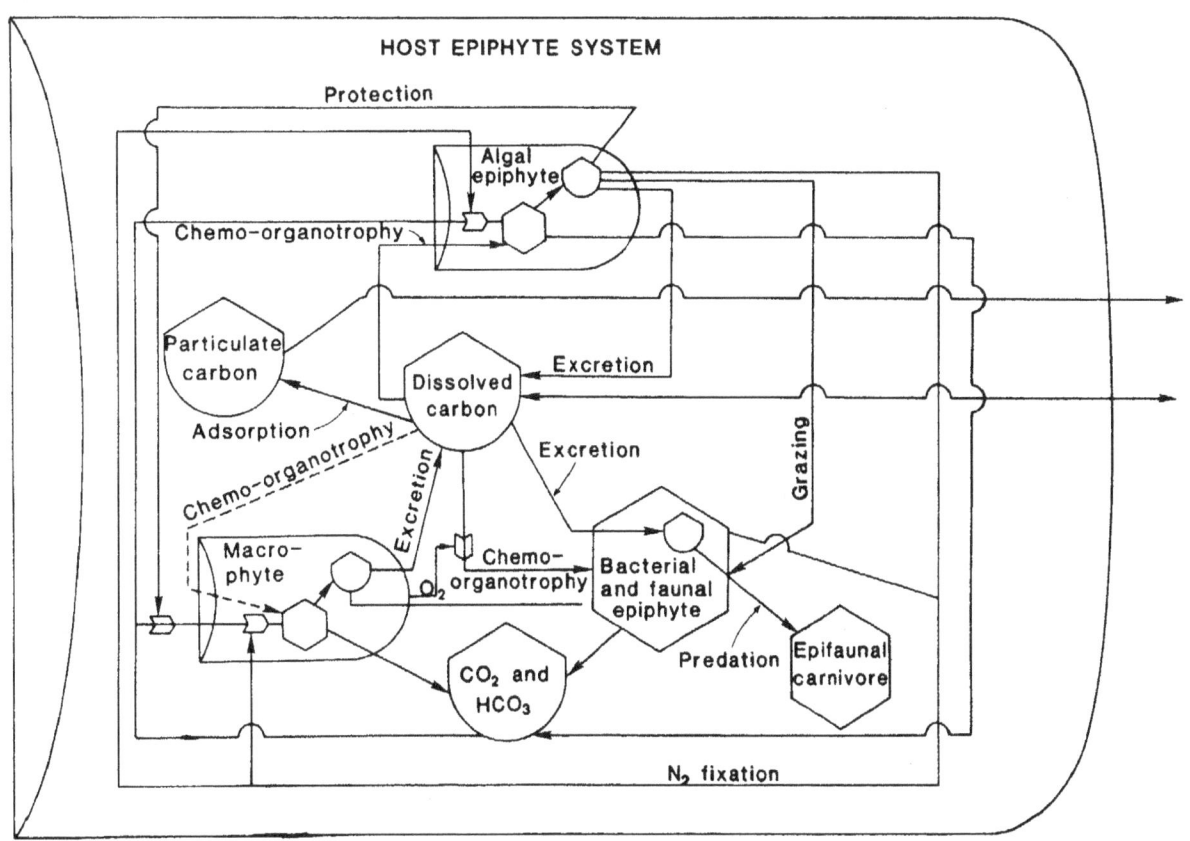

Figure 48. Conceptual diagram of some major trophic relations and host-epiphyte interactions in a seagrass meadow. (Modified from Stevenson and Confer 1978 and based on an original by Allen 1971.)

interrelations and protection functions provided within this portion of the seagrass system. The epibiotic community on eelgrass blades is composed of both autotrophs and heterotrophs, and therefore, can derive its carbon from both inorganic carbon in the overlying water column and from dissolved organic carbon (DOC) released by the plant. Numerous investigators have demonstrated nutrient translocation from the leaf or epiphytic community (Harlin 1973; McRoy and Goering 1974; Penhale and Smith 1977; Kirchman et al. 1984), and Penhale and Smith (1977) showed a significantly higher release of DOC for epiphyte-free leaves than for epiphytized leaves. Further, Thayer et al. (1978), using stable carbon isotope analyses, estimated that about 50% of the carbon present in the epibiotic community on eelgrass blades near Beaufort, North Carolina, could be derived from DOC released by the eelgrass itself. Wilkins (1982) also reported stable carbon isotope ratios of the epiphytic community on widgeon grass and eelgrass blades which closely approximate isotope ratios of the blades themselves.

Our understanding of trophic relations and rate processes in seagrass meadows exists primarily on a qualitative basis. There are quantitative data on primary producer components and rates of production for most of the plant species (see Chapter 2), faunal feeding habits, plant decomposition processes (Zieman 1982), and standing crops of detritus (Thayer et al. 1977). However, the actual fate of the primary production, e.g., how much is consumed directly, how much is deposited and decomposed in situ, or how much is exported to adjacent systems, is not well documented. Many linkages between and among trophic levels remain vague and most are unquantified.

There are numerous sources of primary organic material and many possible trophic interactions within any seagrass meadow. Organic matter formed within the meadow through the production of eelgrass, the associated plant epiphytes, and the benthic micro- and macroalgae is termed autochthonous. Organic matter also may be produced outside the system: phytoplankton, emergent and terrestrial plants, and atmospheric input. These sources are termed allochthonous and are suspended as plankton and detritus in the overlying water column passing through the meadow. Thus, consumer organisms within an eelgrass bed have available a variety of primary organic sources (Figure 49) of both variable quantity and quality. Because of location within the system

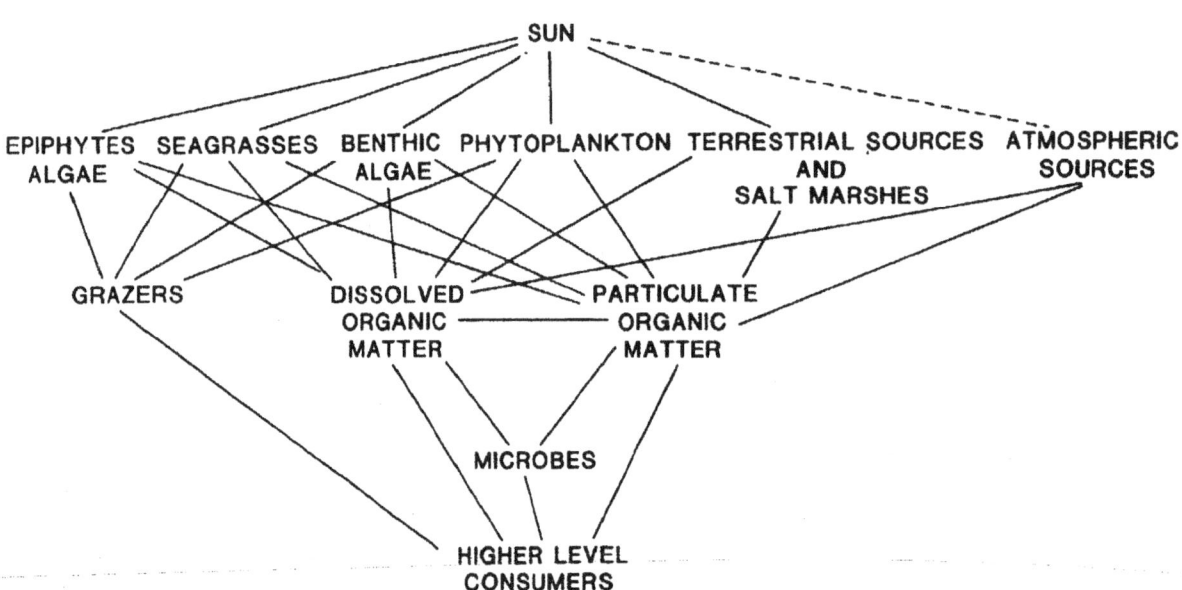

Figure 49. Potential inputs and pathways of organic matter flow in temperate eelgrass systems; not all pathways are included. (Modified from Odum et al. 1982.)

86

(i.e., nearness to sources of terrestrial or marsh input), meadow form, and hydrology of the system, not all meadows will possess equivalent levels or even equivalent sources of primary organic matter. The major source, however, is seagrass (Chapter 2).

Autochthonous and allochthonous inputs of organic matter enter eelgrass faunal food webs either through grazing on living plant tissues or through consumption of detrital material. Until recently, the initial linkage of plant production to fauna through either chain has been based primarily on direct observation of feeding behavior or from food habit or stomach content analyses. More recently, analyses of cellulose digestion capabilities and stable isotope techniques, separately and in combination with stomach content analyses, have proven useful tools to delimit food web relations in eelgrass meadows (Thayer et al. 1978; McConnaughey and McRoy 1979; Weinstein et al. 1982).

Both direct grazing on eelgrass leaves and other forms of herbivory have been considered relatively unimportant as trophic pathways in temperate seagrass meadows. Rather, the detrital pathway (Figure 50) has emerged as a major trophic pathway. Although the list of animals that have been reported to consume eelgrass and other temperate seagrasses includes annelids, molluscs, crustaceans, echinoderms, fishes, reptiles, birds, and mammals, the number of species that directly consume eelgrass are comparatively few (Table 13). With the exception of the larger herbivores, e.g., urchins, birds, and possibly the pinfish (L. rhomboides), the abundance and known or presumed energy demands of the other species indicate that they probably do not place a large demand on plant production. Brant, Canada goose, and black swan do reduce standing crops markedly, frequently causing a shift in diet to less preferred foods (Thayer et al. in press a). We have observed small eelgrass beds reduced to aboveground "stubble" in fall, presumably due to grazing by adult pinfish. Carr and Adams (1973), Adams (1976b), and Stoner (1980) also reported that pinfish $\geq$ 80 mm standard length consume large quantities of seagrasses. Urchins also feed on eelgrass (Table 13) and, given the proper

conditions, could reduce eelgrass standing crops. Although not reported for temperate seagrass communities, the sea urchin Lytechinus variegatus has denuded large seagrass areas in Florida (Camp et al. 1973), and the urchin Strongylocentrotus droebachiensis has overgrazed kelp beds in Nova Scotia (Mann 1977).

The general paucity of species that are direct grazers on seagrass leaves may be a function of several factors, including the availability of nitrogen compounds, the presence of relatively high concentrations of structural cell wall compounds (i.e., celluloses, hemicelluloses, and lignin), and the presence of toxic or inhibitory compounds (Thayer et al. in press a; Harrison in press). The carbon:nitrogen ratio of green leaves of eelgrass generally is less than about 17:1 for most of the year (Harrison and Mann 1975b; Thayer et al. 1977). This value frequently is considered adequate for good animal nutrition (Russell-Hunter 1970), but assumes that the nitrogen concentration is a measure of available protein content. Total nitrogen values, however, may be an overestimate of protein content of the plant and a significant fraction of the nitrogen may be unavailable (Harrison and Mann 1975b; Odum et al. 1979).

Cell wall carbohydrates of eelgrass compose a large percentage of the dry weight of the leaves (Chapter 2). Few organisms that are known to ingest eelgrass possess the endogenous capacity to produce enzymes necessary to digest cell wall constituents or possess a gut flora capable of this digestion (Yokoe and Yasumasu 1964; Crosby and Reid 1971; Lawrence 1975). When present in vertebrates, cellulase activity generally is considered exogenous, i.e., derived from microflora and/or invertebrate fauna consumed along with the plant (Stickney and Shumway 1974; Lindsay and Harris 1980). Weinstein et al. (1982), however, have demonstrated that pinfish apparently possess endogenous cellulolytic activity and may be able to digest the structural cell wall components present in eelgrass.

The presence of phenolic compounds also may inhibit grazing on eelgrass.

87

Phenols are known to inhibit herbivory in many plant groups (Feeny 1976), and Zapata and McMillan (1979) have demonstrated the presence of six phenolic compounds in leaves of eelgrass collected from Washington and Rhode Island. Harrison (1982a) showed that water soluble extracts of green eelgrass leaves, possibly containing phenolic compounds, inhibited grazing by the amphipod *Eogammarus confervicolus* on dead eelgrass leaves; when extracts from leached leaves were used there was no inhibition. In a recent review Harrison (in press) also has shown that phenolics bind proteins and carbohydrates in leaves, making them unavailable to organisms which also may be affected by toxic or unpalatable phenols. Robertson and Mann (1982) reported a 5-week delay between the defoliation of leaves from eelgrass plants in Canada and the onset of amphipod and isopod grazing

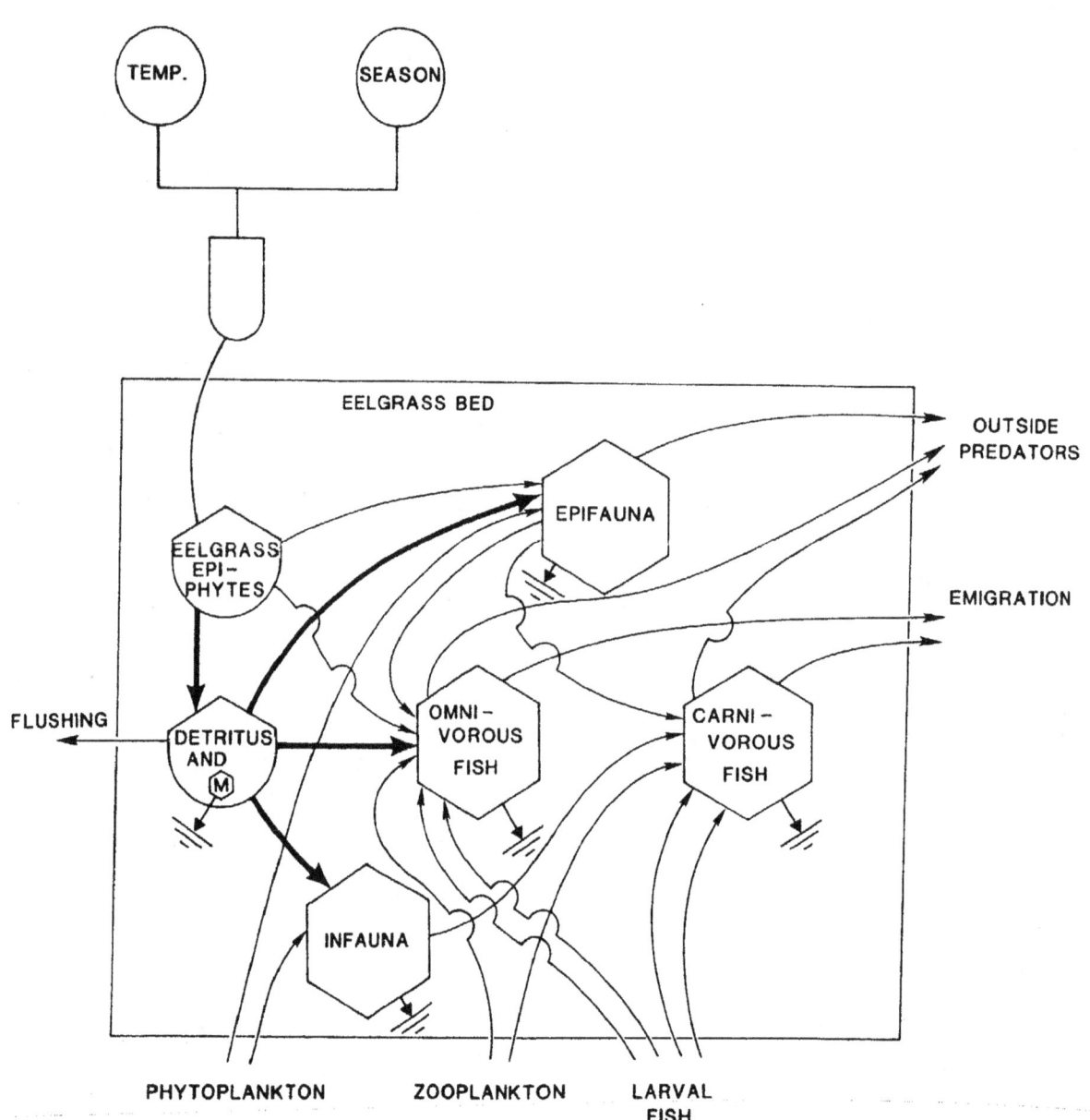

Figure 50. Major flows of carbon for an eelgrass system; M = heterotrophic microbes. (Modified from Ferguson and Adams 1979.)

Table 13. Organisms that reportedly consume temperate seagrasses. Modified from McRoy and Helfferich (1980; Table 1).

Herbivore's scientific name	Common name	Percent seagrass in diet	Location of population	Reference
Annelids				
Capitella capitata	Polychaete	up to 100	Massachusetts	Tenore 1975
Diopatra cuprea	Quill worm		Massachusetts	Mangum et al. 1968
			Chesapeake Bay	
Enchytraeus lineatus	Oligochaete		North Sea	Giere 1975
Hesperonoe adventor	Scaleworm	up to 100	Alaska	McConnaughey, Univ. Alaska; pers. comm.
Lumbricillis lineatus	Oligochaete		North Sea	Giere 1975
Molluscs				
Lacuna variegata	Chink snail	up to 100	Alaska	McConnaughey and McRoy 1979
Lacuna carinata	Chink snail	up to 100	Alaska	McConnaughey, pers. comm.
Lacuna vincta	Chink snail	up to 100	Alaska	McConnaughey, pers. comm.
Littorina sitkana	Snail		Alaska	McConnaughey and McRoy 1979
Quibulla quoyi	Bubble shell		New Zealand	Morton and Miller 1968
Aplysia california (Tethys californicus)	Sea hare		California	Winkler and Dawson 1963 MacGinitie 1935
Bursatella leachii	Sea hare		New Zealand	Morton and Miller 1968
Haminoea zelandiae	Bubble shell		New Zealand	Morton and Miller 1968
Dolabela sp.	-		Australia	Wood 1959
Gibbula sp.	Periwinkle		South Africa	Day 1967
Crustaceans				
Ampithoe vaillanti	Amphipod	16	Black Sea	Greze 1968
A. longimana	Amphipod	18	North Carolina	Nelson 1979b
Callinectes sapidus	Blue crab		U.S. Atlantic coast	Hay 1905
Cancer magister	Dungeness crab	7-15	California	McConnaughey, pers. comm.
Cymadusa compta	Amphipod	5	North Carolina	Nelson 1979b
Dexamine spinosa	Amphipod	1.8	Black Sea	Greze 1968
Gammarus locusta	Amphipod	43	Black Sea	Greze 1968
Idotea baltica	Isopod		Black Sea	Soldatova et al. 1969
Odotea fewkesi	Isopod	up to 100	Black Sea	Soldatova et al. 1969
Ligia pallasii	Isopod		Black Sea	Soldatova et al. 1969
Orchestia sp.	Amphipod		Alaska	McConnaughey, pers. comm.
Pugettia gracilis	Decorator crab		Alaska	McConnaughey, pers. comm.
Telmessus chieragonus	Helmet crab	37	Alaska	McConnaughey and McRoy 1979
Echinoderms				
Psammechinus miliaris	Sea urchin		Denmark	Rasmussen 1973; Lawrence 1975
Strongylocentrotus droebachiensis	Green urchin	up to 100	Alaska	McConnaughey, pers. comm.
			Denmark, Maine	Lawrence 1975
			Puget Sound	
Strongylocentrotus franciscanus	Sea urchin		California	Leighton 1971
Strongylocentrotus intermedius	Sea urchin	10 to 50	Japan	Fuji 1962; Lawrence 1975

(continued)

Table 13. (continued).

Herbivore's scientific name	Common name	Percent seagrass in diet	Location of population	Reference
Echinoderms (cont.)				
Strongylocentrotus purpuratus	Sea urchin	30 to 100	California	McConnaughey, pers. comm.; Lawrence 1975
Lytechinus anamesus	Sea urchin		Gulf of California	Ricketts and Calvin 1962
Lytechinus variegatus	Sea urchin		Beaufort, N.C.	Drifmeyer 1981
Paracentrotus lividus	Sea urchin	up to 100	Marseille, France	Kirkman and Young 1981
Fishes				
Auguilla rostrata	American eel		Chesapeake Bay	Hildebrand and Schroeder 1928
Bairdiella chrysoura	Silver perch	5	North Carolina	Adams 1976b
Hemiramphus australis	Beakie, Sea garfish, Australian garfish		Australia	Wood 1959
Lagodon rhomboides	Pinfish		North Carolina	Adams 1976b; Thayer, unpubl.; Weinstein et al. 1982
Leiostomus xanthurus	Spot	1	North Carolina	Adams 1976b
Monocanthus hispidus	Filefish	12.5	North Carolina	Adams 1976b
Opsanus tau	Toadfish	3.8	North Carolina	Adams 1976b
Reporlampus ardelio	-		Australia	Wood 1959
Rhabdosargus globiceps	White stumpnose		West Africa	Day 1967
Reptiles				
Chelonia mydas	Green sea turtle		Gulf of California	Felger et al. 1980
Birds				
Anus rubripes	American black duck	2 to 5	Southeastern U.S.	Martin et al. 1951
Anas strepera	Gadwall	10 to 25	Southeastern U.S.	Martin et al. 1951
Aythya affinis	Lesser scaup		--	Longcore and Cornwell 1964
		22	--	McMahon 1970
		10 to 25	Southeastern U.S. Northeastern U.S.	Martin et al. 1951
Aythya americana	Redhead		Chesapeake Bay	Stewart 1962
Aythya collaris	Ring-necked	2 to 5	Western U.S.	Martin et al. 1951
Anas platyrhynchos	Mallard	2 to 5	Southeastern U.S.	Martin et al. 1951
Aythya marila	Greater scaup	4	Sweden	Nilsson 1969
		2 to 5		Martin et al. 1951
		2 to 5	Northeastern U.S.	Martin et al. 1951
		10 to 25	Southeastern U.S.	
Aythya valisineria	Canvasback		-	Longcore and Cornwell 1964
		2 to 5	Western U.S.	Martin et al. 1951
Branta bernicla hrota	Atlantic brant	up to 25	North Carolina to Quebec	Martin et al. 1951
		88	North Carolina to Quebec	
Branta bernicla nigricans	Black brant	up to 100	Alaska	McRoy 1966
		50 or more	U.S. Pacific coast	Martin et al. 1951
		2 to 5	U.S. Pacific coast	

(continued)

Table 13. (concluded).

Herbivore's scientific name	Common name	Percent seagrass in diet	Location of population	Reference
Birds (cont.)				
Branta canadensis	Canada goose	< 1 to 100		Martin et al. 1951
Bucephala albeola	Bufflehead	2 to 5	Western U.S.	Martin et al. 1951
Bucephala clangula	Common goldeneye		Sweden	Nilsson 1969
			U.S.	Martin et al. 1951
Bucephala islandica	Barrow goldeneye		-	Martin et al. 1951
Calidris canutus	Red knot	2 to 5	U.S. (migration) U.S. North Atlantic Coast	Martin et al. 1951
Calidris pusilla	Semipalmated sandpiper		U.S. Atlantic Coast	Martin et al. 1951
Calidris melanotos	Pectoral sandpiper		U.S.	Martin et al. 1951
Calidris fuscicollis	White-rumped sandpiper	2 to 5	Eastern U.S.	Martin et al. 1951
Cygnus olor	Mute swan		Rhode Island	pers. observ
Fulica americana	American coot	10 to 25	-	Martin et al. 1951
Himantopus mexicanus	Black-necked stilt		-	Martin et al. 1951
Limnodromus griseus	Shortbilled dowitcher		-	Martin et al. 1951
Limnodromus scolopaceus	Long-billed dowitcher		-	Martin et al. 1951
Anas americana	American wigeon	10-25	U.S. Atlantic and Pacific coasts	Martin et al. 1951
		5-10	U.S. Pacific coast	
Melanitta fusca	White-winged scoter	2-5	U.S. Atlantic and Pacific coasts	Martin et al. 1951
Melanitta perspicillata	Surf scoter	2-5	- U.S. Atlantic and Pacific coasts	Martin et al. 1951
Melanitta nigra	Black scoter	2-5	- U.S. Atlantic and Pacific Coast	Martin et al. 1951
Cygnus columbianus	Tundra (whistling) swan		Rhode Island	Cobb and Harlin, pers. comm.
Oxyura jamaicensis	Ruddy duck	5-10	Western U.S.	Martin et al. 1951
Porphyrula martinica	Purple gallinule		Southeastern U.S.	Martin et al. 1951
Rallus elegans	King rail		Southeastern U.S.	Martin et al. 1951
Anas clypeata	Northern shoveller	2-5	Southeastern U.S.	Martin et al. 1951
Mammals				
Homo sapiens	Man (Seri Indians) (Kwakiutl Indians)		Mexico British Columbia	Felger and Moser 1973 Turner and Bell 1963

on the leaves. If phenolic compounds were present, it is possible that this period is required for the compounds to be reduced to a level that Idotea phosphorea, I. baltica, and Gammarus oceanicus would feed on the leaves. Two of the phenolic compounds found in eelgrass leaves, ferulic acid and p-coumaric acid, inhibit utilization of Spartina alterniflora detritus by snails and amphipods when present at concentrations that are common in living eelgrass (Valiela et al. 1979). Thus, it appears that phenolic compounds could play a role in detering direct grazing on eelgrass leaves.

There are numerous examples, both experimental and observational, suggesting that algal epiphytes on eelgrass are important in the transfer of carbon within a meadow. This organic carbon may be newly synthesized by the micro- and macroalgal epiphytes or be eelgrass-carbon transferred through the loss of DOC from the host plant and then taken up by members of the epiphytic community (Harlin 1973; Penhale and Smith 1977; Thayer et al. 1978). Caine (1980) has shown that the caprellid amphipod Caprella laeviuscula scrapes epiphytes from eelgrass leaves, and is most abundant on the upper quarter of the blade where epiphytes are most dense. Caine noted that the influence of crapellid grazing was enormous; in microcosm experiments, eelgrass blades without C. laeviuscula had a greater than 400% increase in epiphyte biomass compared to blades with caprellids. Van Montfrans et al. (1982) showed that the gastropod Bittium varium (Figure 42) also has a major impact on both epiphyte density and species composition. In some instances, these investigators reported almost total removal of the epiphyte mat and exposure of the eelgrass epithelium, while in other cases the loosely adhering diatom species, such as Amphora sp. and Nitzschia sp., were removed, but the firmly attached species, such as Cocconeis scutellum, were not. Ewald (1969) and Howard (1982), respectively, have reported that the caridean shrimp Tozeuma carolinense and the gammaridean amphipod Tethygeneia nalgo feed on epiphytic algae; Howard noted that I. nalgo cropped the epiphytic material close to the epidermis of the host plant.

There are few quantitative data on the grazing activity. Robertson and Mann (1982) reported that, in microcosms with eelgrass leaves, Idotea phosphorea and I. baltica spent about 40% of the time browsing along the leaf surface. Zimmerman et al. (1979) showed that not only were epiphytic algae consumed by three species of amphipods (Cymadusa compta, Gammarus mucronatus, and Melita nitida) but that their assimilation efficiencies for the algae were high: 48%, 43%, and 75%, respectively. Although this study was carried out in Florida, these amphipods are common components of eelgrass meadows and presumably also consume epiphytes in areas further north.

These herbivores not only gain nutrition from the epiphytic community, potentially influencing the species composition, but they also may enhance the productivity of the eelgrass itself. Sand-Jensen (1977) noted that epiphytes can reduce eelgrass photosynthesis by up to 31% under optimum light conditions. Both light attenuation and reduced bicarbonate diffusion were considered as possible mechanisms by which the epiphytic community interfered with eelgrass photosynthesis. Removal of the epiphytic mat by grazing should reduce shading and, hence, decrease light attentuation; if light is a limiting factor, this may enhance productivity. Both Caine (1980) and Van Montfrans et al. (1982) also suggested that this grazing-associated decrease in light attenuation has allowed, or could allow, eelgrass to grow in areas where it otherwise would be unable to grow because of epiphyte-related light reduction.

Another source of organic matter available in eelgrass meadows is phytoplankton suspended in the overlying water column (Figures 49, 50). Several estimates have been made of the contribution of phytoplankton and eelgrass as well as other producer components to the total productivity of a system (e.g., Thayer et al. 1975a,b; Penhale and Smith 1977; Murray and Wetzel 1982; Lively et al. 1983). Few reports, however, have considered phytoplankton as a major organic source for herbivores in grass beds; e.g., Zieman (1982) in his community profile of tropical seagrass systems, does not consider phytoplankton. Stable isotope studies in eelgrass meadows, however, have shown that phytoplankton carbon is consumed and assimilated by numerous species of invertebrates and directly or indirectly by fishes (Thayer et al. 1978; McConnaughey and McRoy 1979; Van Montfrans 1982). According to Boynton and Heck (1982), stable carbon isotope ratios from grass beds in the lower Chesapeake Bay suggest that seagrass detritus may be exported from beds prior to extensive utilization by fauna, and, therefore, phytoplankton may be a major carbon resource for herbivores in these meadows.

Although the overall importance of phytoplankton to the success of most fauna inhabiting eelgrass beds is poorly understood or totally unknown, one important economic species common to these habitats is dependent to a large degree on phytoplankton as a source of organic matter. The bay scallop, _Argopecten irradians_, is an herbivore that is dependent on phytoplankton as a major carbon source (Kirby-Smith 1972; Kirby-Smith and Barber 1974; Peirson 1983). This organism is found almost exclusively in seagrass meadows. The baffling effect of the eelgrass blades may concentrate phytoplankton and thereby reduce the energy expenditure of the scallop in the food gathering (filter feeding) process. Other suspension/surface feeding invertebrates also may benefit similarly. Thayer et al. (1978), using stable carbon isotope analyses, estimated that _Tellina versicolor, Macoma tenta, M. balthica, Arca ponderosa, A. transversa,_ and _C. cancellata,_ all collected from an eelgrass meadow, could derive between 60%-70% of their tissue carbon from a phytoplankton carbon trophic pathway.

The trophic pathway from benthic micro- and macroalgae has received little attention. Adams (1976b) and Thayer et al. (1980b) noted that algae frequently contributed measurable quantities to the stomach contents of pinfish collected in eelgrass meadows. There also can be little doubt that benthic feeding fish, such as spot and mullet, derive some nutrition from benthic microalgae, although the extent is unknown.

Except in local areas, little of the living seagrass plant is consumed directly by grazers. The majority of the organic matter produced by eelgrass decomposes either in situ or is transported out of the system to decompose and enters the food chain through the detrital pathway elsewhere (Figures 45,50). Studies on benthic communities have shown that decomposer food chains are significant components of shallow estuarine systems (Fenchel 1977; Tenore and Coull 1980), and available literature suggests this to be the case in eelgrass meadows (Thayer et al. 1975a; Kikuchi 1980; McRoy and Lloyd 1981).

The plant source and its chemical composition determine the ultimate availability and utilization of detritus. Godshalk and Wetzel (1978a) showed that the rate of decomposition of aquatic plants differs considerably. Tenore and Rice (1980) noted that the different rates are a function of biochemical composition of the plant (and the age of detritus), and therefore, parts of the detritus pool become available at different times. Boon and Haverkamp (1982) suggested that the decomposition of _Zostera_ may be a function in part of the phenolic compounds present in the plant. Newell (1981) suggested that the efficiency of conversion of detritus through microheterotrophs into a form that can be used by larger organisms may be the key to understanding the high secondary productivity of coastal waters. Detritus consumers in seagrass meadows, and any estuarine area for that matter, have a variety of different physical forms of detritus available: solutes in seawater, particles identifiable as dead plants and plant debris, dead animals and animal debris of wide-ranging sizes, and fecal pellets (Cousins 1980). Amorphous detrital particles whose origin is not evident from visual observation frequently are reported in stomach content analyses and in environmental samples (e.g., LaTouche and West 1980). Sources of this detritus, which is abundant in estuaries, include "reconstructed detritus" (Paerl 1974; Kranck and Milligan 1980) derived from dissolved organic matter and decomposing fecal pellets (Pomeroy and Deibel 1980). Figure 51 is a simplified conceptual diagram of possible major pathways during the formation of detritus

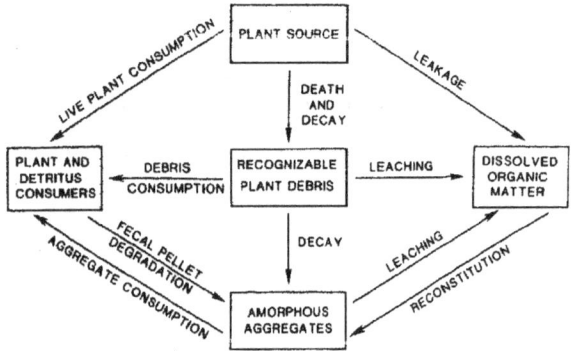

Figure 51. Conceptual diagram of the major events and pathways during the formation and utilization of detritus.

and its subsequent use by heterotrophic organisms. Data frequently are conflicting regarding rates of detritus formation, factors controlling the rates, the leaching of organic matter, and the role of microorganisms in these processes (e.g., Newell 1979, 1981; Peterson and Peterson 1979; Reed 1980; Tenore and Coull 1980). Utilization of detritus by invertebrate and vertebrate organisms is even less well understood.

In a discussion of decomposition of seagrasses, Fenchel (1977) subdivided the animals associated with decomposer food chains into two major categories: microfauna which select their food particles and meiofaunal and macrofaunal organisms which browse on particles or ingest substrate. Fenchel (1977) stated that these larger organisms utilize bacteria and microfauna present on the detritus. Although this may be the case, numerous species are capable of utilizing dead plant material directly (e.g., Yokoe and Yasumasu 1964; Adams and Angelovic 1970; Crosby and Reid 1971; Foulds and Mann 1978), and Cammen (1980) demonstrated that there are insufficient bacteria on detrital particles to meet the energy demands of some organisms. Involvement of these organisms in detrital processing is discussed in Section 4.11. These organisms are not only important in the processing phase, but they also serve as links to higher trophic levels and as major food resources for polychaetes, amphipods, and decapods, which, in turn,

are consumed by fishes, birds, and man (Thayer et al. 1975a,b; Kikuchi 1980).

4.11 DETRITAL PROCESSES AND TRANSFER LINKS

M.L. Robertson (in Zieman 1982, pp. 69-74) summarized the recent literature pertinent to detrital processes and transfer linkages within seagrass meadows in a section entitled "Detrital Processing" (Section 6.3). The processes described are generic and applicable to both eelgrass and turtle grass meadows. The discussion is accurate and sufficiently detailed, covering many of the aspects we have presented briefly and illustrated in Figure 51. Thus, we believe it would be largely redundant to retrace Robertson's discussion. Some of the literature not covered by Robertson has been covered in our discussions in Chapter 3 and Section 4.10.

With permission of Robertson and Zieman, "Detrital Processing" is reproduced below. We have added material or references (indicated by brackets) to update the original. We have modified Robertson's Figure 23 to include eelgrass (Figure 52). We have also added a new Section, "Belowground Organic Detritus," to the end.

"For the majority of animals that derive all or part of their nutrition from seagrasses, the greatest proportion of fresh plant material is not readily used as a food source. For these animals seagrass organic matter becomes a food source of nutritional value only after undergoing decomposition to particulate organic detritus, which is defined as dead organic matter along with its associated microorganisms (Heald 1969).

"The nonavailability of fresh seagrass material to detritus-consuming animals (detritivores) is due to a complex combination of factors. For turtle grass leaves, direct assays of fiber content have yielded values up to 59% of the dry weight (Vicente et al. 1980; in Robertson's report this was cited as 1978). Many animals lack the enzymatic capacity to assimilate this fibrous material. The fibrous components also

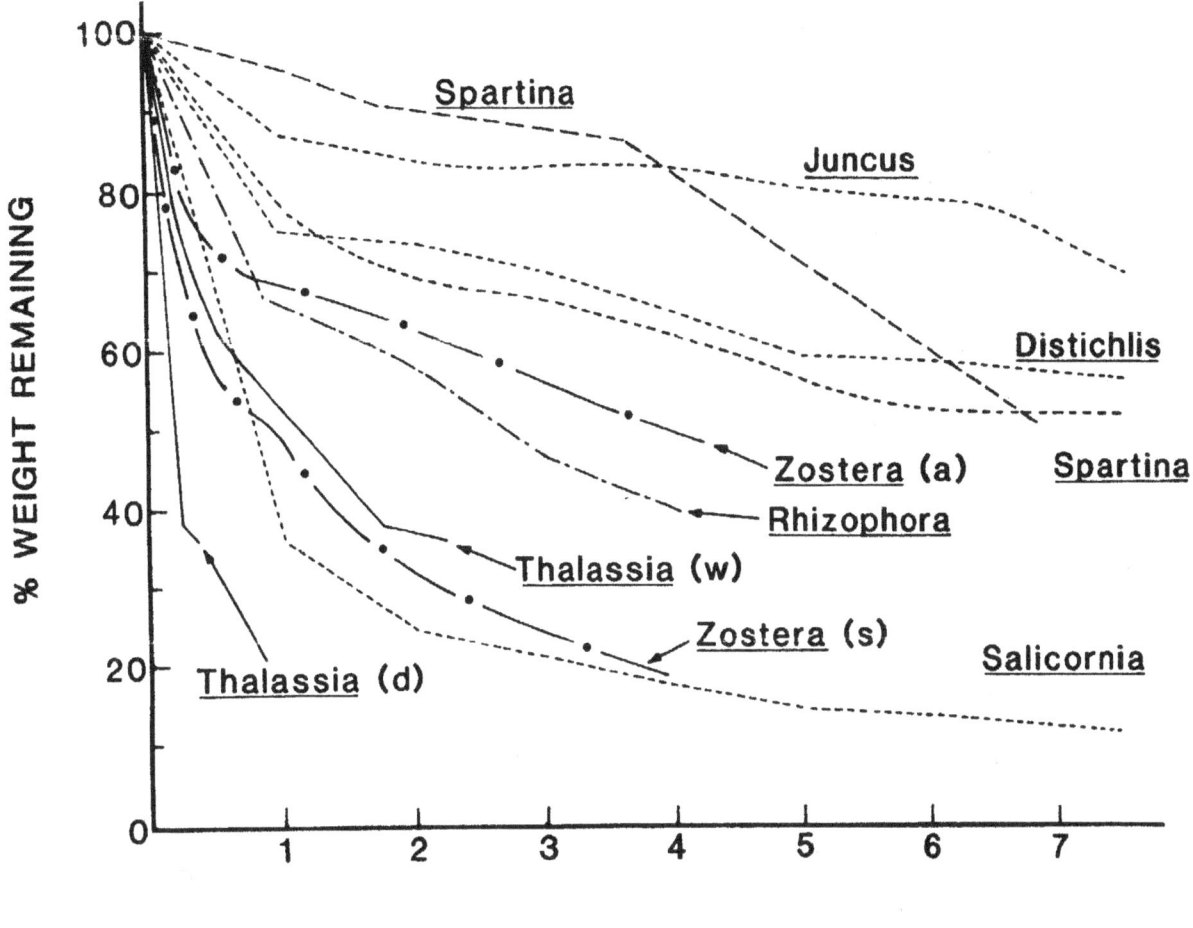

TIME IN MONTHS

Figure 52. Comparative decay rates showing the rapid decomposition of eelgrass compared with other marine and estuarine plants; d = dry, w = wet, s = submerged, a = alternating wet and dry. (Modified from Zieman 1982, data on Zostera from Thayer et al. 1980a).

make fresh seagrass resistant to digestion except by animals (such as parrotfishes and green turtles) with specific morphological or physiological adaptations enabling physical maceration of plant material. Fresh seagrasses also contain phenolic compounds that may deter herbivory by some animals.

"During decomposition of seagrasses, numerous changes occur that result in a food source of greater value to many consumers. Bacteria, fungi, and other microorganisms have the enzymatic capacity to degrade the refractile seagrass organic matter that many animals lack. These microorganisms colonize and degrade the seagrass detritus, converting a portion of

it to microbial protoplasm and mineralizing a large fraction. Whereas nitrogen is typically 2% to 4% dry weight of seagrasses, microflora contain 5% to 10% nitrogen. Microflora incorporate inorganic nitrogen from the surrounding medium - either the sediments or the water column - into their cells during the decomposition process, enriching the detritus with proteins and other soluble nitrogen compounds. In addition, other carbon compounds of the microflora are much less resistant to digestion than the fibrous components of the seagrass matter. Thus, as decomposition occurs there will be a gradual mineralization of the highly-resistant fraction of the seagrass organic matter and corresponding synthesis of microbial biomass that contains a much higher proportion of soluble compounds.

"Microorganisms, because of their diverse enzymatic capabilities, are a necessary trophic intermediary between the seagrasses and detritivorous animals. Evidence (Tenore 1977; Ward and Cummins 1979) suggests that these animals derive the largest portion of their nutritional requirements from the microbial component of detritus. Detritivores typically assimilate the microflora compounds with efficiencies of 50% to almost 100%, whereas plant compound assimilation is less than 5% efficient (Yingst 1976; Lopez et al. 1977; Cammen 1980). [Findlay and Tenore (1982) have shown that microbes are an important nitrogen source for the polychaete Capitella when feeding on marsh grass detritus, but when feeding on detritus of seaweed origin nitrogen derived from the plant is most important.]

"During seagrass decomposition, the size of the particulate matter is decreased, making it available as food for a wider variety of animals. The reduced particle size increases the surface area available for microbial colonization, thus increasing the decomposition rate. The abundant and trophically important deposit-feeding fauna of seagrass beds and adjacent benthic communities, such as polychaete worms, amphipods and isopods, ophiuroids, certain gastropods, and mullet, derive much of their nutrition from fine detrital particles.

"It is important to note that much of the contribution of seagrasses to higher trophic levels through detrital food webs occurs away from the beds. The most decomposed, fine detrital particles (less than 0.5 mm) are easily resuspended and are widely distributed by currents (Fisher et al. 1979). They contribute to the organic detritus pool in the surrounding waters and sediments where they continue to support an active microbial population and are browsed by deposit feeders.

Physical Breakdown

"The physical breakdown and particle size reduction of seagrasses are important for several reasons. First, particle size is an important variable in food selection for a wide range of organisms. Filter feeders and deposit feeders (polychaetes, zooplankton, gastropods) are only able to ingest fine particles (less than 0.5 mm diameter). Second, as the seagrass material is broken up, it has a higher surface area to volume ratio which allows more microbial colonization. This increases the rate of biological breakdown of the seagrass carbon. Physical decomposition rate is an approximate indication of the rate at which the plant material becomes available to the various groups of detritivores and how rapidly it will be subjected to microbial degradation.

"Evidence indicates that turtle grass detritus is physically decomposed at a rate faster than the marsh grass, Spartina alterniflora, and mangrove leaves. Zieman (1975) found a 50% loss of original dry weight for turtle grass leaves after 4 weeks using sample bags of 1-mm mesh size [Figure 52].

"Seagrass leaves are often transported away from the beds. Large quantities are found among the mangroves, in wrack lines along beaches, floating in large mats, and collected in depressions on unvegetated areas of the bottom. Studies have shown that the differences in the physical and biological conditions of these environments resulted in different rates of physical decomposition (Zieman 1975). Turtle grass leaves exposed to alternate wetting and drying or wave action break down rapidly, although this may inhibit microbial growth (Josselyn and Mathieson 1980). [Josselyn and Mathieson (1980) and Thayer et al. (1980a) both have demonstrated a more rapid decay of eelgrass under constant submerged conditions than under alternating wet-dry conditions; this is shown in Figure 52].

"Biological factors also affect the rate of physical decomposition. Animals grazing on the microflora of detritus disrupt and shred the plant substrate, accelerating its physical breakdown. Fenchel (1970) found that the feeding activities of the amphipod Parahyella whelpyi dramatically decreased the particle size of turtle grass detritus.

96

Microbial Colonization and Activities

"Feeding studies performed with various omnivores and detritivores have shown that the nutritional value of macrophyte detritus is limited by the quantity and quality of microbial biomass associated with it. (See Cammen 1980 for other studies of detrital consumption.) The microorganisms' roles in enhancing the food value of seagrass detritus can be divided into two functions. First, they enzymatically convert the fibrous components of the plant material that is not assimilable by many detritivores into microbial biomass which can be assimilated. Second, the microorganisms incorporate constituents such as nitrogen, phosphorus, and dissolved organic carbon compounds from the surrounding medium into their cells and thus enrich the detrital complex. The microorganisms also secrete large quantities of extracellular materials that change the chemical nature of detritus and may be nutritionally available to detritivores. After initial leaching and decay, these processes make microorganisms the primary agents in the chemical changes of detritus.

"The microbial component of macrophyte detritus is highly complex and contains organisms from many phyla. These various components interact and influence each other to such a high degree that they are best thought of as a "decomposer community" (Lee 1980). The structure and activities of this community are influenced by the feeding activities of detritivorous animals and environmental conditions.

Microflora in Detritivore Nutrition

"Microbial carbon constitutes only 10% of the total organic carbon of a typical detrital particle, and microbial nitrogen constitutes no more than 10% of the total nitrogen (Rublee et al. 1978; Lee et al. 1980). Thus, most of the organic components of the detritus are of plant origin and are limited in their availability to detritivores.

"Carbon uptake from a macroalga, Gracilaria, and the seagrass, Zostera marina, by the deposit-feeding polychaete, Capitella capitata, was measured by Tenore (1977). Uptake of carbon in the worms was directly proportional to the microbial activity of the detritus (measured as oxidation rate). The maximum oxidation rate occurred after 14 days for Gracilaria detritus and after 180 days for Zostera detritus. This indicates that the characteristics of the original plant matter affect its availability to the microbes, which, in turn, limits the assimilation of the detritus by consumers.

"Most of the published evidence shows that detritivores do not assimilate significant portions of the non-microbial component of macrophytic detritus. For example, Newell (1965) found that deposit-feeding molluscs removed the nitrogen from sediment particles by removal of the microorganisms but did not measurably reduce the total organic carbon content of the sediments which was presumably dominated by detrital plant carbon. When the nitrogen-poor, carbon-rich feces were incubated in seawater, their nitrogen content increased because of the growth of attached microorganisms. A new cycle of ingestion by the animals again reduced the nitrogen content as the fresh crop of microorganisms was digested. In a study of detrital leaf material, Morrison and White (1980) found that the detritivorous amphipod, Mucrogammarus sp., ingested the microbial component of live oak (Quercus virginica) detritus without altering or consuming the leaf matter.

"While the importance of the microbial components of detritus to detritivores is established, some results have indicated that consumers may be capable of assimilating the plant carbon also. Cammen (1980) found that only 26% of the carbon requirements of a population of the deposit-feeding polychaete Nereis succinea would be met by ingested microbial biomass. The microbial biomass of the ingested sediments could supply 90% of the nitrogen requirements of the studied polychaete population. The mysid, Mysis stenolepsis, commonly found in Zostera beds, was capable of digesting cell wall compounds of plants (Foulds and Mann 1978). These studies raise the possibility that while microbial biomass

97

is assimilated at high efficiencies of 50% to 100% (Yingst 1976; Lopez et al. 1977) and supplies proteins and essential growth factors, the large quantities of plant material that are ingested may be assimilated at low efficiencies (less than 5%) to supply carbon requirements. Assimilation at this low efficiency would not be readily quantified in most feeding studies (Cammen 1980).

"The microbial degradation of seagrass organic matter is greatly accelerated by the feeding activities of detritivores and microfauna, although the exact nature of the effect is not clear. Microbial respiration rates associated with turtle grass and _Zostera_ detritus were stimulated by the feeding activities of animals, apparently as a result of physical fragmentation of the detritus (Fenchel 1970; Harrison and Mann 1975a).

Chemical Changes During Decomposition

"The two general processes that occur during decomposition, loss of plant compounds and synthesis of microbial biomass, can be incorporated into a generalized model of chemical changes. Initially, the leaves of turtle grass, manatee grass, and shoal grass contain 9% to 22% protein, 6% to 31% soluble carbohydrates, and 25% to 44% ash (dry weight basis), depending on species and season (Dawes and Lawrence 1980). Direct assays of crude fiber by Vicente et al. (1980) yielded values of 59% for turtle grass leaves; Dawes and Lawrence (1980) classified this material as "insoluble carbohydrates" and calculated values of 34% to 41% for this species by difference. Initially, losses through translocation and leaching will lead to a decrease in certain components. Thus, the organic carbon and nitrogen content will be decreased, and the remaining material will consist primarily of the highly refractive cell wall compounds (cellulose, hemicellulose, and lignin) and ash (Harrison and Mann 1975b; Thayer et al. 1977).

"As microbial degradation progresses, the nitrogen content will increase through two processes: oxidation of the remaining nitrogen-poor seagrass compounds and

synthesis of protein-rich microbial cells (typically 30% to 50% protein) (Thayer et al. 1977; Knauer and Ayers 1977). The accumulation of microbial debris, such as the chitin-containing hyphal walls of fungi, may also contribute to the increased nitrogen content (Suberkropp et al. 1976; Thayer et al. 1977). Nitrogen for this process is provided by absorption of inorganic and organic nitrogen from the surrounding medium, and fixation of atmospheric N_2. For tropical seagrasses, in particular, there is an increase in ash content during decomposition because of deposition of carbonates during microbial respiration and growth of encrusting algal species, and organic carbon usually continues to decrease (Harrison and Mann 1975a; Knauer and Ayers 1977; Thayer et al. 1977).

Chemical Changes as Indicators of Food Value

"Nitrogen content has long been considered a good indicator of the food value of detritus and has been assumed to represent protein content (Odum and de la Cruz 1967). Subsequent analyses of detritus from many vascular plant species, however, have shown that up to 30% of the nitrogen is not in the protein fraction (Harrison and Mann 1975b; Suberkropp et al. 1976; Odum et al. 1979). As decomposition progresses, the non-protein nitrogen fraction as a proportion of the total nitrogen can increase as the result of several processes: complexing of proteins in the lignin fraction (Suberkropp et al. 1976); production of chitin, a major cell wall compound of fungi (Odum et al. 1979); and decomposition of bacterial exudates (Lee et al. 1980). As a result, actual protein content may be a better indicator of food value. Thayer et al. (1977) found that the protein content of _Zostera_ leaves increased from standing dead to detrital fractions, presumably due to microbial enrichment. The role of the non-protein and protein-nitrogen compounds in detritivore nutrition is not presently understood.

"Like many higher plants, tropical seagrasses contain phenolic acids known as

98

allelochemicals. These compounds are known to deter herbivory in many plant groups (Feeny 1976). Six phenolic acids have been detected in the leaves, roots, and rhizomes of turtle grass, manatee grass, and shoal grass (Zapata and McMillan 1979). In laboratory studies two of these compounds, ferulic acid and p-comuric acid, when present at concentrations found in fresh leaves, inhibited the feeding activities of detritivorous amphipods and snails grazing on S. alterniflora detritus. During decomposition the concentrations of these compounds decreased to levels that did not significantly inhibit the feeding activities of the animals (Valiela et al. 1979).

"Seagrass leaves may also contain compounds that inhibit the growth of microorganisms; this in turn would decrease the usable nutritional value of the detritus. Water soluble extracts of fresh or recently detached Z. marina leaves inhibited the growth of diatoms, phytoflagellates, and bacteria (Harrison and Chan 1980). The inhibitory compounds are not found in older detrital leaves or ones that have been partially desiccated.

Release of Dissolved Organic Matter

"Seagrasses release substantial amounts of dissolved organic carbon (DOC) during growth and decomposition. The DOC fraction is the most readily used fraction of the seagrass organic matter for microorganisms and contains much of the soluble carbohydrates and proteins of the plants. It is quickly assimilated by microorganisms, and is available to consumers as food in significant quantities only after this conversion to microbial biomass. Thus, the utilization of seagrass DOC is functionally similar to detrital food webs based on the particulate fraction of seagrass carbon. Both epiphytes and leaves of Zostera are capable of taking up labelled organic compounds (Smith and Penhale 1980).

"Experiments designed to quantify the release of DOC from growing seagrasses have yielded a wide range of values. The short-term release of recently synthesized photosynthate from blades of turtle grass

was found to be 2% to 10%, using radio-labelled carbon (Wetzel and Penhale 1979; Brylinsky 1977). Losses to the water column from the entire community, including belowground biomass and decomposing portions, may be much higher. Kirkman and Reid (1979) found that 50% of the annual loss of organic carbon from the Posidonia australis seagrass community was in the form of DOC.

"Release of DOC from detrital leaves may also be substantial. In freshwater macrophytes, leaching and autolysis of DOC lead to a rapid 50% loss of weight (Otsuki and Wetzel 1974). [Godshalk and Wetzel (1978b) reported sizeable releases from decaying eelgrass, and we have observed a 20%-30% loss of weight in the first 30 days of litter bag decay experiments (Figure 52).] In laboratory experiments dried turtle grass and manatee grass leaves released 13% and 20%, respectively, of their organic carbon content during leaching under sterile conditions (Robertson et al. 1982).

"The carbon released as DOC is extremely labile and is rapidly assimilated by microorganisms (Otsuki and Wetzel 1974; Brylinsky 1977; [Seki and Yokohoma 1978; Kenworthy and Thayer in press]), which leads to its immediate availability as food for secondary consumers. In 14-day laboratory incubations, the DOC released by turtle grass and manatee grass leaves supported 10 times more microbial biomass per unit carbon than did the particulate carbon fraction (Robertson et al. 1982).

"DOC may also become available to consumers through incorporation into particulate aggregates. Microorganisms attached to particles will assimilate DOC from the water column, incorporating it into their cells or secreting it into the extracellular materials associated with the particles (Paerl 1974, 1975). This microbially mediated mechanism also makes seagrass DOC available for consumers.

"In most marine systems the DOC pool contains 100 times more carbon than the particulate organic carbon pool (Parsons et al. 1977; references therein). The cycling of DOC and its utilization in detrital food webs are complex. The highly labile nature of seagrass DOC suggests that it may play a significant role in supporting secondary productivity.

Role of the Detrital Food Web

"The detrital food web theory represents our best understanding of how the major portion of seagrass organic carbon contributes to secondary productivity. The organic matter of fresh seagrasses is not commonly utilized by many animals because of various factors, including their low concentrations of readily available nitrogen, high concentrations of fiber, and the presence of inhibitory compounds. The particulate and dissolved fractions of seagrass carbon seem to become potential food for animals primarily after colonization by microorganisms. During decomposition the chemical nature of the detritus is changed by two processes: loss of plant compounds and synthesis of microbial products.

"The decomposer community also has the enzymatic mechanisms and ability to assimilate nutrients from the surrounding medium, leading to the enrichment of the detritus as a food source. As a result, the decomposer community represents a readily-usable trophic level between the producers and most animal consumers. In this food web, the consumers derive nutrition largely from the microbial components of the detritus. The decomposer community is influenced by environmental conditions and biological interactions, including the feeding activities of consumers" (M.L. Robertson in Zieman 1982).

Belowground Organic Detritus

This discussion of detrital processes that we have taken from the Florida Bay Seagrass Community Profile neglected to address an aspect of organic detritus processing that is likely to be very important in an eelgrass meadow. Seagrasses are unique since they are the only marine plants that, by virtue of their morphology, produce organic matter that is a direct input into the sediments.

Production and decay of eelgrass roots and rhizomes contributes a large quantity of particulate and dissolved organic matter to the sediments. Estimates of root and rhizome production range between 55 and 180 g C m^{-2} yr^{-1} (Kenworthy and Thayer, in press; see Chapter 2). This organic matter decays more slowly than the leaf material.

Detrital biomass can be quite large, unusually exceeding 100 g dw m^{-2}. Studies using litter bags buried in estuarine sediments (Kenworthy and Thayer in press) have shown that approximately 50% to 60% of the original ash free dry weight is lost in 170 days. During the initial stage of decay the roots and rhizomes leach soluble organic matter that is used by bacteria. The remaining particulate organic matter forms a large pool of organic compounds that reacts with other complex molecules to form humic substances and to provide surfaces for the adsorption of macronutrients, trace elements, and other chemical constituents of the sediment.

The extent to which the belowgound detritus is remineralized and consumed by macrofauna is largely unknown. Estimates of the physical and chemical composition of the organic matter show that it is structurally complex and has a very low nitrogen content (Kenworthy and Thayer in press). It is likely that only very specialized organisms capable of digesting this type of material could utilize the detritus originating from the roots and rhizomes. Since the sediment is predominantly an anaerobic environment, bacteria are probably responsible for most of the decomposition. Potential candidates for the trophic pathway of this material are bacteria → protozoans → subsurface deposit feeders. Many trophic pathways associated with eelgrass meadows originate with benthic secondary production. Seagrass primary production in the form of roots and rhizomes may be an important source of energy for these pathways, as well as a reserve of organic matter that is available during periodic fluctuations in aboveground production by seagrasses and other autotrophs.

CHAPTER 5
INTERSYSTEM COUPLING

Tidal flushing, faunal feeding, and faunal movement extend the sphere of influence of a submerged eelgrass meadow well beyond its physical boundaries. Organic matter produced within the system is passively transported out of the meadow through tidal action (of course, meadows also trap material - Chapters 3, 4) and actively transported in the tissues and in stomach contents of animals that have fed there. Whereas export of detritus from tropical meadows was only recently recognized (Zieman et al. 1979; Zieman 1982), export of eelgrass and its subsequent utilization was recognized in the early 1900's. Peterson (1918) based his trophic model of the fisheries of the Kattegat (Denmark) on this process (see Chapter 1).

Although the export of detritus from eelgrass meadows has been recognized, there are few quantitative data available on how much and in what form material is exported. The paucity of data may be a result of the general tendency of researchers to evaluate the structural and functional aspects of meadows as entities unto themselves rather than as components of the larger estuarine-coastal system. Thayer et al. (1975b, p. 228) stated, "Seagrasses must be considered in terms of their interaction with the other sources of primary production that support the estuarine trophic structure before their significance can be fully appreciated." Although eelgrass meadows vary in the magnitude of their contributions, there is little doubt that they contribute to the overall functioning of the coastal system of which they are a part.

Organic matter produced within a meadow can be transported in several forms. These pathways include: (1) entire plants or whole portions of plants, plus associated and attached epiphytes; (2) recognizable eelgrass detritus; (3) dissolved organic matter (DOM); and (4) tissues and feces of fauna that use an eelgrass-based food chain. Figure 53 is a simplified model of energy flow in an eelgrass meadow near Beaufort, North Carolina, that includes most of these pathways. In developing this model numerous assumptions were made, many trophic interactions were ignored (or were unknown), and computations were simplified. Macrofauna were estimated to consume energy equivalent to roughly 55% of the net production of eelgrass, phytoplankton, and benthic algae in the bed. No attempt was made to partition the energy derived by the fauna from each separate producer component. These and other data on epiphyte production and dissolved organic matter release (Chapter 2), as well as on detrital processes and feeding relations (Chapter 4), not only suggest that eelgrass beds are detrital-based, but also that a large portion of the organic matter produced within the meadow is available for export. This does not imply that epiphytes, for example, are unimportant food resources, but at this time quantitative data are lacking (see Chapter 4).

There have been numerous reports of entire plants, leaves, and recognizable fragments of leaves floating or being deposited onshore (Figure 54), but there are few quantitative data that document the possible extent of export. As early as 1908, Ostenfeld documented (in a chapter titled "Dead Weed") the contribution of eelgrass to the formation of extensive wrack lines and the occurrence

101

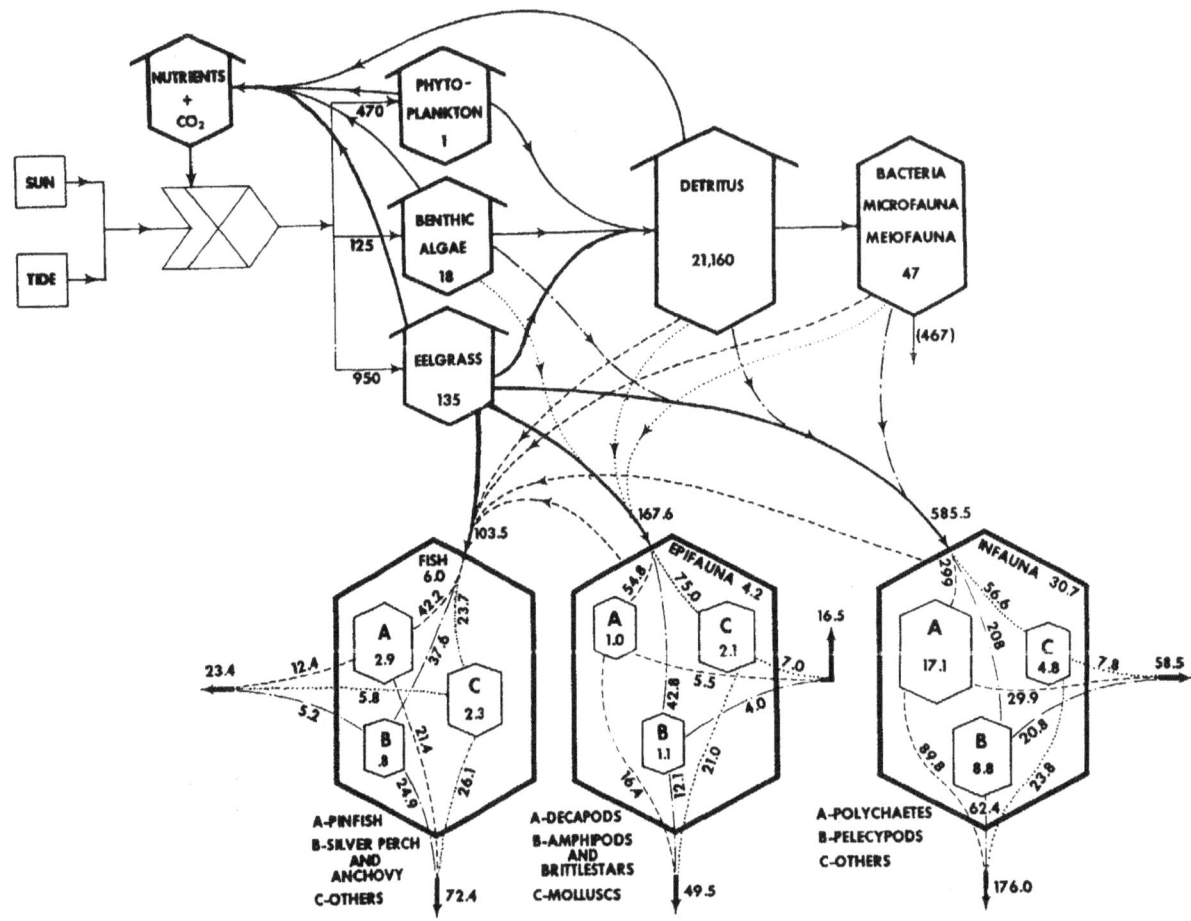

Figure 53. Annual energy flow in a North Carolina eelgrass meadow (Kcal m^{-2} yr^{-1}). Inputs into producer units are net production, and inputs to consumer units are net consumption. Outflows to bottom are metabolic energy requirements; others are secondary production. Different lines are used for each consumer unit. (From Thayer et al. 1975a.)

of senesced leaves on the bottom in deep water areas. Petersen and Boysen-Jensen (1911) concluded that eelgrass was the main input of organic matter to offshore waters in the Kattegat Region of Denmark. Blegvad (1914) reported that great numbers of Zostera blades could be collected directly over a meadow with a plankton net, and Petersen (1918) recorded free-floating eelgrass blades over large areas of the Denmark coast. More recently, Josselyn and Mathieson (1980) stated that floating eelgrass blades were common in summer and fall in Great Bay, New Hampshire. In one of the few attempts to estimate the amount of eelgrass exported, Josselyn and Mathieson (1980) made monthly collections of plant litter from the wrack

line at three locations between Great Bay and Fort Constitution on the open coast of New Hampshire. An annual average of about 600 g dw m^{-2} (range 190-1400 g dw m^{-2}) was deposited in the wrack line within the estuary and about 500 g dw m^{-2} on the open coast. Bach and Thayer (unpubl.) collected floating material adjacent to grass meadows near Beaufort, North Carolina, with surface and bottom drift nets (Table 14). Export ranged from 0.23-0.57 g afdw m^{-2} d^{-1} for an open water, high current meadow and from 0.01-0.26 g afdw m^{-2} d^{-1} from two protected, low-current meadows. These values are similar to those reported for both Syringodium filiforme and Thalassia testudinum for Tague Bay, U.S. Virgin Islands

(Zieman et al. 1979). This export from the open water meadow near Beaufort accounted for 10%-30% of the production of eelgrass; export from embayment habitats represented from < 6% to 80% of the monthly eelgrass production during seasons of maximum growth.

Availability of entire plants or leaves for export is caused by the same

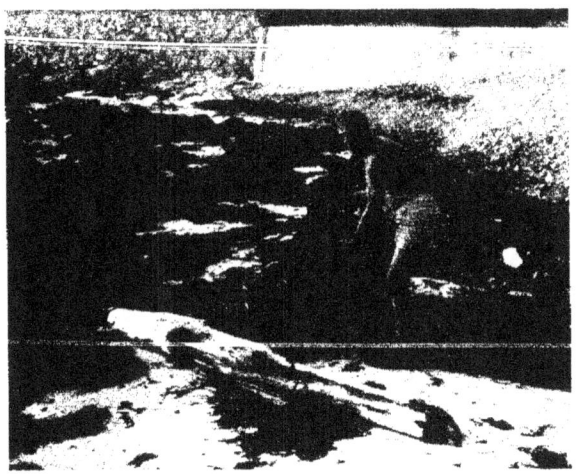

Figure 54. High water mark wrack line of eelgrass, Sakonnet Point, Rhode Island.

events described for tropical seagrasses: herbivores, mortality and dehiscence of shallow growing plants, and storms that uproot entire plants (Zieman 1982). Josselyn and Mathieson (1980) stated that in New Hampshire the largest wrack line accumulations followed major storms, and Bach and Thayer (unpubl.) described how shifts in both wind direction and speed could alter export rates. Ice scour during winter in the northern range of eelgrass growth and summer thermal stress near the southern end of its range also contribute to leaf mortality and export (Chapters 1 and 2). Herbivores such as swans, geese, and ducks tear the grass out of the substrate (Chapter 4 and Figure 46). Drifmeyer (1981) noted that urchins are "sloppy eaters," producing fragments that could be exported, and Thayer et al. (in press a) point out that waterfowl feeding in seagrass meadows cast aside measurable quantities of plant material. Benthic feeders, such as cownose rays, also can uproot entire plants (Chapter 4).

Epiphytes attached to eelgrass also must be considered as part of the flux of material across meadow boundaries. As

Table 14. Comparison of export of seagrass detritus by different species from different geographical areas in North Carolina. (From Bach and Thayer, unpubl.)

Species	Location	Export (g dw/m^2/day)	Production exported %	Biomass exported %
Zostera marina	Phillips Island	0.01 - 0.26[a]	6 - 8[a]	1 - 20[b]
Zostera marina	Middle Marsh	0.05[b]	0.2 - 2.5[b]	0.2 - 2.5[b]
Zostera marina	Harkers Island	0.23 - 0.57[b]	10 - 30[b]	10 - 30[b]
Halodule wrightii	Phillips Island	-	-	-
Halodule wrightii	Middle Marsh	0.04[b]	-	2 - 17[b]
Halodule wrightii	Harkers Island	0.23[b]	-	40 - 75[b]

[a] Annual range.

[b] Maximal summer value.

103

eelgrass grows, dehisces, and senesces, it undergoes a sequence of epiphytism correlated with the life history stage of the plant (Sieburth and Thomas 1973). Patriquin (1972a), Brauner (1973), Penhale (1977), and Borum and Wium-Andersen (1980) demonstrated seasonal and annual contributions of epiphytes to the biomass of the macrophytes. Penhale (1977) and Borum and Wium-Andersen (1980) reported average annual epiphytic biomass of 24.7 and 6.3 g dw·m^{-2}, which represent 23.5% and 35.9% of the eelgrass biomass for areas in North Carolina and Denmark, respectively. Epiphytic coatings sometimes reduce available light by as much as 90% (Borum and Wium-Andersen 1980) and eelgrass photosynthesis by up to 50% (Sand-Jensen 1977). Reduction in light to eelgrass at different times of the year may also exacerbate exfoliation of eelgrass leaves, contributing to material flux from the meadow.

Export of dehiscent or senescent eelgrass parts, together with the epiphytic complex, can lead to a rapid turnover of biomass and to rapid carbon cycling. Since the epiphytic community has fewer refractory compounds than eelgrass, it would decompose more rapidly. Photosynthate and leachate from eelgrass are released from leaves as they grow and die, and presumably some is assimilated by the epiphytic community (McRoy and Goering 1974; Harlin 1975; Penhale and Smith 1977; Thayer et al. 1978; Penhale and Thayer 1980; Kirchman et al. 1984). These aspects should be considered in evaluating energy flow through material flux pathways from eelgrass meadows, since autotrophic and heterotrophic epiphyte conversion of dissolved nutrients into biomass could be as high as 40% of the eelgrass productivity itself. Since the epiphytic complement of eelgrass is an intrinsic portion of the community, epiphytic load must be considered in modeling export processes or much of the reported biomass could be erroneously attributed to eelgrass.

Macroalgae are characteristic but frequently transient components of eelgrass meadows and may be important in the export process. Some macroalgae (especially Gracilaria, Hypnea, and Enteromorpha sp.) thrive in the relatively nutrient-rich and temperature-mediated microhabitat of low-current eelgrass beds (Thorne-Miller et al. 1983). Lappalainen (1973) demonstrated that within a meadow, living and dead autochthonous algae (Fucus) may comprise a substantial fraction of the total plant biomass; she reported a 1:1:1 ratio of living and dead eelgrass and Fucus in a shallow habitat near Ruarminne, Finland. Macroalgae sometimes represent the major part of the biogenic material exported from the meadow (Josselyn and Mathieson 1980; Bach and Thayer unpubl.). Some of the dominant macroalgae contributing to material flux from eelgrass meadows are described by Conover (1964), Josselyn (1978), Bach and Thayer (unpubl.), and Thorne-Miller et al. (1983). They are primarily phaeophyte species (Ascophyllum and Fucus) (Josselyn 1978) in the rocky coastal areas of northern coasts; Rhodophora (Agardhiella, Gracilaria, and Polysiphonia) and Chlorophyta (Chaetomorpha, Cladophora, Enteromorpha, and Ulva) in New England lagoon systems (Conover 1964); and Phaeophyta (Ectocarpus, Dictyota, and Sargassum) and Rhodophyta species (Agardhiella and Gracilaria) in southern temperate lagoon systems (Bach and Thayer unpubl.).

Export of macroalgae also occurs in seasonal cycles that are a function of ice scour (northern range), storms, tidal currents, and natural seasonality of species. Biomass of macroalgae in the wrack line in a New Hampshire estuarine system at times greatly exceeded that of eelgrass (Figure 55), and species composition varied both seasonally and with location (Josselyn and Mathieson 1980). Macroalgal material exported from eelgrass beds near Beaufort also can be an important component of the total plant biomass removed from the system (Figure 56), and one that also displays a seasonal efflux pattern, with maximum values in late summer and fall (Figure 56,57).

Bach and Thayer (unpubl.) also measured the flux of particulate organic matter (POM) through an eelgrass meadow as retained by 250 μm drift nets. This POM was primarily plant matter during all but the winter months when zooplankton made up 90%-95% of the biomass. The plant fraction of the POM, which was fragmented and

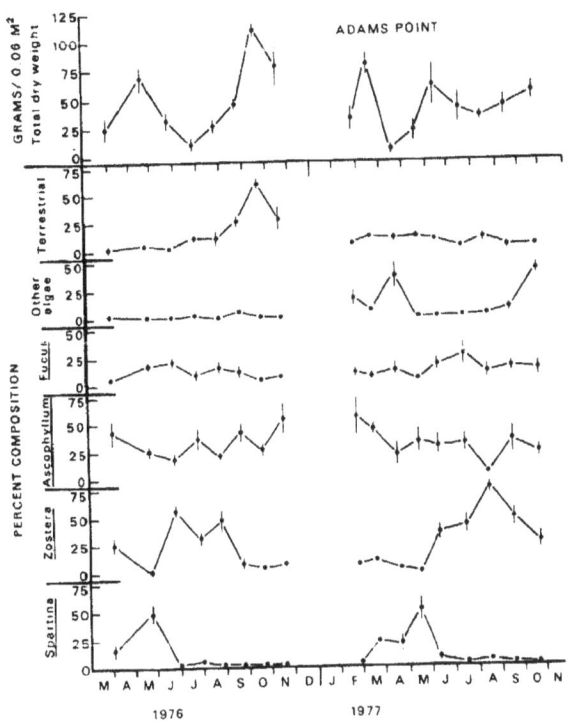

Figure 55. Wrack line composition in grams dry weight per m² of shoreline, Great Bay, New Hampshire. Upper portion is summed total of lower components. Blank in middle is during ice cover. (Redrawn from Josselyn and Mathieson 1980.)

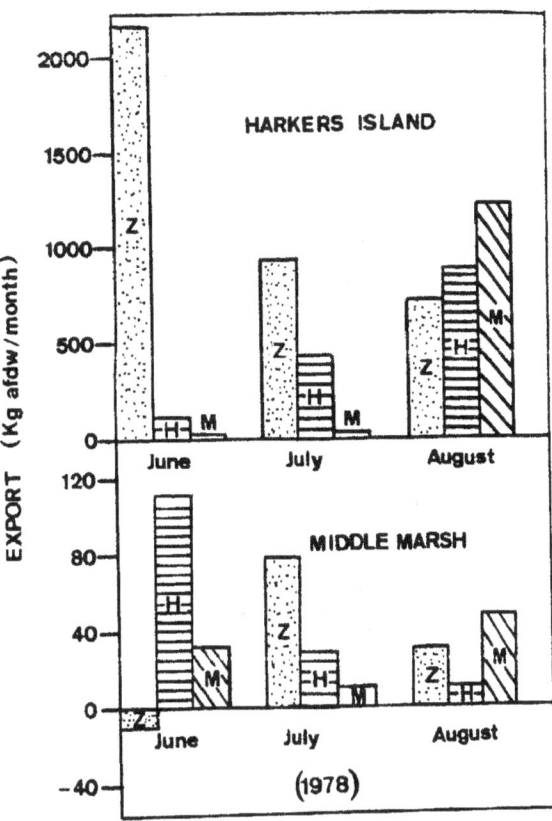

Figure 56. Summer efflux of eelgrass (Z), shoalgrass (H), and macroalgae (M) from an open water seagrass meadow (top) versus an enclosed meadow (bottom) in Back Sound, Carteret County, North Carolina. (From Bach and Thayer, unpubl.)

may have been derived in part from the feeding of herbivores and detritivores (Chapter 4), may be resuspended by wave scour or by benthic gas bubble production. Gas bubbles produced by benthic metabolic activity in a tropical seagrass system suspended about 1 g dw m⁻² of particulate matter daily (Durako et al. 1982).

The species of plant and the site of deposition, in part, control decomposition rates and nutrient exchange rates between eelgrass meadows and adjacent systems. Macroalgae possess fewer refractory compounds and, therefore, decompose more rapidly than seagrasses (Josselyn and Mathieson 1980; Rice and Tenore 1981). Fucus and Ascophyllum appear to decompose faster if submerged than if exposed to alternating wet-dry conditions characteristic of the wrack line (Josselyn and Mathieson 1980). Harrison and Mann (1975b) found little difference in the

rate of decomposition of eelgrass under similar conditions in Canada. Experiments in New Hampshire (Josselyn 1978; Josselyn and Mathieson 1980) and North Carolina (Thayer et al. 1980a), however, demonstrated rates that were ordered according to deposition site: submerged > wrack line ≥ within a salt marsh (see Figure 52). The general sequence of events observed under five environmental conditions in North Carolina are shown in Table 15. The increased decomposition rate when eelgrass is continuously submerged may result from faunal shredding of the plants and a continuous supply of nutrients for microbes as opposed to a pulsed supply which would occur during alternating wet-dry conditions in the wrack line. Desiccation during exposure also reduces microbial activity in the

105

wrack line significantly. Thus, active export of algae and eelgrass to inter- and supratidal systems may not cycle the material as rapidly as if it were maintained within the meadow.

In addition to measurable fluxes of organic and inorganic matter as identifiable eelgrass, epiphytes, macroalgae, and finer fractions of particulate organic matter, there is considerable evidence that eelgrass directly exports and mediates movement of various essential nutrients in a dissolved form. McRoy et al. (1972) demonstrated that eelgrass in an Alaskan lagoon excreted about 60 mg phosphorus$\cdot$m^{-2} d^{-1} into the water column. They estimated that about 3 metric tons of phosphorus, or more than 40% of the reactive phosphorus excreted, was exported to the Bering Sea. The volcanic sediments of southern Alaska are phosphorus-rich and this "pumping" may be important in maintaining the high concentrations of phosphorus characteristic of these lagoon waters. Near Beaufort, North Carolina, where only 3% of the phosphorus taken up by the root-rhizome system was excreted, eelgrass appears to contribute little to the phosphorus content of the overlying water (Penhale and Thayer 1980). Carbon also is liberated to the water column (Harlin 1973; Brylinsky 1977; Penhale and Smith 1977), although epiphytes apparently absorb large quantities of DOC before it reaches the water column (Penhale and Smith 1977). The role that excretion of dissolved carbon plays, depicted in Figure 48, is more thoroughly discussed in Chapter 4. Excess ammonium-nitrogen also could be translocated from the sediment ammonium reservoir through eelgrass shoots to epiphytes and the overlying water column (Patriquin 1972b; McRoy and Goering 1974; Smith 1981) and be exported. Extensive research on gaseous exchange in eelgrass communities also has been conducted. Murray and Wetzel (1982) reported that approximately 40% of macrophyte-epiphyte oxygen production was available for export. Some of these excreted dissolved nutrients, both as organic compounds and gases, are available for uptake by other plant-epiphyte combinations or other autotrophs such as plankton, some bacteria, and benthic microalgae.

Although trace metals, too, can be exported, most are associated with particulate phases of the eelgrass detrital material, and concentrations of dissolved metals are naturally low (Chapter 2). Wolfe et al. (1976) and Drifmeyer et al. (1980) have described pathways of metal element cycling in eelgrass systems (Figure 36). Drifmeyer et al. (1980), who described eelgrass as being one of the largest biological reservoirs of several

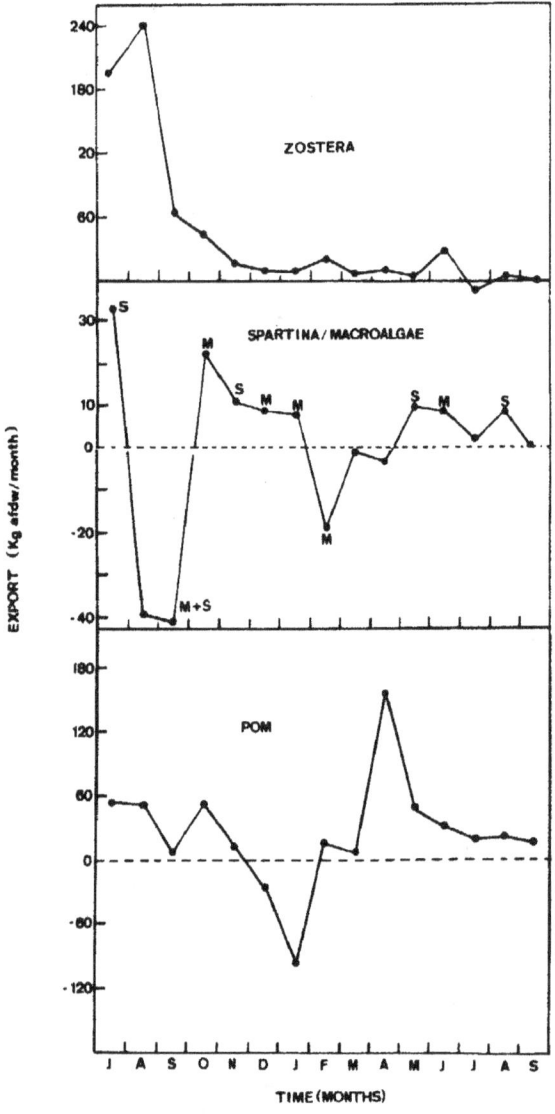

Figure 57. Seasonal efflux of surface material estimated for a semi-enclosed North Carolina eelgrass meadow. Each point is an average of 8 to 20 observations for that time. (Redrawn from Bach and Thayer, unpubl.)

106

Table 15. General sequence of events observed during decomposition of eelgrass blades under five environmental conditions in North Carolina. Bleached leaves refer to naturally colorless and senesced leaves, due to exposure.

Location	Days from initiation					
	17	31	46	67	85	123
Low intertidal	Leaves intact	Leaves intact and bleached				
Low intertidal-buried	"	Leaves intact			Some polychaetes present, leaves intact	
High intertidal	"	Leaves intact and bleached				
Low energy-subtidal	"	Partial fragmentation, amphipods present	Fragmentation, amphipods present	Epibiota present fragmentation high		
High energy subtidal	Partial fragmentation	Epibiota present high degree of fragmentation				

trace elements in a North Carolina lagoon system, stated that senescence and decomposition of Zostera constituted the major flux pathway through the system.

A fourth pathway by which organic and inorganic matter leaves a meadow is in the tissues and stomach contents of animals that feed in the eelgrass meadow. Herbivory and detrital feeding were discussed in detail in Chapter 4. Since few organisms feed directly on the whole, fresh parts of eelgrass, most of the plant passes through a series of decompositional stages before the complex cellulose, hemicellulose, and lignin components are available for use by lower trophic level organisms. Gut studies, observations, and stable isotope analyses have revealed, however, that eelgrass carbon is a gut and tissue component of a large portion of the higher trophic level fauna that utilize seagrass beds. As discussed in Chapter 4, few consumers are exclusively eelgrass meadow dwellers. Their movements form conspicuous links between vegetated and unvegetated habitats. Considering that gut evacuation rates for many species probably exceed the foraging period, fecal material is probably deposited some distance from the meadow. Even if it were not, there is a high likelihood of it being exported on a subsequent tide; we have observed green "cigar-shaped" feces of brant on the water surface after the brant have fed in an eelgrass meadow. This connection of habitats through feeding and subsequent off-site coprophagy was suggested for green turtles (Chelonia mydas) (Thayer et al. 1982) and other tropical seagrass bed herbivores (Ogden 1980), and has been discussed in a recent review of seagrass herbivory by large fauna (Thayer et al. in press a). Robertson (1982) has demonstrated the importance of coprophagous feeding to coral reef fishes. The importance of this process in temperate seagrass systems, however, is virtually unknown.

107

The degree of coupling a given eelgrass meadow may have with other areas depends on its setting and geographic location. Depth determines the frequency of wave scour, which suspends material in the water column in the meadow, as well as the frequency of ice scour and summertime foliage desiccation. Wave and ice scour and exposure and desiccation are all important pathways for material flux from the meadow (Chapter 2). Water depth also determines the mode of faunal interactions with other systems. For example, in shallow-water meadows, wading birds prey on local invertebrates; and ducks, swans, and geese feed directly on the grasses themselves (Wilkins 1982; Thayer et al. in press a). In deep-water meadows, the coupling to other areas via waterfowl is less direct. Otherwise, subtidal trophic interactions (fish, crustaceans, molluscs) dominate the immediate utilization of the eelgrass meadow (Chapter 4).

Hydrodynamic conditions, such as waves and currents, determine the amounts of dehiscent foliar material that either are incorporated into the sediments or are swept away (Chapter 3). Local hydrodynamic conditions also are correlated with the quantity of roots and rhizomes exported. Unless roots and rhizomes are ripped out of the sediment by humans, large herbivores, or storms, they rarely are moved directly to other systems. As noted earlier, geographic location and climatological conditions also influence coupling between systems through seasonal storms, waves, ice conditions, heat stress, and desiccation.

In summary, the export or exchange of materials between eelgrass meadows and adjacent systems occurs as whole plant parts with associated epiphytes, particulate organic matter, dissolved organics, dissolved gases, or as living tissue and feces of grazing fauna. Where submerged meadows exist, seagrass, epiphytes, and associated macroalgae dominate the flux of biogenic material. Therefore eelgrass meadows cannot be considered simply as isolated systems. Because of their generally shallow water existence in close proximity to fisheries activities, shoreline development, and nearshore pollution, eelgrass meadows are susceptible to both acute and sometimes chronic perturbation. As a consequence, information on their contribution to coastal systems beyond a direct nursery function is necessary to develop a reliable information base for making decisions regarding protection and management of these habitats.

CHAPTER 6
CONSIDERATIONS FOR MANAGEMENT

6.1 INTRODUCTION

The first chapters of this profile have provided an awareness of the ecological significance of the eelgrass community. To maintain its vital functions in the larger ecosystem, careful consideration must be given to its management.

Degradation of these essential and sensitive areas, which has cumulative effects, is expected to accelerate as our population grows. The major anthropogenic activities that impact eelgrass communities are: (1) dredging and filling, (2) commercial fishery harvest techniques and recreational vehicles, (3) modification of normal temperature and salinity regimes, and (4) addition of organic and inorganic chemical wastes. Natural perturbations (e.g., hurricanes, rain-induced salinity fluctuations, ice scour) are superimposed over those caused by man and are beyond human control.

Resource managers need reliable information on which to base decisions regarding protection and management of eelgrass meadows from harmful human activities. In a recent publication, Odum (1982) pointed out that we may avoid the cumulative environmental impacts that result from "small environmental decisions" by incorporating a holistic approach in planning for both scientific research and for decisions that are environmentally related. Present policies for managing coastal systems do not incorporate this holistic approach. As a consequence, numerous relatively small-scale impacts on seagrass meadows are occurring without benefit of conservation and mitigation to offset the cumulative losses.

Until a holistic approach is taken, such unmitigated alteration will continue.

The development of a holistic (Odum 1982) or ecosystem-level (Ashe 1982) viewpoint on the management of eelgrass communities is required to adequately preserve both their structure and function. Although much is known about the productivity and life history of the eelgrass itself, little consideration is given to incorporating facts about its dynamics as a community into its management, and much less is known about the requirements of eelgrass-associated fauna. Ultimately, the economic value of the system is measured by the production of recreationally and commercially valuable fish and shellfish that depend on eelgrass meadows. Some human activities that introduce toxic material, such as pesticides, may be extremely injurious to these species but not affect the eelgrass at all (Thayer et al. 1975b).

The dynamics and community structure of fauna in natural meadows are being researched intensively, but little is known about the recovery of fauna in perturbed or restored meadows (Homziak et al. 1982; Thayer et al. in press b). Virtually nothing is known about the quality of the ecosystem level functions which restored eelgrass meadows are theorized to support (see Race and Christie [1982] for a parallel argument on marsh creation).

6.2 SUSCEPTIBILITY AND VULNERABILITY OF EELGRASS MEADOWS

Man's multifaceted dependence on estuaries includes food production, energy development, transportation, waste disposal, living space, recreation, and aesthetic pleasure. As pointed out by Ferguson et al. (1980), not all of these uses are compatible and in many cases they are mutually exclusive (Figure 58). Some of the uses may be beneficial, others detrimental, while still others may have no measurable impact on environmental quality (Figure 59). The impacts of some of the activities shown in Figures 58-59 are discussed below with special reference to the means of degradation.

6.3 DREDGE AND FILL

Dredging and filling are probably the most deleterious of man's impacts on eelgrass meadows that have yet been identified. Of the two, direct removal of eelgrass by dredging is probably the most readily observable meadow disruption.

Dredges may be of various designs, but generally are either hydraulic or scoop types. Hydraulic dredges use a stream of pressurized sea water, either as suction to remove sediment in suspension or as a jet-like exhaust. Suction types characteristically are used to dredge channels,

and exhaust types generally are utilized in shellfishing operations. Scoop-type dredges do just that; they mechanically lift out sections of sediment as would a shovel. Typical dredge designs are draglines or clamshell scoops.

In addition to physically removing eelgrass, dredges often deposit the dredged material onto bay bottom areas containing eelgrass. Although eelgrass can orient its rhizome development vertically, it rarely can match the rate at which sediment from these operations accumulate. As the photosynthetically active blades become covered with sediment, light reception is impaired, further depriving the rhizomes of energy needed to compensate for sedimentation. The plants are probably better able to cope with rapid sediment erosion than with sediment accretion (Figure 60).

The high turbidity produced by dredging and filling reduces the productivity of grasses, and if severe enough, eventually kills them. Depending on the hydraulic stability of the site, elevated turbidity and off-site drift of dredged material can be chronic or acute. The use of silt curtains to contain suspended material offers only limited protection, since the curtains usually are removed along with the other equipment when dredging is terminated. Chronic elevated turbidity or the covering of eelgrass either intentionally by direct deposition

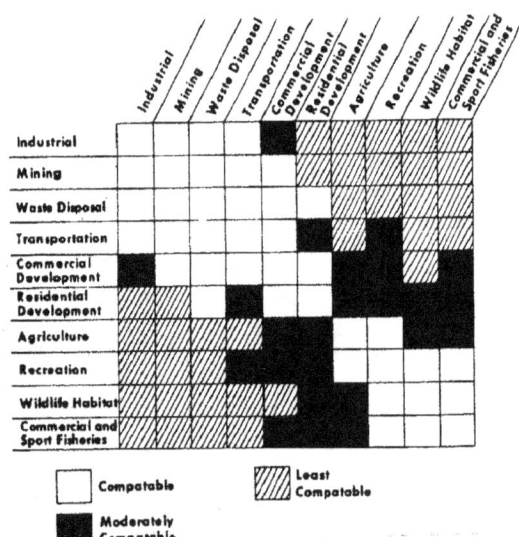

Figure 58. Compatibility of uses of the marine environment. (From Ferguson et al. 1980.)

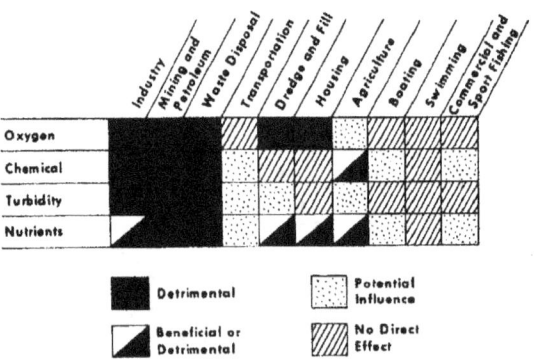

Figure 59. Actual and potential impacts of man's use of the marine environment on water quality. (From Ferguson et al. 1980.)

or from drift off the immediate impact zone, means that production of those areas is either substantially diminished or totally eliminated. Many of these sites remain biologically unproductive because of high fluid energy at the disposal site. Successful replanting of eelgrass onto these areas, however, enhances the stability of the substrate and thus promotes development of an extensive faunal component. Replanting of eelgrass can provide a major mitigation of the dredging impact. Stabilizing the site also could reduce the need for frequent dredging of the nearby channel, thus reducing the time-averaged impact on local biota and decreasing the cost of channel maintenance.

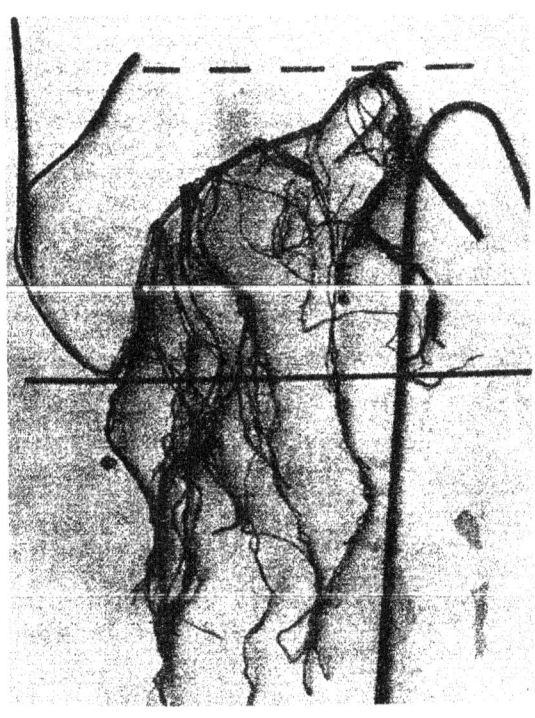

Figure 60. Photograph of the response of a transplanted eelgrass shoot to erosion. The sediment surface was slightly above the anchor when planted (dashed line). A storm eroded approximately 10 cm of sediment with the resultant geotrophic growth response of the root-rhizome. The shoot had reached the new sediment surface (solid line) in approximately 90 days when this photograph was taken.

6.4 COMMERCIAL HARVEST/RECREATIONAL VEHICLES

The direct impact of man's use of seagrass meadows is readily observable. Zieman (1976) described the lasting impact (time in years) of motorboat cuts through tropical seagrass meadows. Detonations for geological surveys off Belize and silted-in bomb craters of Vieques, Puerto Rico, have remained visible after 2 to 3 decades (Zieman and Ogden; Zieman and Fonseca, pers. observ. respectively). Eelgrass meadows also have suffered from impacts on a scale similar to that for tropical seagrasses. For example, eelgrass has been dynamited in the Niantic River of Connecticut to improve water circulation (M. Ludwig, NMFS, Environmental Assessment Branch, Milford, Connecticut; pers. comm.). Resource managers have since come to new wisdom and no longer condone such actions. Eelgrass, because of the way it grows (Chapter 2), recolonizes damaged areas more rapidly than some tropical species, but this process still requires years (Kenworthy et al. 1980).

The activity of commercial and recreational vessels in eelgrass meadows removes the shoots by various methods. Most common is the slicing and uprooting of shoots by boat propellers. Based on qualitative observations, the most deleterious equipment next to boat propellers are toothed rakes or dredges towed behind a power boat to harvest shellfish. Their use in submerged vegetation (such as eelgrass) is outlawed in most coastal states. Large hand-operated toothed rakes and tongs, which can uproot eelgrass in substantial quantities, should be guarded against, but hand rakes ("pea diggers") are more selective and less disruptive (Peterson et al. 1983). Thayer and Stuart (1974) demonstrated that commercial dredging reduced both scallop and eelgrass density in an area near Beaufort, North Carolina. Fonseca et al. (1979) reported the denudation of an eelgrass meadow by scallop harvesting and its subsequent restoration. These two papers described eelgrass meadows sustaining scallop harvesting impact, but they did not describe the mechanism of impact other than the uprooting of entire shoots. In a more recent study, Fonseca et al. (in press) demonstrated that scallop dredging significantly reduced biomass and surface area as well as shoot density of eelgrass growing in both soft bottom and hard bottom substrates. Eelgrass was more susceptible in soft than in hard bottom substrates (Figure 61). The authors hypothesized that areas of low eelgrass biomass (less than 50 g dw m^{-2}) and areas dominated by seedlings will be most susceptible to harvesting impacts.

Any overboard activity, whether using rakes or simple hand collections, often tramples the grasses into the soft bottom. Footprint holes through the rhizome layer are often quickly enlarged by crabs (especially Callinectes and Limulus sp.)

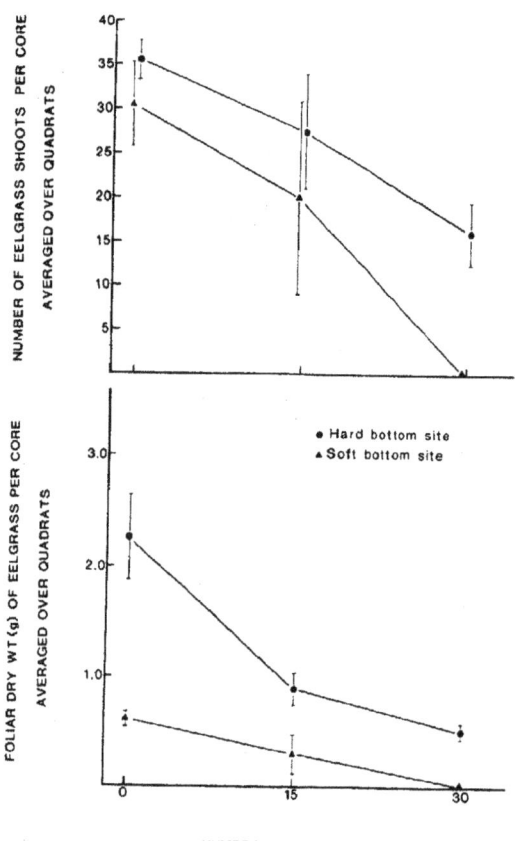

Figure 61. Decrease in average eelgrass shoot number per core (top) and foliar biomass (bottom) as a function of scallop harvest effort. Bars represent + 1 SE and are offset for readability. (Redrawn from Fonseca et al., in press.)

searching for shellfish and can become an erosion face for currents and waves. Orth (1975) reported meadow disruption through a similar but natural effect of cownose rays in Chesapeake Bay, and Wilkins (1982) documented loss of both invertebrates and eelgrass by feeding birds (Chapter 4).

6.5 TEMPERATURE/SALINITY

The tolerances of eelgrass to temperature and salinity variations is discussed in detail in Chapter 2. High temperatures are alluded to in Chapter 1 as a possible cause of the "wasting disease." Only a few of man's activities could alter either parameter sufficiently to impact eelgrass directly. Thermal effluent from power plants can induce local eelgrass mortalities. Creation of groins, jetties, and dikes may alter circulation patterns and stagnate water that could elevate the ambient temperature of a local eelgrass meadow. Impoundment and stagnation of estuarine waters also can lead to increased salinity by evaporation. Conversely, freshwater discharge by canal opening or agricultural and sewage discharge can dilute estuarine waters, making them less saline and less than optimal for existing eelgrass.

Temperatures and/or salinities above or below optimum limits might not necessarily destroy a meadow, but they might inhibit metabolism and thus decrease the plant's productivity. Weakening the plants also could make them less competitive with invading species. As pointed out in Chapter 2, eelgrass is relatively euryhaline and eurythermal, so that any changes in salinity or temperature would have to be large for the effects to be severe and chronic to make a large or noticeable impact.

There also may be secondary effects of temperature and salinity fluctuations in grass beds. It was noted by Orth (Virginia Institute of Marine Science, Gloucester Point, Virginia; pers. comm.) that a dramatic reduction in salinity in Chesapeake Bay during hurricanes was accompanied by a die-off of eelgrass. He theorizes that the grass was not directly damaged by the lower salinity, but that the ubiquitous, epiphyte-grazing gastropod

Bittium varium (Figure 42) may have been adversely affected. A massive mortality of _Bittium_, according to Orth, could have lead to a rapid increase in epiphytism in the absence of their grazing, thereby reducing light to the eelgrass blades and exacerbating the plant's demise.

6.6 ORGANIC AND INORGANIC POLLUTANTS

The influence of organic and inorganic pollutants on growth and survival of eelgrass is presently the most poorly understood aspect of man's impact on this system. The general paucity of information most likely has been due to a combination of technical/analytical deficiencies and ignorance of potential hazards. Recent awareness of the value of eelgrass meadows has prompted investigations of their reactions to acute, catastrophic events, such as the _Amoco Cadiz_ oil spill in France, and to insidious and chronic events, such as the eelgrass demise in Chesapeake Bay.

The major organic pollutants impacting eelgrass meadows identified to date are petroleum and related compounds, herbicides, and pesticides. McRoy and Williams (1977) detected the suppression of eelgrass phytosynthesis by kerosene, and Jacobs (1980) noted adverse impacts on the intertidal eelgrass after the _Amoco Cadiz_ spill. In the same spill area, Calder et al. (1978) traced petroleum impacts on seagrass systems and stated that they had been minimal, except where the grass had been smothered by thick layers of oil (Foster et al. 1971; Nadeau and Berquist 1977; den Hartog and Jacobs 1980). An extensive review of the effects of oil on seagrass systems is provided by Zieman et al. (in press).

Although eelgrass is apparently tolerant of short-term exposure to petroleum hydrocarbons, there is no quantitative information as to how its physiology or reproductive success are affected by long-term exposure. Acute episodes of petroleum release also may affect eelgrass seed recruitment in a given year. Seed recruitment plays a significant role in the maintenance of eelgrass populations in some environments (Chapter 2).

The fauna react much more negatively, particularly to massive, short-term exposures. Den Hartog and Jacobs (1980), Nadeau and Berquist (1977), Chan (1977), and Diaz-Piferrer (1962) all document mass mortalities of fauna following oil spills, although the effects appeared to be species-specific and dependent on a number of environmental factors. Among these factors are the amount of wave energy present, the kind of oil, and the manner in which oil is distributed by tides. Wave action, while possibly accelerating the natural release of the more toxic aromatics from the oil, rapidly spreads the oil deeper into the canopy and across tidal zones. Den Hartog and Jacobs (1980) noted that the laid-over eelgrass canopy at low tide, by providing a physical buffer from the oil mass for the fauna and for the sediment, probably reduced mortality of indigenous species.

A point of concern that requires further investigation is whether carcinogenic or mutagenic compounds incorporated into the eelgrass itself would be harmful to higher trophic levels. Since eelgrass grows rapidly and sloughs leaf material, which forms the base of an extensive food web, this high productivity becomes a mechanism for mobilizing and distributing potentially dangerous compounds upward and throughout the food chain. By and large, this brief discussion of petroleum hydrocarbons is generally applicable to the mobilization and effects of pesticides, herbicides, and inorganic elements, especially metals.

Excessive discharges of inorganic nutrients such as nitrates, phosphates or ammonia from farm drainage, residential construction, and septic systems can cause dramatic shifts in the community structure of coastal systems. Causes and effects of eutrophication are well documented (Neilson and Cronin 1981). Green and blue-green algae, some of which are toxic and often noxious in large quantities, take advantage of excess nutrient loading by increasing their production. High rates of algal production, followed by algal decay and its consequent high oxygen demand may result in an anoxic water column, as well as measureable decreases in light penetration; both factors may reduce eelgrass productivity.

In a recent study, Harlin and Thorne-Miller (1981) reported that fertilizers dispensed in the water column of an eelgrass bed in the form of ammonia, nitrate, and phosphate stimulated the growth of the endemic green algae (Enteromorpha plumosa and Ulva lactuca) far more than it did the growth of eelgrass. The authors argued that excess nutrients released into semi-closed shallow marine systems would result in heavy blooms of green algae. In the same lagoon studied by Harlin and Thorne-Miller, Kenworthy (pers. observ.) has observed an increase in green algae and steady decline of eelgrass for nearly a decade. It is therefore important that the potential degradation of eelgrass meadows by eutrophication be considered in the future management of eelgrass systems.

So many unknowns remain that the only prudent course is to assume that all types of organic and inorganic compounds are potential hazards. A massive study, recently completed on the influence of some of these compounds on eelgrass in the Chesapeake Bay, indicated that pesticides and metals alone caused no significant reduction of eelgrass shoot populations in that area (United States Environmental Protection Agency: Chesapeake Bay Report 1982). These compounds are often strongly correlated with nonpoint source runoff, elevated suspended solid loading (hence decreased light penetration), and other deleterious compounds. The major concerns are that metals may be accumulated by the eelgrass (Drifmeyer et al. 1980; USEPA: Chesapeake Bay Report 1982) and mobilized up the food chain and that a persistent depression of faunal assemblages by the pesticide loading may occur. Even though nonpoint source runoff and atmospheric inputs of these compounds both contribute to loading from anthropogenic sources, in the estuary the compounds follow hydrodynamic pathways and can be found where fine sediments accumulate. One major habitat that enhances fine sediment accumulation is the eelgrass meadow, characteristically inhabited by large numbers of estuarine organisms. A point raised by USEPA (1982, p. 347) succinctly summarizes the problem: "... most bioconcentrations have been treated as static levels in tissues or organisms. Some organisms, however, accumulate toxicants quickly, whereas others that metabolize slowly can accumulate toxicants slowly but to high levels. Therefore, bioaccumulation needs to be examined as a dynamic equilibrium determined by the (organisms') metabolic rate."

The most practically oriented submerged aquatic/herbicide study to date is one done in Chesapeake Bay (USEPA: Chesapeake Bay Report 1982). The bay was surveyed for the distribution of two major herbicides, atrazine and linuron, and for their effect on some submerged aquatic vegetation (SAV). The herbicides were found to significantly reduce photosynthesis in SAV's at concentrations of 20 ppb. Although the Chesapeake Bay study concludes that herbicides did not appear to directly cause the loss of SAV's in the system, the study concluded that the effects of daughter products of herbicide degradation are not known.

Frequent reductions in photosynthetic levels due to elevated turbidity and agricultural runoff definitely add to existing stresses on plants from both natural and anthropogenic sources. The herbicide atrazine has been demonstrated to accumulate linearly in eelgrass with increased concentration (L. Gabanski, Biology Dept., Old Dominion University; pers. comm.). Root/rhizome uptake was less than 10% of leaf uptake, most likely due to bacterial metabolism of atrazine in the sediments. Cunningham and Kemp (University of Maryland, Horn Point Laboratories, Cambridge, Maryland; pers. comm.) studied the effects over an 8-week period of atrazine in physiological and morphological responses of Potamogeton perfoliatus, a submerged vascular plant typically found in fresh or low-salinty areas. The plant responded by increasing leaf length and chlorophyll a concentration while decreasing weight per unit length, a response similar to shade adaptations for this species. They also noted that after addition of the herbicide ceased, there was a significant recovery of photosynthetic activity within two weeks. The authors contend that not only short-term, but long-term effects of herbicide additions to the system should now be considered. Cunningham and Kemp and authors of the Chesapeake Bay Study conclude that herbicide-related reductions in productivity have potential for developing conditions intolerable to SAV survival.

6.7 PLANNING AND UTILIZATION

Management Needs

In this profile we have tried to relate the function of eelgrass meadows in the larger estuarine ecosystem. To maintain their contribution to nearshore productivity, eelgrass meadows should be managed as part of the ecosystem. Ideally, avoidance of impact and total conservation of this system would be the best strategy to ensure its continued productivity. Top priority must be given to making the public aware of the qualities and economic value of the system. All too often the public becomes isolated from the pertinent scientific information because it is published in technical journals. This leads to skepticism of the bureaucracy and diminishes public participation in the exchange of information between scientists and resource managers.

There are several ways that resources can be managed to protect them from damage. First, legislation can prohibit specific activities that degrade the resource. For this approach, applied research programs are needed to identify and study the potential problems.

Basic scientific information must be coordinated with major coastal projects so that potential disturbances can be identified and appropriate preventive action taken. An example of such a process occurred in a lagoon vegetated with eelgrass in southern New England. The New England Power Company proposed to open a new inlet through a barrier island to a coastal lagoon in order to allow passage of a barge carrying a reactor vessel. A hydrodynamic model coupled with studies of the eelgrass system predicted that the opening of the inlet would severely damage the eelgrass meadows (Short et al. 1974). The information was made available to the scientific, industrial, and public sectors and became an integral part of the decisionmaking process. In the existing inlet of this same lagoon, extensive amounts of sediment have been naturally transported through the inlet and deposited onto a large portion of an eelgrass meadow (Harlin et al. 1982). The sediment has thus formed a flood-tide delta, choking the flow of water between the lagoon and adjacent oceanic waters. Decreased flushing is likely to cause dramatic changes in water quality and possibly detrimental effects to the eelgrass in its communities (Harlin and Thorne-Miller 1981). Such impacts can be far reaching and long term. A recent article in the *Salt Water Sportsman* (June 1983) surveyed the best striped bass fishing spots on the south shore of Rhode Island. In the article it was noted that the inlet at Charlestown Pond (the same lagoon as noted above) was once one of the best surf fishing spots, but that a reduction in water flow from the lagoon had decreased its fishing productivity. Thus, even the recreational fishery was impacted and in a very short time. This is a good example of the type of information necessary for planning effective management.

Mitigation

Policy may be established without legislation if there is reason to believe a potential impact exists. But establishing such a policy requires interaction between scientists and managers at all levels of government and in the private sector. Such interaction, however, is unusual. Numerous authors have pointed out the conflict that arises between coastal zone development and the need to preserve eelgrass (and other seagrass) meadows (Thorhaug 1976; Lindall et al. 1979; Zieman 1982; Thayer et al. in press b, and references cited therein). Those charged with managing these systems are continually faced with trying to ameliorate disturbances ex post facto. It is unfortunate that restoration of eelgrass meadows often is included as a viable alternative in planning processes. Such a priori consideration of restoration tends to concede the point of conservation and preservation. As demonstrated by Race and Christie (1982), there is insufficient evidence to conclude that restored systems provide the same ecosystem functions as natural ones. Ashe (1982), in a timely paper, promulgated a definition of mitigation totally applicable to eelgrass systems: "Fish and wildlife [eelgrass] mitigation is a process resulting in specific actions, designed to compensate for the unavoidable loss of fish and wildlife resources which accompany human activity." This definition relegates the disruption of eelgrass meadows to the appropriate position in the decision process, an ex post facto consideration when all realistic alternatives to impact avoidance have been exhausted (after Race and Christie 1982).

Even after a decision has been made to allow the destruction of eelgrass habitat, two important points must be considered. The first is that if eelgrass habitat (or any natural, biologically productive habitat) is destroyed, the productivity of the entire system can never be returned to what it had been originally. Once a segment of an ecosystem is lost, the biological and chemical links within the entire system are permanently disrupted, even if new habitat is created elsewhere within the system. The second point, really a caveat of the first that is based on an application of the ecosystem theory, is that mitigation rarely creates new habitat. This leads us to reflect on the nature of mitigation itself. Let us say a segment of an eelgrass meadow is replaced by a man-made structure and a new area is sought for planting. The most desirable area is typically a natural, unvegetated bottom. This also poses two problems. One, it may be unvegetated because it is unsuitable for eelgrass growth, or two, it is a temporary space in an existing community of eelgrass. The fact is that there probably exist few suitable areas that eelgrass has not already reached and colonized on the east coast of the United States. This is where an ecosystem-level knowledge must be applied to facilitate true mitigation.

Since eelgrass meadows are extremely dynamic plant systems, they exhibit seasonal fluctuations in their density and distribution within the system. Thus, apparently barren, unvegetated areas well may be eelgrass habitat. We have observed large acreages in the Beaufort, North Carolina, area oscillate from being totally unnavigable due to thick eelgrass cover, to barren, and back to lush cover in three years. Planting these areas

would not constitute mitigation, since no long-term additions to the system would have been realized. Only a temporary enhancement would be achieved. If new areas were engineered, e.g., upland areas lowered and flooded and then planted, a like amount of habitat would have been artificially created to mitigate that which was artificially lost. Only creation of truly new, previously unvegetated aquatic habitat (that has not been created at the expense of another biologically productive habitat) can be allowed as mitigation. Otherwise, cumulative small-scale losses of eelgrass habitat will continue along with a concomitant loss of irreplaceable fishery resources.

6.8 RESTORATION

As early as 1947, Addy developed an eelgrass planting guide. The basic criteria developed are still valid and continue to be the subject of far-ranging research. Reports by Goforth and Peeling (1979) and Fonseca et al. (1979) review most of the pertinent literature on eelgrass transplanting. Restoration techniques, which have included the use of seeds (Churchill et al. 1978) and vegetative material, have produced viable transplants, but few have been cost effective. Seeds of eelgrass are collectable but are difficult to anchor because of their small size (approx. 5 mm long by 2 mm diameter). Presently, any holding or culturing of seeds and seedlings on a scale suitable for most restoration projects appears unnecessary and would probably increase cost. Transplanting mature, vegetative sprigs is less labor intensive and has received more attention, but research is continuing into the use of seeds for planting this species (R.J. Orth, pers. comm.). Vegetative transplanting techniques can be broken into two categories: (1) sediment-attached and (2) sediment-free. Early transplanting attempts used cored-out plugs or turfs (Figure 62) of eelgrass, but there is no indication that eelgrass requires native sediment for propagation. Sediment-free techniques, pioneered by Phillips (1974a) and later used by Riner (1976), Churchill et al. (1978), and Fonseca et al. (1982a), circumvent the incredible logistic problems associated with moving an

116

Figure 62. Photograph of a turf or plug of eelgrass taken with a corer (right).

estimated 5 to 30 metric tons of sediment and plants per hectare of bottom planted. Actually, much more sediment must be displaced because holes must be created at the planting site to accommodate the plugs. On a small scale, either approach is probably workable. But plug techniques have not been reliable in high-current areas. Vegetative shoots washed free of sediment and, where necessary, anchored to the bottom have allowed more flexibility in movement, less disturbance to the donor site, and high survival even in areas of high current velocities (+ 50 cm/sec) (Fonseca et al. 1982a; Thayer et al. in press b).

Preparation of planting units (PU's) by this technique is a four-step procedure: (1) eelgrass is dug up and rinsed free of sediment at the site, care being taken to maintain the integrity of the root-rhizome complex; (2) shoots are removed from dug-up mats to make planting units, care being taken to hold the clump of shoots upright; (3) a clump of shoots is wound with a plastic-coated wire and secured to an anchor made from one-third of a metal coathanger, bent to an L or J-shape; and (4) the planting units are then covered with seawater for transportation to the field (Figure 63).

Transplanting has restored some functions lost when the original meadow was disturbed (specifically, infauna and primary productivity). Homziak et al. (1982) (Figure 64) and Thayer et al. (in press b) (Table 16) provide the only quantitative information on the functional values of restored eelgrass meadows. Homziak et al. (1982) demonstrated that within one growing season after planting (203 days), the number of infauna species and taxa increased asymptotically, paralleling eelgrass regrowth. Thayer et al. (in press b) estimated the production (g C m^{-2}) of eelgrass leaves, roots, rhizomes, and associated epiphytes at the same restoration site as Homziak et al. (1982) and found that 60% to 70% of the production of these components as compared to ambient meadows were recovered within 250 days after planting.

These data comprise only a few experimental plots and need verification by other workers in different geographic locations. Particular attention should be paid to the recolonization of these restored meadows by the fauna. Although the data look promising, such information can be a two-edged sword. Such evidence can be and has been used as an excuse to allow habitat degradation because a technology exists to "replace" it. As we emphasized earlier, however, such arguments are illogical and without basis in fact. The restoration of eelgrass or any seagrass meadows should be used as a last resort to salvage portions of these fragile ecosystems only when a consensus of public interest is served by their destruction and no realistic alternative for their preservation is available. It is no longer sufficient to assume that successful restoration of the primary producer component means concomitant replacement of habitat functions and consumer organisms. The restored primary production must be utilized in maintaining the system either as a source of protection, substrate for attachment, and a direct or indirect food resource, or the effect has not been valuable.

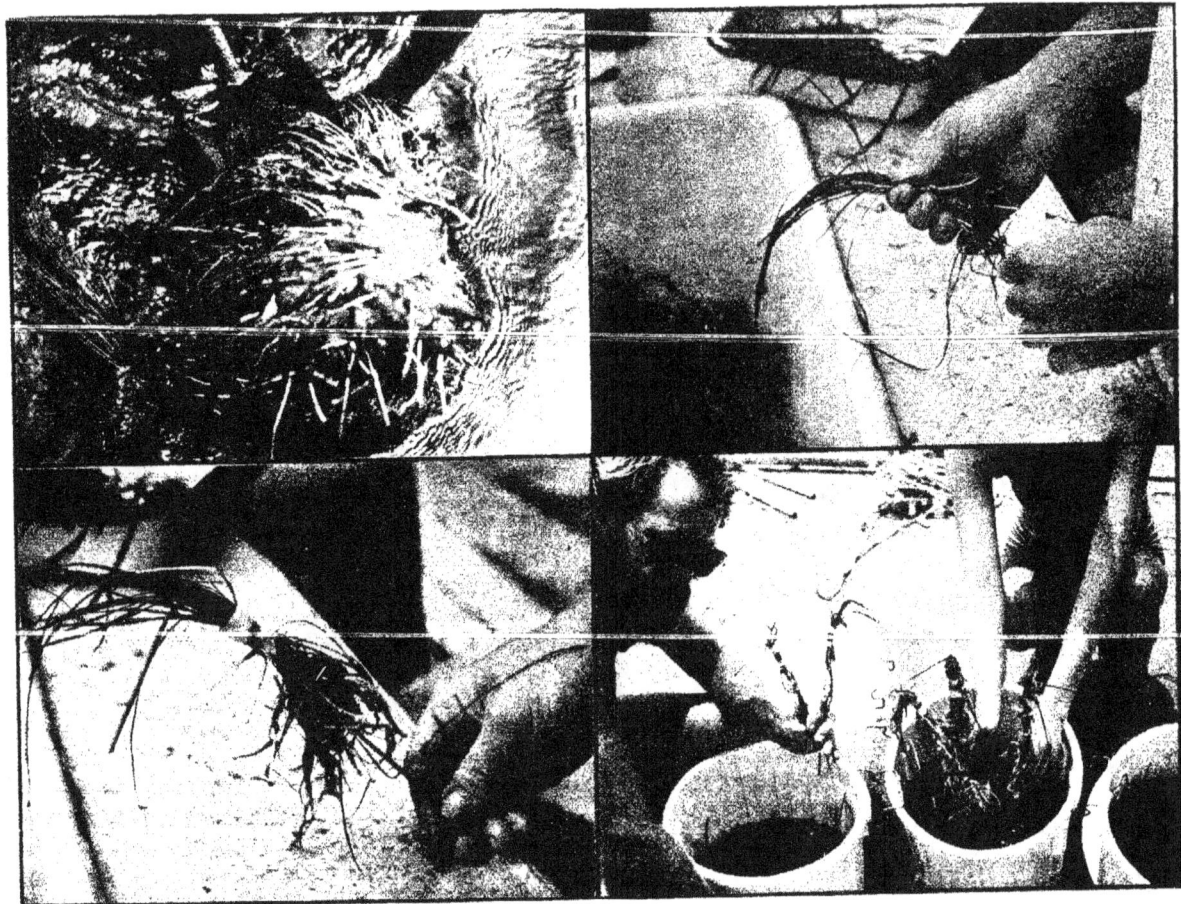

Figure 63. Photographs of the four-step planting unit creation process: (1) upper left - selection and harvest of plants, (2) upper right - isolation of sediment-free shoots, (3) lower left - attachment to anchors, and (4) lower right - deployment in seawater-filled containers.

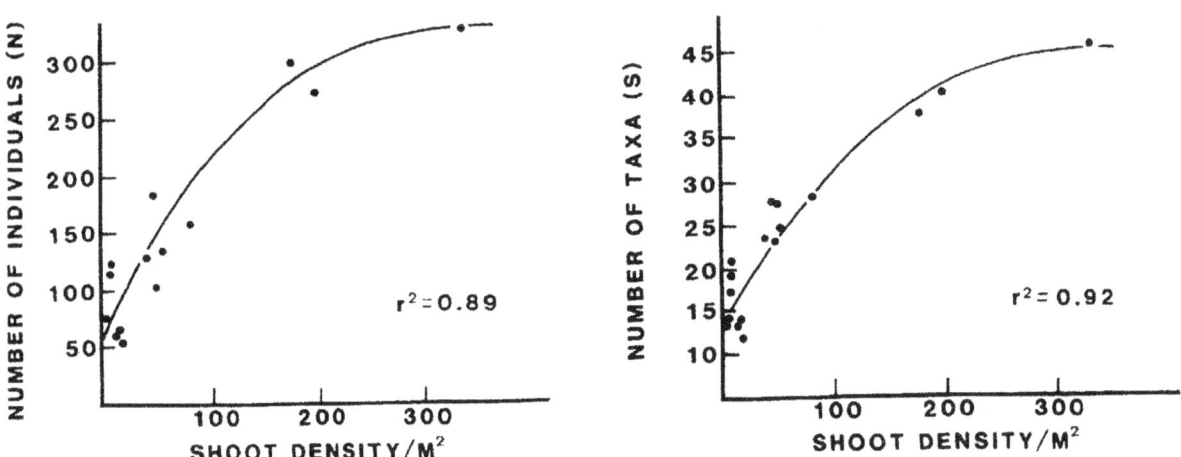

Figure 64. Asymptotic regressions of number of infaunal individuals (left) and taxa per core (right) in a transplanted eelgrass meadow in North Carolina. (Redrawn from Homziak et al. 1982.)

Table 16.   Estimates of the average net carbon production in undisturbed and transplanted meadows of <u>Zostera marina</u> for a 250-day growing season in North Carolina. (From Thayer et al., in press b.)

Component	Carbon production ($gC \cdot m^{-2}$)	
	Undisturbed	Transplanted
Leaves	310	182
Roots and rhizomes	52	31
Epiphytes	68	40

REFERENCES

Adams, S.M. 1976a. The ecology of eelgrass, _Zostera marina_ (L.), fish communities. I. Structural analysis. J. Exp. Mar. Biol. Ecol. 22: 269-291.

Adams, S.M. 1976b. The ecology of eelgrass, _Zostera marina_ (L.), fish communities. II. Functional analysis. J. Exp. Mar. Biol. Ecol. 22: 293-311.

Adams, S.M., and J.W. Angelovic. 1970. Assimilation of detritus and its associated bacteria by three species of estuarine animals. Chesapeake Sci. 11: 249-254.

Addy, C.E. 1947a. Eelgrass planting guide Md. Conserv. 24: 16-17.

Addy, C.E. 1947b. Germination of eelgrass seed. J. Wildl. Manage. 11: 279.

Aioi, K. 1980. Seasonal changes in the standing crop of eelgrass (_Zostera marina_ L.) in Odawa Bay, Central Japan. Aquat. Bot. 8: 343-354.

Aioi, K., H. Mukai, I. Koike, M. Ohtsu, and A. Hattori. 1981. Growth and organic production of eelgrass (_Zostera marina_ L.) in temperate waters of the Pacific coast of Japan. II. Growth analysis in winter. Aquat. Bot. 10: 175-182.

Allen, H.L. 1971. Primary productivity, chemo-organotrophy, and nutritional interactions of epiphytic algae and bacteria on macrophytes in the littoral of a lake. Ecol. Monogr. 41: 97-127.

Aller, R.C. 1978. The effects of animal-sediment interactions on geochemical processes near the sediment-water interface. Pages 157-172 _in_ M. L. Wiley, ed.

Estuarine interactions. Academic Press, New York.

Anderson, R.R. 1970. The submerged vegetation of Chincoteague Bay. Pages 136-155 _in_ Assateague ecological studies. Univ. Md. Chesapeake Biol. Lab. Ref. 446.

Arasaki, M. 1950. Studies on the ecology of _Zostera marina_ and _Zostera nana_. Bull. Jpn. Soc. Sci. Fish. 16: 70-76.

Ashe, D.M. 1982. Fish and wildlife mitigation: Description and analysis of estuarine applications. Coastal Zone Manage. J. 10: 1-52.

Backman, T.W., and D.C. Barilotti. 1976. Irradiance reduction: Effects on standing crops of the eelgrass _Zostera marina_ in a coastal lagoon. Mar. Biol. 34: 33-40.

Bagnold, R.A. 1963. Mechanics of marine sedimentation. Pages 507-528 _in_ M. N. Hill, ed. The sea, vol. 3. Interscience Publishers, New York.

Bak, H.P. 1980. Age populations and biometrics in eelgrass, _Zostera marina_ L. Ophelia 19: 155-162.

Bayer, R.D. 1979. Intertidal zonation of _Zostera marina_ in the Yaquina estuary, Oregon. Syesis 12: 147-154.

Biebel, R., and C.P. McRoy. 1971. Plasmatic resistance and rate of respiration and photosynthesis of _Zostera marina_ at different salinities and temperatures. Mar. Biol. 8: 48-56.

Bigley, R.E. 1981. The population biology of two intertidal seagrasses, _Zostera_ *japonica* and *Ruppia maritima*, at Roberts Bank, British Columbia. M.S. Thesis. University of British Columbia, Vancouver. 206 pp.

Billen, G. 1978. A budget of nitrogen cycling in North Sea sediments off the Belgian coast. Estuarine Coastal Mar. Sci. 7: 127-146.

Bjorndal, K.A. 1980. Nutrition and grazing behavior of the green turtle, *Chelonia mydas*. Mar. Biol. 56: 147-154.

Blackburn, T.H. 1979. Method for measuring rates of NH$_4$ turnover in anoxic marine sediments using a ^{15}H-NH$_4$ dilution technique. Appl. Environ. Microbiol. 37: 760-765.

Blegvad, H. 1914. Food and condition of nourishment among the communities of invertebrate animals found on or in the sea bottom in Danish waters. Rep. Dan. Biol. Stn. 22: 41-78.

Blodgett, L.A. 1980. General summary of weather conditions. NOAA (Natl. Ocean. Atmos. Admin.) Environ. Data Info. Serv. Climatol. Data Natl. Summary 31(13): 50-52.

Blois, J.C., J.M. Francaz, S. Gaudichon, and L. Lebris. 1961. Observations sur les herbiers de Zosteres de la region de Roscoff. Cah. Biol. Mar. 2: 223-262.

Boon, J.J., and J. Haverkamp. 1982. Pyrolysis mass spectrometry of intact and decomposed leaves of *Nuphar variegatum* and *Zostera marina*, and some archeological eelgrass samples. Hydrobiol. Bull. 16: 71-82.

Borum, J., and S. Wium-Andersen. 1980. Biomass and production of epiphytes on eelgrass (*Zostera marina* L.) in the Oresund, Denmark. Ophelia, Suppl. 1:57-61.

Boynton, W.R., and K.L. Heck, Jr. 1982. Ecological role and value of submerged macrophyte communities: A scientific summary. Pages 429-502 in E.G. Macalaster, D.A. Barber, and M. Kasper, eds. Chesapeake Bay Program technical studies: A synthesis. U.S. Environmental Protection Agency, Washington, D.C.

Brauner, J.F. 1973. Seasonality of epiphytic algae on *Zostera marina* in the vicinity of Beaufort, North Carolina. M.A. Thesis. Duke University, Durham, N.C. 137 pp.

Brauner, J.F. 1975. Seasonality of epiphytic algae on *Zostera marina* at Beaufort, North Carolina. Nova Hedwigia 26: 125-133.

Briggs, P.T., and J.S. O'Connor. 1971. Comparison of shore-zone fishes over naturally vegetated and sand-filled bottoms in Great South Bay. N.Y. Fish Game J. 18: 15-41.

Brinkhuis, B.H., W.F. Penello, and A.C. Churchill. 1980. Cadmium and manganese flux in eelgrass, *Zostera marina*. II. Metal uptake by leaf and root-rhizome tissues. Mar. Biol. 58: 187-196.

Brown, C.L. 1962. On the ecology of aufwuchs of *Zostera marina* in Charlestown Pond, Rhode Island. M.S. Thesis. University of Rhode Island, Kingston. 52 pp.

Brylinsky, M. 1977. Release of dissolved organic matter by some marine macrophytes. Mar. Biol. 39: 213-220.

Burkholder, P.R., and T.E. Doheny. 1968. The biology of eelgrass with special reference to Hempstead and South Oyster Bays, Nassau County, Long Island, New York. Lamont Geol. Observatory, Contrib. 1227. 120 pp.

Burrell, D.C., and J.R. Schubel. 1977. Seagrass ecosystem oceanography. Pages 196-225 in C.P. McRoy and C. Helfferich, eds. Seagrass ecosystems, a scientific perspective. Marcel Dekker, New York.

Caine, E.A. 1980. Ecology of two littoral species of caprellid amphipods (Crustacea) from Washington, U.S.A. Mar. Biol. 56: 327-335.

Calder, J.A., J. Lake, and J. Laseter. 1978. Chemical composition of selected environmental and petroleum samples from the Amoco Cadiz oil spill. Pages 21-82 in W.N. Hess, ed. The Amoco Cadiz oil spill, a preliminary scientific report. U.S. Department of Commerce and U.S.

Environmental Protection Agency, Washington, D.C.

Cammen, L.M. 1980. The significance of microbial carbon in the nutrition of the deposit feeding polychaete Nereis succinea. Mar. Biol. 61: 9-20.

Camp, D.K., S.P. Cobb, and J.F. Van Breedveld. 1973. Overgrazing of seagrasses by a regular urchin, Lytechinus variegatus. Bioscience 23(1): 37-38.

Capone, D.G. 1982. Nitrogen fixation (acetylene reduction) by rhizosphere sediments of the eelgrass, Zostera marina. Mar. Ecol. Prog. Ser. 10: 67-75.

Capone, D.G., and J.M. Budin. 1982. Nitrogen fixation associated with rinsed roots and rhizomes of the eelgrass Zostera marina. Plant Physiol. 70: 1601-1604.

Carr, W.E.S., and C.A. Adams. 1973. Food habits of juvenile marine fishes occupying seagrass beds in the estuarine zone near Crystal River, Florida. Trans. Am. Fish. Soc. 102: 511-540.

Chan, E.I. 1977. Oil pollution and tropical littoral communities: Biological effects of the 1975 Florida Keys oil spill. Pages 539-542 in Proceedings of the 1977 Oil Spill Conference, New Orleans, La. American Petroleum Institute, Washington, D.C.

Choat, J.H., and P.D. Kingett. 1982. The influence of fish predation on the abundance cycles of an algal turf invertebrate fauna. Oecologia 54: 88-95.

Christiansen, C., H. Christofferson, J. Dalsgaard, and P. Nornberg. 1981. Coastal and near-shore changes correlated with die-back in eelgrass (Zostera marina L.). Sediment. Geol. 28: 163-173.

Churchill, A.C. 1983. Field studies on seed germination and seedling development in Zostera marina L. Aquat. Bot. 16: 21-29.

Churchill, A.C., and M.I. Riner. 1978. Anthesis and seed production in Zostera marina L. from Great South Bay, New York, U.S.A. Aquat. Bot. 4: 83-93.

Churchill, A.C., A.E. Cok, and M.I. Riner. 1978. Stabilization of subtidal sediments by the transplantation of the seagrass Zostera marina L. N.Y. Sea Grant Rep. NYSSGP-RS-78-15. 48 pp.

Congdon, R.A., and A.J. McComb. 1979. Productivity of Ruppia: seasonal changes and dependence on light in an Australian estuary. Aquat. Bot. 6: 121-132.

[Conover, J.T.] 1964. Environmental relationships of benthos in salt ponds (plant relationships). R.I. Grad. Sch. Oceanogr. Tech. Rep. 3. 2 vols.

Conover, J.T. 1968. The importance of natural diffusion gradients and transport of substances related to benthic plant metabolism. Bot. Mar. 11: 1-9.

Conover, J.T., and E. Gough. 1964. The importance of stem and leaf vs. root assimilation in Ruppia maritima L. and Zostera marina L. related to seasonal growth. R.I. Grad. Sch. Oceanogr. Tech. Rep. 3: 6-1 - 6-19.

Cosgrove, D.J. 1977. Microbial transformations in the phosphorus cycle. Adv. Microbiol. Ecol. 1: 95-134.

Cottam, C. 1934. Past periods of eelgrass scarcity. Rhodora 36: 261-264.

Cottam, C., and D.A. Munro. 1954. Eelgrass status and environmental relations. J. Wildl. Manage. 18: 449-460.

Cottam, C., J.F. Lynch, and A.L. Nelson. 1944. Food habits and management of American sea brant. J. Wildl. Manage. 82: 36-56.

Cousins, S.H. 1980. A trophic continuum derived from plant structure, animal size and a detritus cascade. J. Theor. Biol. 82: 607-618.

Craven, P.A., and S. Hayasaka. 1982. Inorganic phosphate solubilization by rhizosphere bacteria in a Zostera marina community. Can. J. Microbiol. 28: 605-610.

Crosby, N.D., and R.G.B. Reid. 1971. Relationships between food, phylogeny and cellulose digestion in bivalvia. Can. J. Zool. 49: 617-622.

Davies, J.L. 1964. A morphologenic approach to world shorelines. Z. Geomorphol. 8: 27-42.

Dawes, C.J., and J.M. Lawrence. 1980. Seasonal changes in the proximate constituents of the seagrasses, Thalassia testudinum, Halodule wrightii, and Syringodium filiforme. Aquat. Bot. 8: 371-380.

Day, J.H. 1967. The biology of Knysna estuary, South Africa. Pages 397-407 in G. H. Lauff, ed. Estuaries. Am. Assoc. Adv. Sci. Publ. 83.

DeCock, A.W.A.M. 1980. Flowering, pollination and fruiting in Zostera marina L. Aquat. Bot. 9: 201-220.

DeCock, A.W.A.M. 1981a. Development of the flowering shoot of Zostera marina L. under controlled conditions in comparison to the development in two different natural habitats in the Netherlands. Aquat. Bot. 10: 99-113.

DeCock, A.W.A.M. 1981b. Influence of light and dark on flowering in Zostera marina L. under laboratory conditions. Aquat. Bot. 10: 115-123.

den Hartog, C. 1970. The seagrasses of the world. North-Holland Publishing Co., Amsterdam. 275 pp.

den Hartog, C. 1971. The dynamic aspect in the ecology of seagrass communities. Thalassia Jugosl. 7: 101-112.

den Hartog, C. 1977. Structure, function and classification in seagrass communities. Pages 89-122 in C.P. McRoy and C. Helfferich, eds. Seagrass ecosystems, a scientific perspective. Marcel Dekker, New York.

den Hartog, C., and R.P.W.M. Jacobs. 1980. Effects of the "Amoco Cadiz" oil spill on an eelgrass community at Roscoff (France) with special reference to the mobile benthic fauna. Helgol. Meeresunters. 33: 182-191.

Dennison, W.C. 1979. Light adaptations of plants: a model based on the seagrass Zostera marina L. M.S. Thesis. Univ. of Alaska, Fairbanks. 70 pp.

Dennison, W.C., and R.S. Alberte. 1982. Photosynthetic responses of Zostera marina L. (eelgrass) to in situ manipulations of light intensity. Oecologia 55: 137-144.

Dexter, R.W. 1947. The marine communities of a tidal inlet at Cape Ann, Massachusetts: A study in bio-ecology. Ecol. Monogr. 17: 261-294.

Diaz-Piferrer, M. 1962. The effects of an oil spill on the shore of Guanica, Puerto Rico. Assoc. Isl. Mar. Lab. Meet. 4: 12-13.

Dietz, C.G. 1982. Ammonium fluxes from estuarine sediments: Great South Bay, New York. M.S. Thesis. State Univ. of New York, Stony Brook. 128 pp.

Dillon, C.R. 1971. A comparative study of the primary productivity of estuarine phytoplankton and macrobenthic plants. Ph.D. Dissertation. Univ. of North Carolina, Chapel Hill. 112 pp.

Dodd, C.A. 1966. Epiphytic diatoms of Zostera marina in Great South Bay. M.S. Thesis. Adelphi Univ., Adelphi, N.Y. 208 pp.

Drew, E.A. 1980. Soluble carbohydrate composition of seagrasses. Pages 247-260 in R.C. Phillips and C.P. McRoy, eds. Handbook of seagrass biology, an ecosystem perspective. Garland STPM Press, New York.

Drifmeyer, J.E. 1981. Urchin Lytechinus variegatus grazing on eelgrass, Zostera marina. Estuaries 4: 374-375.

Drifmeyer, J.E., G.W. Thayer, F.A. Cross, and J.C. Zieman. 1980. Cycling of Mn, Fe, Cu and Zn by eelgrass, Zostera marina L. Am. J. Bot. 67: 1089-1096.

Durako, M.J., R.A. Medlyn, and M.D. Moffler. 1982. Particulate matter resuspension via metabolically produced gas bubbles from benthic estuarine microalgae communities. Limnol. Oceanogr. 27: 752-756.

Dykhouse, J.D. 1976. Seasonal dynamics of dominant epiphytic invertebrates on eelgrass (Zostera marina L.) in South Humboldt Bay. M.A. Thesis. Humboldt State Univ., Arcata, Calif. 45 pp.

Emery, A.R. 1968. Preliminary observations of coral reef plankton. Limnol. Oceanogr. 13: 293-303.

Ewald, J.J. 1969. Observations on the biology of Tozeuma carolinense (Decapoda, Hippolyidae) from Florida, with special reference to larval development. Bull. Mar. Sci. 19: 510-549.

Feeny, P. 1976. Plant apparency and chemical defense. Recent Adv. Phytochem. 10: 1-40.

Felger, R.S., and C.P. McRoy. 1975. Seagrasses as potential food plants. Pages 62-68 in G.F. Sommers, ed. Seed bearing halophytes as food plants. Univ. of Delaware, Newark.

Felger, R., and M.B. Moser. 1973. Eelgrass (Zostera marina L.) in the Gulf of California: discovery of its nutritional value by the Seri Indians. Science 181: 355-356.

Felger, R.S., M.B. Moser, and E.W. Moser. 1980. Seagrasses in Seri Indian culture. Pages 260-276 in R.C. Phillips and C.P. McRoy, eds. Handbook of seagrass biology, an ecosystem perspective. Garland STPM Press, New York.

Fenchel, T. 1970. Studies on the decomposition of organic detritus derived from turtle grass, Thalassia testudinum. Limnol. Oceanogr. 15: 14-20.

Fenchel, T. 1977. Aspects of the decomposition of seagrasses. Pages 123-145 in C.P. McRoy and C. Helfferich, eds. Seagrass ecosystems, a scientific perspective. Marcel Dekker, New York.

Fenchel, T., and T.H. Blackburn. 1979. Bacteria and mineral cycling. Academic Press, New York. 225 pp.

Fenchel, T., and R.J. Riedl. 1970. The sulfide system: A new biotic community underneath the oxidized layer of marine sand bottoms. Mar. Biol. 7: 225-268.

Fenchel, T.M., C.P. McRoy, J.C. Ogden, P. Parker, and W.E. Rainey. 1979. Symbiotic cellulose degradation in green turtles, Chelonia mydas L. Appl. Environ. Microbiol. 37: 348-350.

Ferguson, R.L., and S.M. Adams. 1979. A mathematical model of trophic dynamics in estuarine seagrass communities. Pages 41-70 in Richard F. Dame, ed. Marsh-estuarine systems simulation. Univ. of South Carolina Press, Columbia.

Ferguson, R.L., G.W. Thayer, and T.R. Rice. 1980. Marine primary producers. Pages 9-69 in F.J. Vernberg and W. Vernberg, eds. Functional adaptations of marine organisms. Academic Press, New York.

Findlay, S., and K. Tenore. 1982. Nitrogen source for a detritivore: detritus substrate versus associated microbes. Science 218: 371-373.

Fisher, J.S., J. Pickral, and W.E. Odum. 1979. Organic detritus particles: initiation of motion criteria. Limnol. Oceanogr. 24: 529-532.

Fonseca, M.S., W.J. Kenworthy, J. Homziak, and G.W. Thayer. 1979. Transplanting of eelgrass and shoalgrass as a potential means of economically mitigating a recent loss of habitat. Pages 279-326 in D.P. Cole, ed. Proceedings of the Sixth Annual Conference on Restoration and Creation of Wetlands. Hillsborough Community College, Tampa, Fla.

Fonseca, M.S., W.J. Kenworthy, G.W. Thayer, and D.Y. Heller. 1982a. Transplanting of the seagrasses Zostera marina and Halodule wrightii for the stabilization of subtidal dredge material. Annual Report of the National Marine Fisheries Service, Southeast Fisheries Center, Beaufort Laboratory, Division of Estuarine and Coastal Ecology, Beaufort, N.C., to the U.S. Army Corps of Engineers, Coastal Engineering Research Center, Fort Belvoir, Va. 61 pp.

Fonseca, M.S., J.J. Fisher, J.C. Zieman, and G.W. Thayer. 1982b. Influence of the seagrass, Zostera marina L., on current flow. Estuarine Coastal Shelf Sci. 15: 351-364.

Fonseca, M.S., J.C. Zieman, G.W. Thayer, and J.S. Fisher. 1983. The role of current velocity in structuring eelgrass (Zostera marina L.) meadows. Estuarine Coastal Shelf Sci. 17: 367-380.

Fonseca, M.S., W.J. Kenworthy, G.W. Thayer, D.Y. Heller, and K.M. Cheap. 1984. Transplanting of the seagrasses Zostera marina and Halodule wrightii for sediment stabilization and habitat development on the East Coast of the United States. Tech. Rep. EL-84-14, U.S. Army Engineer Waterways Experiment Station, Vicksburg, Miss. [14] pp.

Fonseca, M.S., G.W. Thayer, A.J. Chester, and C. Foltz. In press. Impact of scallop harvesting on eelgrass (Zostera marina L.) meadows: implications for management. N. Am. J. Fish. Manage.

Foster, M., M. Neushul, and R. Zingmark. 1971. The Santa Barbara oil spill, Part 2. Initial effects on intertidal and kelp bed organisms. Environ. Pollut. 2: 115-134.

Foulds, J.B., and K.H. Mann. 1978. Cellulose digestion in Mysis stenolepsis and its ecological implications. Limnol. Oceanogr. 23: 760-766.

Fuji, A. 1962. Ecological studies on the growth and food consumption of Japanese common littoral sea urchin, Strongylocentrotus intermedius. Mem. Fac. Fish. Hokkaido Univ. 15(2): 1-160.

Fulton, R.S., III. 1982. Predation and the organization of an estuarine copepod community. Ph.D. Diss. Duke Univ., Durham, N.C. 421 pp.

Gagnon, P.S., R.L. Vadas, D.B. Burdick, and B.P. May. 1980. Genetic identity of annual and perennial forms of Zostera marina L. Aquat. Bot. 8: 157-162.

Giere, O. 1975. Population structure, food relations and ecological role of marine oligochaetes with special reference to meiobenthic species. Mar. Biol. 31: 139-157.

Ginsberg, R.N., and H.A. Lowenstam. 1958. The influence of marine bottom communities on the deposition environment of sediments. J. Geol. 66: 310-318.

Glude, J.B. 1954. The effects of temperature and predators on the abundance of the soft-shell clam, Mya arenaria, in New England. Trans. Am. Fish. Soc. 84: 13-26.

Godshalk, G.L., and R.G. Wetzel. 1978a. Decomposition in the littoral zone of lakes. Pages 131-143 in R.E. Good, D.F. Whigham and R.L. Simpson, eds. Fresh water wetlands: Production processes and management potentials. Academic Press, New York.

Godshalk, G.L., and R.G. Wetzel. 1978b. Decomposition of aquatic angiosperms. III. Zostera marina L. and a conceptual model of decomposition. Aquat. Bot. 5: 329-354.

Goforth, H.W., and T.J. Peeling. 1979. Intertidal and subtidal eelgrass (Zostera marina L.) transplant studies in San Diego Bay, California. Pages 324-356 in D. P. Cole, ed. Proceedings of the Sixth Annual Conference on the Restoration and Creation of Wetlands. Hillsborough Community College, Tampa, Fla.

Gosner, K.L. 1971. Guide to identification of marine and estuarine invertebrates, Cape Hatteras to the Bay of Fundy. John Wiley and Sons, Inc., New York. 693 pp.

Grant, J. 1981. Sediment transport and distribution on an intertidal sandflat: infaunal distribution and recolonization. Mar. Ecol. Prog. Ser. 6: 249-255.

Grant, W.D., and O.S. Madsen. 1979. Combined wave and current interaction with a rough bottom. J. Geophys. Res. 84: 1797-1807.

Greening, H.S., and R.J. Livingston. 1982. Diel variation in the structure of seagrass-associated epibenthic macroinvertebrate communities. Mar. Ecol. Prog. Ser. 7: 147-156.

Greze, I.I. 1968. Feeding habits and food requirements of some amphipods in the Black Sea. Mar. Biol. 1: 316-321.

Gutsell, J.S. 1930. Natural history of the bay scallop. Bull. U.S. Bur. Fish. 45: 569-632.

Hamner, W.M., and J.H. Carleton. 1979. Copepod swarms: Attributes and role in coral reef ecosystems. Limnol. Oceanogr. 24: 1-14.

Harlin, M.M. 1973. Transfer of products between epiphytic marine algae and host plants. J. Phycol. 9: 243-248.

Harlin, M.M. 1975. Epiphyte-host relations in seagrass communities. Aquat. Bot. 1: 125-131.

Harlin, M.M. 1980. Seagrass epiphytes. Pages 117-151 in R.C. Phillips and C.P. McRoy, eds. Handbook of seagrass biology, an ecosystem perspective. Garland STPM Press, New York.

Harlin, M.M., and B. Thorne-Miller. 1981. Nutrient enrichment of seagrass beds in a Rhode Island coastal lagoon. Mar. Biol. 65: 221-229.

Harlin, M.M., B. Thorne-Miller, and J.C. Boothroyd. 1982. Seagrass-sediment dynamics of a flood-tidal delta in Rhode Island (U.S.A.). Aquat. Bot. 14: 127-138.

Harms, J.C. 1969. Hydraulic significance of some sand ripples. Bull. Geol. Soc. Am. 80: 363-396.

Harrison, P.G. 1982a. Control of microbial growth and of amphipod grazing by water-soluble compounds from leaves of Zostera marina. Mar. Biol. 67: 225-230.

Harrison, P.G. 1982b. Spatial and temporal patterns in abundance of two intertidal seagrasses, Zostera americana den Hartog and Zostera marina L. Aquat. Bot. 12: 305-320.

Harrison, P.G. In press. Phenolic compounds in seagrasses: bane or boon to decomposers? Bull. Mar. Sci.

Harrison, P.G., and A.T. Chan. 1980. Inhibition of growth of microalgae and bacteria by extracts of eelgrass (Zostera marina) leaves. Mar. Biol. 61: 21-26.

Harrison, P.G., and B.J. Harrison. 1980. Interactions of bacteria, microalgae, and copepods in a detritus microcosm: through a flask darkly. Pages 373-385 in K.R. Tenore and B.C. Coull, eds. Marine benthic dynamics. University of South Carolina Press, Georgetown.

Harrison, P.G., and K.H. Mann. 1975a. Detritus formation from eelgrass (Zostera marina L.): the relative effects of fragmentation, leaching, and decay. Limnol. Oceanogr. 20: 924-934.

Harrison, P.G., and K.H. Mann. 1975b. Chemical changes during the seasonal cycle of growth and decay in eelgrass (Zostera marina L.) on the Atlantic coast of Canada. J. Fish. Res. Board Can. 32: 615-621.

Hay, W.P. 1905. The life history of the blue crab (Callinectes sapidus). Rep. U.S. Bur. Fish. 1904: 395-413.

Hayes, M.O. 1975. Morphology of sand accumulations in estuaries. Pages 3-22 in L.E. Cronin, ed. Estuarine research, vol. 2. Academic Press, New York.

Heald, E.J. 1969. The production of organic detritus in a south Florida estuary. Ph.D. Diss. Univ. of Miami, Coral Gables, Fla. 110 pp.

Heck, K.L., Jr., and R.J. Orth. 1980a. Structural components of eelgrass (Zostera marina) meadows in the lower Chesapeake Bay - Decapod Crustacea. Estuaries 3: 289-295.

Heck, K.L., Jr., and R.J. Orth. 1980b. Seagrass habitats: the roles of habitat complexity, competition and predation in structuring associated fish and motile macroinvertebrate assemblages. Pages 449-464 in V.S. Kennedy, ed. Estuarine perspectives. Academic Press, New York.

Heck, K.L., and T.A. Thoman. 1981. Experiments on predator-prey interactions in vegetated aquatic habitats. J. Exp. Mar. Biol. Ecol. 53: 125-134.

Hildebrand, S.F., and W.C. Schroeder. 1928. Fishes of Chesapeake Bay. Bull. U.S. Bur. Fish. 43(1): 1-366.

Homziak, J., M.S. Fonseca, and W.J. Kenworthy. 1982. Macrobenthic community structure in a transplanted eelgrass (Zostera marina) meadow. Mar. Ecol. Prog. Ser. 9: 211-221.

Howard, R.K. 1982. Impact of feeding activities of epibenthic amphipods on surface-fouling of eelgrass leaves. Aquat. Bot. 14: 91-97.

Hungate, R.E. 1966. The rumen and its microbes. Academic Press, New York. 533 pp.

Iizumi, H., A. Hattori, and C.P. McRoy. 1980. Nitrate and nitrite in interstitial waters of eelgrass beds in relation to the rhizosphere. J. Exp. Mar. Biol. Ecol. 47: 191-201.

Iizumi, H., A. Hattori, and C.P. McRoy. 1982. Ammonium regeneration and assimilation in eelgrass (Zostera marina) beds. Mar. Biol. 66: 59-65.

Jacobs, R.P.W.M. 1979. Distribution and aspects of the production and biomass of eelgrass, Zostera marina L., at Roscoff, France. Aquat. Bot. 7: 151-172.

Jacobs, R.P.W.M. 1980. Effects of the "Amoco Cadiz" oil spill on the seagrass community at Roscoff with special reference to the benthic infauna. Mar. Ecol. Prog. Ser. 2: 207-212.

Jacobs, R.P.W.M. 1982. Reproductive strategies of two seagrass species (Zostera marina L. and Zostera noltii [Hosnen]) along west European coasts. Pages 150-155 in J.J. Lymoens, S.S. Hooper, and P. Compere, eds. Studies on aquatic vascular plants. Royal Botanical Society of Belgium, Brussels.

Jacobs, R.P.W.M., and E.S. Pierson. 1981. Phenology of reproductive shoots of eelgrass, Zostera marina L., at Roscoff (France). Aquat. Bot. 10: 45-60.

Jacobs, R.P.W.M., C. den Hartog, B.F. Braster, and F.C. Carriere. 1981. Grazing of the seagrass Zostera noltii by birds at Terschelling (Dutch Wadden Sea). Aquat. Bot. 10: 241-259.

Johannes, R.E. 1964. Phosphorus excretion as related to body size in marine animals: microzooplankton and nutrient regeneration. Science 146: 923-924.

Jorgensen, B.B., and T. Fenchel. 1974. The sulfur cycle of a marine sediment model system. Mar. Biol. 24: 189-201.

Josselyn, M.N. 1978. The contribution of marine macrophytes to the detrital pool of the Great Bay estuarine system, N.H. Ph.D. Diss. Univ. of New Hampshire, Durham. 129 pp.

Josselyn, M.N., and A.C. Mathieson. 1980. Seasonal influx and decomposition of autochthonous macrophyte litter in a north temperate estuary. Hydrobiologia 71: 197-208.

Jumars, P.A., A.R. Nowell, and R.L. Self. 1981. A simple model of flow-sediment organism interaction. Mar. Geol. 42: 155-172.

Keddy, J., and D.G. Patriquin. 1978. An annual form of eelgrass in Nova Scotia. Aquat. Bot. 5: 163-170.

Keller, M. 1963. Growth and distribution of eelgrass (Zostera marina L.) in Humboldt Bay, California. M.S. Thesis. Humboldt State College, Arcata, Calif. 53 pp.

Kemp, W.M., W.R. Boynton, J.C. Stevenson, R.R. Twilky, and J.C. Means. In press. The decline of submerged vascular plants in Chesapeake Bay: summary of results concerning possible causes. Mar. Technol. Soc. J.

Kentula, M.E. 1983. Production dynamics of a Zostera marina L. bed in Netarts Bay, Oregon. Ph.D. Diss. Oregon State Univ., Corvallis. 158 pp.

Kenworthy, W.J. 1981. The interrelationship between seagrasses, Zostera marina and Halodule wrightii, and the physical and chemical properties of sediments in a mid-Atlantic coastal plain estuary near Beaufort, North Carolina (U.S.A.). M.S. Thesis. Univ. of Virginia, Charlottesville, 114 pp.

Kenworthy, W.J., and M.S. Fonseca. 1977. Reciprocal transplant of the seagrass, Zostera marina L. effect of substrate on growth. Aquaculture 12: 197-213.

Kenworthy, W.J., and G.W. Thayer. In press. Aspects of the production and decomposition of the roots and rhizomes of seagrasses, Zostera marina and Thalassia testudinum, in temperate and subtropical marine ecosystems. Bull. Mar. Sci.

Kenworthy, W.J., M.S. Fonseca, J. Homziak, and G.W. Thayer. 1980. Development of a transplanted seagrass (Zostera marina L.) meadow in Back Sound, Carteret County, North Carolina. Pages 175-193 in D.P. Cole, ed. Proceedings of the Seventh Annual Conference on the Restoration and Creation of Wetlands. Hillsborough Community College, Tampa, Fla.

Kenworthy, W.J., J.C. Zieman, and G.W. Thayer. 1982. Evidence for the influence of seagrass on the benthic nitrogen cycle in a coastal plain estuary near Beaufort, North Carolina (USA). Oecologia 54: 152-158.

Kenworthy, W.J., M.S. Fonseca, and G.W. Thayer. In preparation. Aspects of the population biology of eelgrass, Zostera marina L.

Khailov, K.M., and Z.Z. Finenko. 1970. Organic macromolecular compounds dissolved in seawater and their inclusion in marine food chains. Pages 6-18 in J.H. Steele, ed. Marine food chains. University of California Press, Berkeley.

Kikuchi, T. 1961. An ecological study on animal community of Zostera belt, in Tomioka Bay, Amakusa, Kyushu (I). Community composition (1) Fish fauna. Rec. Oceanogr. Works Jpn. Spec. No. 5: 211-219.

Kikuchi, T. 1962. An ecological study on animal community of Zostera belt, in

Tomioka Bay, Amakusa, Kyushu (II). Community composition (2) Decapod crustaceans. Rec. Oceanogr. Works Jpn. Spec. No. 6: 135-146.

Kikuchi, T. 1966. An ecological study on animal communities of the Zostera marina belt in Tomioka Bay, Amakusa, Kyushu. Publ. Amakusa Mar. Biol. Lab. Kyushu Univ. 1: 1-106.

Kikuchi, T. 1980. Faunal relationships in temperate seagrass beds. Pages 153-172 in R.C. Phillips and C.P. McRoy, eds. Handbook of seagrass biology, an ecosystem perspective. Garland STPM Press, New York.

Kikuchi, T., and J.M. Peres. 1977. Consumer ecology of seagrass beds. Pages 147-193 in C.P. McRoy and C. Helfferich, eds. Seagrass ecosystems, a scientific perspective. Marcel Dekker, New York.

Kirby-Smith, W.W. 1972. Growth of the bay scallop, the influence of experimental water currents. J. Exp. Mar. Biol. Ecol. 8: 7-18.

Kirby-Smith, W.W., and R.T. Barber. 1974. Suspension-feeding aquaculture systems: effects of phytoplankton concentration and temperature on the growth of the bay scallop. Aquaculture 3: 135-145.

Kirchman, D., and R. Mitchell. 1982. Contribution of particle-bound bacteria to total microheterotrophic activity in five ponds and two marshes. Appl. Environ. Microbiol. 43: 200-209.

Kirchman, D.L., L. Mazzella, R. Mitchell, and R.S. Alberte. 1980. Bacterial epiphytes on Zostera marina surfaces. Biol. Bull. (Woods Hole) 159: 461-462.

Kirchman, D.L., L. Mazella, R.S. Alberte, and R. Mitchell. 1984. Epiphytic bacterial production on Zostera marina. Mar. Ecol. Prog. Ser. 15: 117-123.

Kirkman, H., and D.D. Reid. 1979. A study of the role of the seagrass Posidonia australis in the carbon budget of an estuary. Aquat. Bot. 7: 173-183.

Kirkman, H., and P.C. Young. 1981. Measurement of health and echinoderm grazing on Posidonia oceanica (L.) Delile. Aquat. Bot. 10: 329-338.

Kita, T., and E. Harada. 1962. Studies on the epiphytic communities. I. Abundance and distribution of microalgae and small animals on the Zostera blades. Publ. Seto Mar. Biol. Lab. 10: 245-247.

Klug, M.J. 1980. Detritus-decomposition relationships. Pages 225-246 in R.C. Phillips and C.P. McRoy, eds. Handbook of seagrass biology, an ecosystem perspective. Garland STPM Press, New York.

Knauer, G.A., and A.V. Ayers. 1977. Changes in carbon, nitrogen, adenosine triphosphate and chlorophyll in decomposing Thalassia testudinum leaves. Limnol. Oceanogr. 22: 408-414.

Knutson, P.L., W.N. Seelig, and M.R. Inskeep. 1982. Wave dampening in Spartina alterniflora marshes. Wetlands 2: 87-104.

Koike, I., and A. Hattori. 1978. Denitrification and ammonium formation in anaerobic coastal sediments. Appl. Environ. Microbiol. 35: 278-282.

Kranck, K., and T. Milligan. 1980. Macroflocs: production of marine snow in the laboratory. Mar. Ecol. Progr. Ser. 3: 19-24.

Kuenzler, E.J. 1961. Phosphorus budget of a mussel population. Limnol. Oceanogr. 6: 400-415.

Lamounette, R. 1977. A study of the germination and viability of Zostera marina L. seed. M.S. Thesis. Adelphi Univ., Garden City, N.Y. 41 pp.

Lappalainen, A. 1973. Biotic fluctuations in a Zostera marina community. Oikos 15 (Suppl.): 1-7.

Lascara, V.J. 1981. Fish predator-prey interactions in areas of eelgrass (Zostera marina). M.S. Thesis. College of William and Mary, Williamsburg, Va. 80 pp.

LaTouche, R.W., and A.B. West. 1980. Observations on the food of Antedon bifida (Echinodermata: Crinoidea). Mar. Biol. 60: 39-46.

Lawrence, J.M. 1975. On the relationships between marine plants and sea urchins. Oceanogr. Mar. Biol. Annu. Rev. 13: 213-286.

Ledoyer, M. 1962. Etude de la faune vagile de herbiers superficiels de Zosteracees et de quelques biotopes d'algues littorales. Recl. Trav. Stn. Mar. Endoume-Mars. 25: 117-225.

Lee, C., R.W. Howarth, and B.L. Howes. 1980. Sterols in decomposing Spartina alterniflora and the use of ergosterol in estimating the contribution of fungi to detrital nitrogen. Limnol. Oceanogr. 25: 290-303.

Lee, J.E. 1980. A conceptual model of marine detrital decomposition and the organisms associated with the process. Pages 257-291 in M.R. Droop and H.W. Jannasch, eds. Advances in microbial ecology, vol. 2. Academic Press, New York.

Leighton, D.L. 1971. Grazing activities of benthic invetebrates in southern California kelp beds. Beih. Nova Hedwigia 32: 421-453.

Lindall, W.N., A. Mager, G.W. Thayer, and D.R. Ekberg. 1979. Estuarine habitat mitigation planning in the southeast. Pages 129-135 in G.A. Swanson, tech. coord. The mitigation symposium. U.S. For. Serv. Rocky Mtn. For. Range Exp. Stn. Gen. Tech. Rep. RM-65.

Lindsay, G.J.H., and J.E. Harris. 1980. Carboxymethyl-cellulase activity in the digestive tracts of fish. J. Fish. Biol. 16: 219-233.

Lindsay, S.O. 1975. Mycetozoans. Academic Press, New York. 293 pp.

Linley, E.A.S., R.C. Newell, and S.A. Bosma. 1981. Heterotrophic utilization of mucilage released during fragmentation of kelp (Eklonia maxima and Laminaria pallida). I. Development of microbial communities associated with the degradation of kelp mucilage. Mar. Ecol. Prog. Ser. 4: 31-41.

Lively, J.S., Z. Kaufman, and E.J. Carpenter. 1983. Phytoplankton ecology of a barrier island estuary: Great South Bay, New York. Estuarine Coastal Shelf Sci. 16: 51-68.

Longcore, J.R., and G.W. Cornwell. 1964. The consumption of natural foods by captive canvasback and lesser scaups. J. Wildl. Manage. 28: 527-530.

Lopez, G.R., S. Levinton, and L.B. Slobodkin. 1977. The effect of grazing by the detritivore Orchestia grillus on Spartina litter and its associated microbial community. Oecologia 30: 111-127.

Lyngby, J.E., and H. Brix. 1982. Seasonal and environmental variation in cadmium, copper, lead and zinc concentrations in eelgrass (Zostera marina L.) in the Limfjord, Denmark. Aquat. Bot. 14: 59-74.

Lyngby, J.E., H. Brix, and H.H. Schierup. 1982. Adsorption and translocation of zinc in eelgrass (Zostera marina L.). J. Exp. Mar. Biol. Ecol. 58: 259-270.

MacGinitie, G.E. 1935. Ecological aspects of a California marine estuary. Am. Midl. Nat. 16: 629-765.

Main, S.P., and C.D. McIntire. 1974. The distribution of epiphytic diatoms in Yaquilla estuary, Oregon (U.S.A.). Bot. Mar. 17: 88-99.

Mangum, C.P., S.L. Santos, and W.R. Rhodes. 1968. Distribution and feeding on the onuychid polychaete Diopatra cuprea. Mar. Biol. 2: 33-40.

Mann, K.H. 1977. Destruction of kelp-beds by sea-urchins: a cyclical phenomenon or reversible degradation? Helgol. Wiss. Meeresunters. 30: 455-467.

Marsh, G.A. 1973. The Zostera epifaunal community in the York River, Virginia. Chesapeake Sci. 14: 87-97.

Marshall, N., and K. Lukas. 1970. Preliminary observations on the properties of bottom sediments with and without eelgrass, Zostera marina cover. Proc. Natl. Shellfish. Assoc. 60: 107-112.

Martin, A.C., H.S. Zim, and A.L. Nelson. 1951. American wildlife and plants, a guide to wildlife food habits. Dover, New York. 50 pp.

Mazzella, L., D. Mauzerall, H. Lyman, and R.S. Alberte. 1981. Protoplast isolation and photosynthetic characteristics of Zostera marina L. (eelgrass). Bot. Mar. 24: 285-290.

McConnaughey, T., and C.P. McRoy. 1979. ^{13}C label identifies eelgrass (Zostera marina) carbon in an Alaskan estuarine food web. Mar. Biol. 53: 263-269.

McMahon, C.A. 1970. Food habits of ducks wintering in Laguna Madre, Texas. J. Wildl. Manage. 34: 946-949.

McMillan, C., and F.N. Moseley. 1967. Salinity tolerances of five marine spermatophytes of Redfish Bay, Texas. Ecology 48: 503-506.

McRoy, C.P. 1966. The standing stock and ecology of eelgrass (Zostera marina L.) in Izembek Lagoon, Alaska. M.S. Thesis. Univ. of Washington, Seattle. 137 pp.

McRoy, C.P. 1969. Eelgrass under the Arctic winter ice. Nature 224: 818-819.

McRoy, C.P. 1970. Standing stocks and related features of eelgrass populations in Alaska. J. Fish. Res. Board Can. 27: 1811-1821.

McRoy. C.P. 1974. Seagrass productivity: carbon uptake experiments in eelgrass, Zostera marina. Aquaculture 4: 131-137.

McRoy, C.P., and R.J. Barsdate. 1970. Phosphate absorption in eelgrass. Limnol. Oceanogr. 15: 6-13.

McRoy, C.P., and J.J. Goering. 1974. Nutrient transfer between the seagrass Zostera marina and its epiphytes. Nature 248: 173-174.

McRoy, C.P., and C. Helfferich. 1980. Applied aspects of seagrasses. Pages 297-343 in R.C. Phillips and C.P. Mc-

Roy, eds. Handbook of seagrass biology, an ecosystem perspective. Garland STPM Press, New York.

McRoy, C.P., and D.S. Lloyd. 1981. Comparative function and stability of macrophyte-based ecosystems. Pages 473-489 in A.R. Longhurst, ed. Analysis of marine ecosystems. Academic Press, New York.

McRoy, C.P., and C. McMillan. 1977. Production ecology and physiology of seagrasses. Pages 53-88 in C.P. McRoy and C. Helfferich, eds. Seagrass ecosystems, a scientific perspective. Marcel Dekker, New York.

McRoy, C.P., and S.L. Williams. 1977. Sublethal effects (of hydrocarbons) on seagrass photosynthesis. Final report to NOAA Outer Continental Shelf Environmental Assessment Program, Contract #03-5-022-56, Task Order #17, Research Unit #305. 35 pp.

McRoy, C.P., R.J. Barsdate, and M. Nebert. 1972. Phosphorus cycling in an eelgrass (Zostera marina L.) ecosystem. Limnol. Oceanogr. 17: 58-67.

Merriner, J.V., and G.W. Boehlert. 1979. Higher level consumer interactions. Pages 89-142 in R.L. Wetzel, K.L. Webb, P.A. Penhale, R.J. Orth, D.F. Boesch, G.W. Boehlert, and J.V. Merriner. The functional ecology of submerged aquatic vegetation in the lower Chesapeake Bay. EPA/CBP Grant R805974.

Meyer, C.E. 1982. Zooplankton communities in Chesapeake Bay seagrass systems. M.A. Thesis. College of William and Mary, Williamsburg, Va. 96 pp.

Milne, L.J., and M.J. Milne. 1951. The eelgrass catastrophe. Sci. Am. 184 (1): 52-55.

Molinier, R., and J. Picard. 1952. Recherches sur les herbiers de phanerogames marines du littoral Mediterranean francais. Ann. Inst. Oceanogr. 27(3): 157-234.

Morisita, M. 1959. Measurement of interspecific association and similarity between communities. Mem. Fac. Sci. Kyushu Univ. Ser. E (Biol.) 3: 65-80.

Morrison, S.J., and D.C. White. 1980. Effects of grazing by estuarine gammaridean amphipods on the microbiota of allochthonous detritus. Appl. Environ. Microbiol. 40: 659-671.

Morton, J., and M. Miller. 1968. The New Zealand sea shore. Collins, London. 638 pp.

Mukai, H., K. Aioi, I. Koike, H. Iizumi, M. Ohtsu, and A. Hattori. 1979. Growth and organic production of eelgrass (Zostera marina L.) in temperate waters of the Pacific coast of Japan. I. Growth analysis in spring-summer. Aquat. Bot. 7: 47-56.

Murray, L., and R.L. Wetzel. 1982. Oxygen metabolism of a temperate seagrass (Zostera marina L.) community: plant-epiphyte, plankton and benthic microalgae productivity and respiration. Pages 108-129 in R.L. Wetzel, ed. Structural and functional aspects of the ecology of submerged aquatic macrophyte communities in the lower Chesapeake Bay, vol. 1. Va. Inst. Mar. Sci. Spec. Rep. Appl. Mar. Sci. Ocean Eng. 267.

Nadeau, R.J., and E.T. Berquist. 1977. Effects of the March 18, 1973 oil spill near Cabo Rojo, Puerto Rico on tropical marine communities. Pages 535-538 in Proceedings of the 1977 Oil Spill Conference, New Orleans, La. American Petroleum Institute, Washington, D.C.

Nagle, J.S. 1968. Distribution of the epibiota of macroepibenthic plants. Contrib. Mar. Sci. 13: 105-114.

Neilson, B.J., and L.E. Cronin, eds. 1981. Estuaries and nutrients. Humana Press, Clifton, N.J. 643 pp.

Nelson, W.G. 1979a. Experimental studies of selective predation on amphipods: consequences for amphipod distribution and abundance. J. Exp. Mar. Biol. Ecol. 38: 225-245.

Nelson, W.G. 1979b. An analysis of structural pattern in an eelgrass (Zostera marina L.) amphipod community. J. Exp. Mar. Biol. Ecol. 39: 231-264.

Nelson, W.G.. 1981. Experimental studies of decapod and fish predation on seagrass macrobenthos. Mar. Ecol. Prog. Ser. 5: 141-149.

Neushul, M. 1972. Functional interpretation of benthic marine algal morphology. Pages 47-74 in I.A. Abbott and M. Kurogi, eds. Contributions to the systematics of benthic marine algae of the North Pacific. Japanese Society of Phycology, Kobe.

Newell, R. 1965. The role of detritus in the nutrition of two marine deposit feeders, the prosobranch Hydrobia ulvae and the bivalve Macoma balthica. Proc. Zool. Soc. Lond. 144: 24-45.

Newell, R.C. 1979. Biology of intertidal animals. 3rd ed. Marine Ecology Surveys, Feversham, Kent, England. 555 pp.

Newell, R.C. 1981. Utilization of plant material through the detritus food web in coastal waters. Environs, Duke Univ. Biomed. Prog. Newsl. 4. 10 pp.

Newell, S.Y. 1982. Fungi and bacteria in or on leaves of eelgrass (Zostera marina L.) from Chesapeake Bay. Pages 152-164 in R.L. Wetzel, ed. Structural and functional aspects of the ecology of submerged aquatic macrophyte communities in the lower Chesapeake Bay, vol. 1. Va. Inst. Mar. Sci. Spec. Rep. Appl. Mar. Sci. Ocean Eng. 267.

Nienhuis, P.H., and B.H.H. deBree. 1977. Production and ecology of eelgrass (Zostera marina L.) in the Grevelingen estuary, the Netherlands, before and after closure. Hydrobiologia 52: 55-56.

Nilsson, L. 1969. Food consumption of diving ducks wintering at the coast of south Sweden in relation to food resources. Oikos 20: 128-135.

Nissenbaum, A., N.J. Baedecker, and I.R. Kaplan. 1972. Organic geochemistry of Dead Sea sediments. Geochim. Cosmochim. Acta 36: 709-727.

Nixon, S.W. 1981. Remineralization and nutrient cycling in coastal marine ecosystems. Pages 111-138 in B.J. Nelson and L.E. Cronin, eds. Estuaries and nutrients. Humana Press, Clifton, N.J.

Nixon, S.W., and C.A. Oviatt. 1972. Preliminary measurements of mid-summer metabolism in beds of eelgrass, Zostera marina. Ecology 53: 150-153.

Odum, E.P. 1969. The strategy of ecosystem development. Science 164: 262-270.

Odum, E.P., and A.A. de la Cruz. 1967. Particulate organic detritus in a Georgia salt marsh-estuarine ecosystem. Pages 383-388 in G.H. Lauff, ed. Estuaries. Am. Assoc. Adv. Sci. Publ. 83.

Odum, W.E. 1982. Environmental degradation and the tyranny of small decisions. Bioscience 32: 728-729.

Odum, W.E., P.W. Kirk, and J.C. Zieman. 1979. Non-protein nitrogen compounds associated with particles of vascular plant detritus. Oikos 32: 363-367.

Odum, W.E., C.C. McIvor, and T.J. Smith, III. 1982. The ecology of mangroves of south Florida: A community profile. U.S. Fish Wildl. Serv. Biol. Serv. Program FWS/OBS-81/24. 144 pp.

Ogden, J.C. 1980. Faunal relations in Caribbean seagrass beds. Pages 173-198 in R.C. Phillips and C.P. McRoy, eds. Handbook of seagrass biology, an ecosystem perspective. Garland STPM Press, New York.

Ogilvie, M.A., and A.K.M. St. Joseph. 1976. Dark-bellied brant geese in Britain and Europe, 1955-76. Br. Birds 69: 422-439.

O'Gower, A.K., and J.W. Wacasey. 1967. Animal communities associated with Thalassia, Diplanthera, and sand beds in Biscayne Bay. I. Analysis of communities in relation to water movements. Bull. Mar. Sci. 17: 175-210.

Orth, R.J. 1973. Benthic infauna of eelgrass, Zostera marina beds. Chesapeake Sci. 14: 258-269.

Orth, R.J. 1975. Destruction of eelgrass, *Zostera marina* by the cownose ray, *Rhinoptera bonasus*, in the Chesapeake Bay. Chesapeake Sci. 16: 205-208.

Orth, R.J. 1977. The importance of sediment stability in seagrass communities. Pages 281-300 in B.C. Coull, ed. Ecology of marine benthos. University of South Carolina Press, Columbia.

Orth, R.J., and D.F. Boesch. 1979. Interactions involving resident consumers. Pages 44-88 in R.L. Wetzel, K.L. Webb, P.A. Penhale, R.J. Orth, D.F. Boesch, G.W. Boehlert, and J.V. Merriner. The functional ecology of submerged aquatic vegetation in the lower Chesapeake Bay. EPA/CBP Grant No. R805974.

Orth, P.J., and K.A. Heck, Jr. 1980. Structural components of eelgrass (*Zostera marina*) meadows in the lower Chesapeake Bay - Fishes. Estuaries 3: 278-288.

Orth, R.J., and K.A. Moore. 1981. Submerged aquatic vegetation of the Chesapeake Bay: past, present and future. Trans. N. Am. Wildl. Nat. Resour. Conf. 46: 271-283.

Orth, R.J., and K.A. Moore. 1982a. The biology and propagation of *Zostera marina*, eelgrass, in the Chesapeake Bay, Virginia. Va. Inst. Mar. Sci. Spec. Rep. Appl. Mar. Sci. Ocean Eng. 265. 187 pp.

Orth, R.J., and K.A. Moore. 1982b. Distribution and abundance of submerged aquatic vegetation in Chesapeake Bay: a scientific summary. Pages 381-427 in E.G. Macalaster, D.A. Barber, and M. Kasper, eds. Cheaspeake Bay Program technical studies: a synthesis. U.S. Environmental Protection Agency, Washington, D.C.

Orth, R.J., and K.A. Moore. 1983. Seed germination and seedling growth of *Zostera marina* L. (eelgrass) in the Chesapeake Bay. Aquat. Bot. 15: 117-131.

Ostenfeld, C.H. 1905. Preliminary remarks on the distribution and biology of the *Zostera* of the Danish seas. Bot. Tidsskr. 27: 123-125.

Ostenfeld, C.H. 1908. On the ecology and distribution of grass wrack (*Zostera marina*) in Danish waters. Rep. Dan. Biol. Stn. 16: 1-62.

Osterhout, W.J.V. 1917. Tolerance of fresh water by marine plants and its relation to adaptations. Bot. Gaz. 63: 146-149.

Otsuki, A., and R.G. Wetzel. 1974. Release of dissolved organic matter by autolysis of a submerged macrophyte, *Scirpus subterminalis*. Limnol. Oceanogr. 19: 842-845.

Paerl, H.W. 1974. Bacterial uptake of dissolved organic matter in relation to detrital aggregation in marine and freshwater systems. Limnol. Oceanogr. 19: 966-972.

Paerl, H.W. 1975. Microbial attachment to particles in marine and freshwater systems. Microb. Ecol. 2: 73-83.

Palmer, R.S. 1976. Handbook of North American birds, vol. 3. Yale University Press, New Haven. 560 pp.

Parsons, T.R. 1963. Suspended organic matter in seawater. Prog. Oceanogr. 1: 205-239.

Parsons, T.R., M. Takahashi, and B. Hargrave. 1977. Biological oceanographic processes. 2nd ed. Pergamon Press, New York. 332 pp.

Patriquin, D.G. 1972a. Carbonate mud production by epibionts on *Thalassia*: an estimate based on leaf growth rate data. J. Sediment. Petrol. 42: 687-689.

Patriquin, D.G. 1972b. The origin of nitrogen and phosphorus for growth of the marine angiosperm *Thalassia testudinum*. Mar. Biol. 15: 35-46.

Patriquin, D.G. 1973. Estimation of growth rate, production and age of the marine angiosperm *Thalassia testudinum* König. Carib. J. Sci. 13: 111-123.

Patriquin, D.G. 1975. "Migration" of blowouts in seagrass beds at Barbados and Carriacou, West Indies and its ecological and geological applications. Aquat. Bot. 1: 163-189.

Patriquin, D.G., and C.R. Butler. 1976. Marine resources of Kouchibouguac National Park. Applied Ocean Systems Ltd., Dartmouth, N.S., Parks Canada Contract No. 75-19. 423 pp.

Patriquin, D.G., and R. Knowles. 1972. Nitrogen fixation in the rhizosphere of marine angiosperms. Mar. Biol. 16: 49-58.

Peirson, W.M. 1983. Utilization of eight algal species by the bay scallop, Argopecten irradians concentricus (Say). J. Exp. Mar. Biol. Ecol. 68: 1-11.

Penhale, P.A. 1976. Primary productivity, dissolved organic carbon excretion, and nutrient transport in an epiphyte-eelgrass (Zostera marina) system. Ph.D. Diss. North Carolina State Univ., Raleigh. 83 pp.

Penhale, P.A. 1977. Macrophyte-epiphyte biomass and productivity in an eelgrass (Zostera marina L.) community. J. Exp. Mar. Biol. Ecol. 26: 211-224.

Penhale, P.A., and W.O. Smith, Jr. 1977. Excretion of dissolved organic carbon by eelgrass (Zostera marina) and its epiphytes. Limnol. Oceanogr. 22: 400-407.

Penhale, P.A., and G.W. Thayer. 1980. Uptake and transfer of carbon and phosphorus by eelgrass (Zostera marina) and its epiphytes. J. Exp. Mar. Biol. Ecol. 42: 113-123.

Penhale, P.A., and R.G. Wetzel. 1983. Structural and functional adaptations of eelgrass (Zostera marina L.) to the anaerobic sediment environment. Can. J. Bot. 61: 1421-1428.

Petersen, C.G.J. 1891. Fiskenes biologiske forhold i Holbaek fjord 1890-91. Beret. Dan. Biol. Stn. 1: 121-184.

Petersen, C.G.J. 1918. The sea bottom and its production of fish food: a summary of the work done in connection with valuation of Danish waters from 1883 to 1917. Rep. Dan. Biol. Stn. 25: 1-82.

Petersen, C.G.J., and P. Boysen-Jensen. 1911. Valuation of the sea. I. Animal life of the sea bottom, its food and quantity. Rep. Dan. Biol. Stn. 20: 1-81.

Peterson, C.H. 1982. Clam predation by whelks (Busycon spp.): experimental tests on the importance of prey size, prey density, and seagrass cover. Mar. Biol. 66: 159-170.

Peterson, C.H., and N.M. Peterson. 1979. The ecology of intertidal flats of North Carolina: a community profile. U.S. Fish Wildl. Serv. Biol. Serv. Program FWS/OBS-79/39. 73 pp.

Peterson, C.H., H.C. Summerson, and S.R. Fegley. 1983. The relative efficiency of two clam rakes and their contrasting impacts on seagrass biomass. U.S. Natl. Mar. Fish. Serv. Fish. Bull. 81: 429-434.

Phillips, R.C. 1972. Ecological life history of Zostera marina L. (eelgrass) in Puget Sound, Washington. Ph.D. Diss. Univ. of Washington, Seattle. 154 pp.

Phillips, R.C. 1974a. Transplantation of seagrasses with special emphasis on eelgrass, Zostera marina L. Aquaculture 4: 161-176.

Phillips, R.C. 1974b. Temperate grass flats. Pages 244-299 in H.T. Odum, B.J. Copeland, and E.A. McMahan, eds. Coastal ecological systems of the United States: a source book for estuarine planning, vol. 2. Conservation Foundation, Washington, D.C.

Phillips, R.C., W.S. Grant, and C.P. McRoy. 1983a. Reproductive strategies of eelgrass (Zostera marina L.). Aquat. Bot. 16: 1-20.

Phillips, R.C., C. McMillan, and K.W. Bridges. 1983b. Phenology of eelgrass, Zostera marina L., along latitudinal gradients in North America. Aquat. Bot. 15: 145-156.

Pomeroy, L.R., and D. Deibel. 1980. Aggregation of organic matter by pelagic tunicates. Limnol. Oceanogr. 25: 643-652.

Porter, D. 1967. Observations on the cytology and motility of Labyrinthula. Ph.D. Diss. Univ. of Washington, Seattle. 139 pp.

Pulich, W.M. 1982a. Edaphic factors related to shoalgrass (Halodule wrightii Aschers.) production. Bot. Mar. 25: 467-475.

Pulich, W.M. 1982b. Culture studies of Halodule wrightii Aschers. Edaphic requirements. Bot. Mar. 25: 477-482.

Race, M.S., and D.R. Christie. 1982. Coastal zone development: mitigation, marsh creation and decision-making. Environ. Manage. 6: 317-328.

Rasmussen, E. 1973. Systematics and ecology of the Isef Fjord marine fauna (Denmark) with a survey of the eelgrass (Zostera) vegetation and its communities. Ophelia 11(2-3): 1-507.

Rasmussen, E. 1977. The wasting disease of eelgrass (Zostera marina) and its effect on environmental factors and fauna. Pages 1-51 in C.P. McRoy and C. Helfferich, eds. Seagrass ecosystems, a scientific perspective. Marcel Dekker, New York.

Reed, J.P. 1980. A bioenergetic model of anaerobic decomposition: sulfate reduction. Pages 173-182 in V.S. Kennedy, ed. Estuarine perspectives. Academic Press, New York.

Renn, C.E. 1934. Wasting disease of Zostera in American waters. Nature 134: 416.

Rice, D.L. 1982. The detritus nitrogen problem: new observations and perspectives from organic geochemistry. Mar. Ecol. Prog. Ser. 9: 153-162.

Rice, D.L., and K.R. Tenore. 1981. Dynamics of carbon and nitrogen during the decomposition of detritus derived from estuarine macrophytes. Estuarine Coastal Shelf Sci. 13: 681-690.

Ricketts, E.F., and J. Calvin. 1962. Between Pacific tides. Stanford University Press, Stanford, Calif. 516 pp.

Riggs, S.A., and R.A. Fralick. 1975. Zostera marina L., its growth and distribution in the Great Bay Estuary, New Hampshire. Rhodora 77: 456-466.

Riner, M.I. 1976. A study on methods, techniques and growth characteristics for transplanted portions of eelgrass (Zostera marina). M.S. Thesis. Adelphi Univ., Garden City, N.Y. 104 pp.

Robertson, A.I. 1980. The structure and organization of an eelgrass fish fauna. Oecologia 47: 76-82.

Robertson, A.I., and K.H. Mann. 1982. Population dynamics and life history adaptations of Littorina neglecta Bean in an eelgrass meadow (Zostera marina L.) in Nova Scotia. J. Exp. Mar. Biol. Ecol. 63: 151-171.

Robertson, A.I., and K.H. Mann. 1984. Disturbance by ice and life-history adaptations of the seagrass Zostera marina. Mar. Biol. 80:131-142.

Robertson, D.R. 1982. Fish feces as fish food on a Pacific coral reef. Mar. Ecol. Prog. Ser. 7: 253-265.

Robertson, M.L., A.L. Mills, and J.C. Zieman. 1982. Microbial synthesis of detritus-like particulates from dissolved organic carbon released by tropical seagrasses. Mar. Ecol. Prog. Ser. 7: 279-285.

Rosenfeld, J.K. 1979a. Ammonium adsorption in nearshore anoxic sediments. Limnol. Oceanogr. 24: 356-364.

Rosenfeld, J.K. 1979b. Amino acid diagenesis and adsorption in nearshore anoxic sediments. Limnol. Oceanogr. 24: 1014-1021.

Rublee, P., L. Cammen, and J. Hobbie. 1978. Bacteria in a North Carolina salt marsh: standing crop and importance in the decomposition of Spartina alterniflora. N.C. Univ. Sea Grant Publ. UNC-SG-78-11. 80 pp.

Russell-Hunter, W.D. 1970. Aquatic productivity, an introduction to some basic aspects of biological oceanography and limnology. Collier-MacMillian, London. 306 pp.

Sand-Jensen, K. 1975. Biomass, net production and growth dynamics in an eelgrass (Zostera marina L.) population in Vellerup Vig, Denmark. Ophelia 14: 185-201.

Sand-Jensen, K. 1977. Effect of epiphytes on eelgrass photosynthesis. Aquat. Bot. 3: 55-63.

Sand-Jensen, K., and J. Borum. 1983. Regulation of growth in eelgrass (Zostera marina L.) in Danish waters. Mar. Technol. Soc. J. 17: 15-21.

Sauvageau, C. 1891. Sur les feuilles de quelques Monocotyledones aquatiques. Ann. Soc. Nat. Bot. ser 7, 13: 103-296.

Scoffin, T.P. 1970. The trapping and binding of subtidal carbonate sediments by marine vegetation in Bimini Lagoon, Bahamas. J. Sediment. Petrol. 40: 249-273.

Sculthorpe, C.D. 1967. The biology of aquatic vascular plants. Arnold, London. 618 pp.

Seki, H., and Y. Yokohama. 1978. Experimental decay of eelgrass (Zostera marina) into detrital particles. Arch. Hydrobiol. 84: 109-119.

Setchell, W.A. 1929. Morphological and phenological notes on Zostera marina L. Univ. Calif. Publ. Bot. 14: 389-452.

Sharp, J.H. 1973. Size classes of organic carbon in seawater. Limnol. Oceanogr. 18: 441-447.

Short, F.T. 1975. Eelgrass production in Charlestown Pond: an ecological analysis and simulation model. M.S. Thesis. University of Rhode Island, Kingston. 180 pp.

Short, F.T. 1980. A simulation model of the seagrass production system. Pages 277-298 in R.C. Phillips and C.P. McRoy, eds. Handbook of seagrass biology, an ecosystem perspective. Garland STPM Press, New York.

Short, F.T. 1981. Nitrogen resource analysis and modelling of an eelgrass (Zostera marina L.) meadow in Izembek Lagoon, Alaska. Ph.D. Diss. Univ. of Alaska, Fairbanks. 173 pp.

Short, F.T. 1983a. The response of interstitial ammonium in eelgrass (Zostera marina L.) beds to environmental perturbations. J. Exp. Mar. Biol. Ecol. 68: 195-208.

Short, F.T. 1983b. The seagrass, Zostera marina L.: plant morphology and bed structure in relation to sediment ammonium in Izembek Lagoon, Alaska. Aquat. Bot. 16: 149-161.

Short, F.T., S.W. Nixon, and C.A. Oviatt. 1974. Field studies and simulation with a fine grid hydrodynamic model. Pages VIB1-VIB27 in An environmental study of a nuclear power plant at Charlestown, Rhode Island. Univ. R.I. Coastal Resour. Cent. Mar. Tech. Rep. 33.

Sieburth, J.M., and C.D. Thomas. 1973. Fouling on eelgrass. J. Phycol. 9: 46-50.

Siglio, A.C., T.C. Hoering, and G.R. Helz. 1982. Composition of estuarine colloidal material: organic components. Geochim. Cosmochim. Acta 46: 1619-1626.

Silberhorn, G.M., R.J. Orth, and K.A. Moore. 1983. Anthesis and seed production in Zostera marina L. (eelgrass) from the Chesapeake Bay. Aquat. Bot. 15: 133-144.

Smith, G.W. 1981. Microbiology of the seagrass rhizosphere. Ph.D. Diss. Clemson Univ., Clemson, S.C. 73 pp.

Smith, G.W., and S.S. Hayasaka. 1982. Nitrogenase activity associated with Zostera marina from a North Carolina estuary. Can. J. Microbiol. 28: 448-451.

Smith, G.W., S.S. Hayasaka, and G.W. Thayer. 1979. Root surface area measurements of Zostera marina and Halodule wrightii. Bot. Mar. 22: 347-358.

Smith, G.W., A.M. Kozucki, and S.S. Hayasaka. 1982. Heavy metal sensitivity of seagrass rhizoplane and sediment bacteria. Bot. Mar. 25: 19-24.

Smith, W.O., and P.A. Penhale. 1980. The heterotrophic uptake of dissolved organic carbon by eelgrass (Zostera marina L.) and its epiphytes. J. Exp. Mar. Biol. Ecol. 48: 233-242.

Soldatova, I.N., Ye. A. Tsikhon-Lukanina, G.G. Nikolayeve, and T.A. Lukasheva. 1969. The conversion of food energy by marine crustaceans. Okeanologiya 9(6): 875-882.

Stauffer, R.C. 1937. Changes in the invertebrate community of a lagoon after disapperance of the eelgrass. Ecology 18: 427-431.

Stevenson, J.C., and N.M. Confer. 1978. Summary of available information on Chesapeake Bay submerged vegetation. U.S. Fish Wildl. Serv. Biol. Serv. Program FWS/OBS-78/66. 335 pp.

Stewart, R.E. 1962. Waterfowl populations in the upper Chesapeake Region. U.S. Fish Wildl. Serv. Spec. Sci. Rep. Wildl. 65. 208 pp.

Stickney, R.R., and S.E. Shumway. 1974. Occurrence of cellulase activity in the stomachs of fish. J. Fish. Biol. 6: 779-790.

Stirban, M. 1968. Relationship between the assimilation pigments, the intensity of chlorophyll fluorescence and the level of the photosynthesis zone in Zostera marina L. Rev. Roum. Biol. Ser. Bot. 13: 291-295.

Stoner, A.W. 1980. Perception and choice of substratum by epifaunal amphipods associated with seagrasses. Mar. Ecol. Prog. Ser. 3: 105-111.

Stuart, H.H. 1975. Distribution and summer energetics of invertebrate epifauna in an eelgrass (Zostera marina) bed. M.S. Thesis. North Carolina State Univ., Raleigh. 76 pp.

Stuart, H.H. 1982. Effects of physical and biological disturbance of Zostera marina L. macrobenthos. Ph.D. Diss. North Carolina State Univ., Raleigh. 84 pp.

Stumm, W., and J.J. Morgan. 1970. Aquatic chemistry. John Wiley and Sons, Inc., New York. 583 pp.

Suberkropp, K.F., G.L. Godshalk, and M.J. Klug. 1976. Changes in the chemical composition of leaves during processing in a woodland stream. Ecology 57: 720-727.

Summerson, H.C. 1980. The effects of predation on the marine benthic invertebrate community in and around a shallow subtidal seagrass bed. M.S. Thesis. Univ. of North Carolina, Chapel Hill. 118 pp.

Summerson, H.C., and C.H. Peterson. 1984. The role of predation in organizing benthic communities in and around a temperate zone seagrass bed. Mar. Ecol. Prog. Ser. 15: 63-77.

Swinchatt, J.P. 1965. Significance of constituent composition, texture and skeletal breakdown in some recent carbonate sediments. J. Sediment. Petrol. 35(1): 71-90.

Taylor, A.R.A. 1957. Studies on the development of Zostera marina L. II. Germination and seedling development. Can. J. Bot. 35: 681-695.

Tenore, K.R. 1975. Detrital utilization by the polychaete, Capitella capitata. J. Mar. Res. 33: 261-274.

Tenore, K.R. 1977. Growth of the polychaete, Capitella capitata, cultured on different levels of detritus derived from various sources. Limnol. Oceanogr. 22: 936-941.

Tenore, K.R., and B.C. Coull, eds. 1980. Marine benthic dynamics. University of South Carolina Press, Columbia. 451 pp.

Tenore, K.R., and D.L. Rice. 1980. A review of trophic factors affecting secondary production of deposit feeders. Pages 325-340 in K.R. Tenore and B.C. Coull, eds. Marine benthic dynamics. University of South Carolina Press, Columbia.

Thayer, G.W., and H.H. Stuart. 1974. The bay scallop makes its bed of eelgrass. U.S. Natl. Mar. Fish. Serv. Mar. Fish. Rev. 36(7): 27-39.

Thayer, G.W., S.M. Adams, and M.W. LaCroix. 1975a. Structural and functional aspects of a recently established Zostera marina community. Pages 517-540 in L.E. Cronin, ed. Estuarine research, vol. 1. Academic Press, New York.

Thayer, G.W., D.A. Wolfe, and R.B. Williams. 1975b. The impact of man on seagrass systems. Am. Sci. 63: 288-296.

Thayer, G.W., D.W. Engel, and M.W. LaCroix. 1977. Seasonal distribution and changes in the nutritional quality of living, dead, and detrital fractions of Zostera marina L. J. Exp. Mar. Biol. Ecol. 30: 109-127.

Thayer, G.W., P.L. Parker, M.W. LaCroix, and B. Fry. 1978. The stable carbon isotope ratio of some components of an eelgrass, Zostera marina, bed. Oecologia 35: 1-12.

Thayer, G.W., H.H. Stuart, W.J. Kenworthy, J.F. Ustach, and A.B. Hall. 1979. Habitat values of salt marshes, mangroves, and seagrasses for aquatic organisms. Pages 235-247 in P.E. Greeson, J.R. Clark and J.E. Clark, eds. Wetland functions and values: the state of our understanding. American Water Resources Association, Minneapolis.

Thayer, G.W., M.S. Fonseca, M.W. LaCroix, and M.B. Murdoch. 1980a. Decomposition of Zostera marina leaves under different environmental conditions. Pages 64-78 in Annual report to the U.S. Department of Energy. U.S. National Marine Fisheries Service, Southeast Fisheries Center, Beaufort Laboratory, Beaufort, N.C.

Thayer, G.W., T.J. Price, and M.W. LaCroix. 1980b. Observation on estuarine habitat utilization by juvenile and adult fish. Pages 254-292 in Annual report to the U.S. Department of Energy. U.S. National Marine Fisheries Service, Southeast Fisheries Center, Beaufort Laboratory, Beaufort, N.C.

Thayer, G.W., D.W. Engel, and K.A. Bjorndal. 1982. Evidence for short-circuiting of the detritus cycle of seagrass beds by the green turtle, Chelonia mydas L. J. Exp. Mar. Biol. Ecol. 62: 173-183.

Thayer, G.W., K.A. Bjorndal, J.C. Ogden, S.L. Williams, and J.C. Zieman. In press a. Role of larger herbivores in seagrass communities. Estuaries.

Thayer, G.W., M.S. Fonseca, and W.J. Kenworthy. In press b. Restoration of seagrass meadows for enhancement of nearshore productivity. In International symposium on the utilization of the coastal zone. Planning, pollution and productivity. Rio Grande, Brazil, 1982.

Thorhaug, A. 1976. Symposium on restoration of major plant communities in the United States. Environ. Conserv. 4(1): 49-50.

Thorne-Miller, B., M.M. Harlin, G.B. Thursby, M.M. Brady-Campbell, and B.A. Dworetzky. 1983. Variations in the distribution and biomass of submerged macrophytes in five coastal lagoons in Rhode Island, U.S.A. Bot. Mar. 26: 231-242.

Thursby, G.B., and M.M. Harlin. 1982. Leaf-root interaction in the uptake of ammonia by Zostera marina. Mar. Biol. 72: 109-112.

Tietjen, J.H. 1969. The ecology of shallow water meiofauna in two New England estuaries. Oecologia 2: 251-291.

Tomlinson, P.B. 1974. Vegetative morphology and meristem dependence - the foundation of productivity in seagrasses. Aquaculture 4: 107-130.

Tomlinson, P.B. 1980. Leaf morphology and anatomy in seagrasses. Pages 7-28 in R.C. Phillips and C.P. McRoy, eds. Handbook of seagrass biology, and ecosystem perspective. Garland STPM Press, New York.

Trocine, R.P., J.D. Rice, and G.N. Wells. 1981. Inhibition of seagrass photosynthesis by ultraviolet-B radiation. Plant Physiol. 68: 74-81.

Tubbs, C.R., and J.M. Tubbs. 1982. Brant geese Branta bernicla bernicla and their food in the Solent, southern England. Biol. Conserv. 23: 33-54.

Tubbs, C.R., and J.M. Tubbs. 1983. The distribution of Zostera and its exploitation by wildfowl in the Solent, southern England. Aquat. Bot. 15: 223-239.

Turner, N.C., and A.M. Bell. 1963. The ethnobotany of the southern Kwakiutl Indians of British Columbia. Econ. Bot. 27(3): 257-310.

Tutin, T.G. 1938. The autecology of Zostera marina in relation to its wasting disease. New Phytol. 37: 50-71.

Tutin, T.G. 1942. Zostera. J. Ecol. 30: 217-226.

Uphof, J.C.T. 1941. Halophytes. Bot. Rev. 7: 1-58.

U.S. Environmental Protection Agency (US EPA). 1982. Chesapeake Bay Program technical studies: a synthesis. U.S. Environmental Protection Agency, Washington, D.C. 635 pp.

Valiela, I., L. Konmjian, T. Swain, J.M. Teal, and J.E. Hobbie. 1979. Cinnamic acid inhibition of detritus feeding. Nature 280: 55-57.

Van Montfrans, J., R.J. Orth, and S.A. Vay. 1982. Preliminary studies of grazing by Bittium varium on eelgrass periphyton. Aquat. Bot. 14: 75-89.

Vicente, V.P., J.A. Arroyo Aguilu, and J.A. Rivera. 1980. Thalassia as a food source: importance and potential in the marine and terrestrial environments. J. Agric. Univ. P.R. 64(1): 107-120.

Vogel, S. 1981. Life in moving fluids. Willard-Grant Press, Boston. 352 pp.

Ward, G.M., and K.W. Cummins. 1979. Effects of food quality on growth of a stream detritivore Paratendipes albimanus (Meigen) (Dioptera: Chironomidae). Ecology 60: 57-64.

Warwick, R.M., and R.J. Uncles. 1980. Distribution of benthic macrofauna associations in the Bristol Channel in relation to tidal stress. Mar. Ecol. Prog. Ser. 3: 97-103.

Wayne, C.J. 1975. Sea and marsh grasses: their effect on wave energy and nearshore sand transport. M.S. Thesis. Florida State Univ., Tallahasee. 135 pp.

Weinstein, M.P., and H.A. Brooks. 1983. Comparative ecology of nekton residing in a tidal creek and adjacent seagrass meadow: community composition and structure. Mar. Ecol. Prog. Ser. 12: 15-27.

Weinstein, M.P., K.L. Heck, Jr., P.E. Giebel, and J.E. Gates. 1982. The role of herbivory in pinfish (Lagodon rhomboides): a preliminary investigation. Bull. Mar. Sci. 32: 791-795.

Wetzel, R.L., ed. 1982. Structural and functional aspects of the ecology of submerged aquatic macrophyte communities in the lower Chesapeake Bay. Va. Inst. Mar. Sci. Spec. Rep. Appl. Mar. Sci. Ocean Eng. 267. 187 pp.

Wetzel, R.G., and P.A. Penhale. 1979. Transport of carbon and excretion of dissolved organic carbon by leaves and roots/rhizomes in seagrasses and their epiphytes. Aquat. Bot. 6: 149-158.

Wetzel, R.L., and P.A. Penhale. 1983. Production ecology of seagrass communities in the lower Chesapeake Bay. Mar. Technol. Soc. J. 17: 22-31.

Wildish, D.J., and D.D. Kristmanson. 1979. Tidal energy and sublittoral macrobenthic animals in estuaries. J. Fish. Res. Board Can. 36: 1197-1206.

Wilkins, E.W. 1982. Waterfowl utilization of a submerged vegetation (Zostera marina and Ruppia maritima) bed in the lower Chesapeake Bay. M.A. Thesis, College of William and Mary, Williamsburg, Va. 83 pp.

Williams, A.B. 1965. Marine decapod crustaceans of the Carolinas. U.S. Fish Wildl. Serv. Fish. Bull. 65: 1-298.

Wilson, D.P. 1949. The decline of _Zostera marina_ L. at Salcombe and its effects on the shore. J. Mar. Biol. Assoc. U.K. 28: 395-412.

Winkler, L.R., and E.Y. Dawson. 1963. Observations and experiments on the food habits of California sea hares of the genus _Aplysia_. Pac. Sci. 17: 102-105.

Wolfe, D.A., F.A. Cross, and C.D. Jennings. 1973. The flux of Mn, Fe, and Zn in an estuarine ecosystem. Pages 159-175 _in_ Radioactive contamination of the marine environment. International Atomic Energy Agency, Vienna.

Wolfe, D.A., G.W. Thayer, and S.M. Adams. 1976. Manganese, iron, copper and zinc in an eelgrass (_Zostera marina_) community. Pages 256-270 _in_ C.E. Cushing, Jr., ed. Radioecology and energy resources. Dowden, Hutchinson & Ross, Stroudsburg, Pa.

Wood, D.C., and S.S. Hayasaka. 1981. Chemotaxis of rhizoplane bacteria to amino acids comprising eelgrass (_Zostera marina_ L.) root exudate. J. Exp. Mar. Biol. Ecol. 50: 153-161.

Wood, E.J.F. 1953. Reducing substances in _Zostera_. Nature 172: 916.

Wood, E.J.F. 1959. Some Australian seagrass communities. Proc. Limnol. Soc. N.S.W. 84: 218-226.

Wood, E.J.F., W.E. Odum, and J.C. Zieman. 1969. Influence of sea grasses on the productivity of coastal lagoons. Pages 495-502 _in_ A. Ayala Castañares and F.B. Phleger, eds. Coastal lagoons. Universidad Nacional Autónoma de Mexico, Ciudad Universitaria, México, D.F.

Yingst, J.Y. 1976. The utilization of organic matter in shallow marine sediments by an epibenthic deposit-feeding holothurian. J. Exp. Mar. Biol. Ecol. 23: 55-69.

Yokoe, Y., and I. Yasumasu. 1964. The distribution of cellulase in invertebrates. Comp. Biochem. Physiol. 13: 223-238.

Young, D.K., and M.W. Young. 1977. Community structure of the macrobenthos associated with seagrasses of the Indian River estuary, Florida. Pages 359-382 _in_ B.C. Coull, ed. Ecology of marine benthos. University of South Carolina Press, Columbia.

Young, E.L. 1938. _Labyrinthula_ on Pacific coast eelgrass. Can. J. Res. 16 (2): 115-117.

Zapata, O., and C. McMillan. 1979. Phenolic acids in seagrasses. Aquat. Bot. 7: 307-317.

Zieman, J.C. 1972. Origin of circular beds of _Thalassia testudinum_ in south Biscayne Bay, Florida and their relationships to mangrove hammocks. Bull. Mar. Sci. 22: 559-574.

Zieman, J.C. 1975. Quantitative and dynamic aspects of the ecology of turtle grass, _Thalassia testudinum_. Pages 541-562 _in_ L.E. Cronin, ed. Estuarine research, vol. 1. Academic Press, New York.

Zieman, J.C. 1976. The ecological effects of physical damage from motorboats on turtle grass beds in southern Florida. Aquat. Bot. 2: 127-139.

Zieman, J.C. 1982. The ecology of the seagrasses of South Florida: a community profile. U.S. Fish Wildl. Serv. Biol. Serv. Program FWS/OBS-82/25. 124, 26 pp.

Zieman, J.C., and R.G. Wetzel. 1980. Productivity in seagrasses: methods and rates. Pages 87-116 _in_ R.C. Phillips and C.P. McRoy, eds. Handbook of sea grass biology, an ecosystem perspective. Garland STPM Press, New York.

Zieman, J.C., G.W. Thayer, M.B. Roblee, and R.T. Zieman. 1979. Production and export of seagrasses from a tropical bay. Pages 21-34 _in_ R.J. Livingston, ed. Ecological processes in coastal and marine systems. Plenum Press, New York.

Zieman, J.C., R. Orth, R.C. Phillips, G.W. Thayer, and A. Thorhaug. In press. The effects of oil on seagrass ecosystems. _In_ J. Cairns and A. Buykema, eds. Recovery and restoration of marine ecosystems. Ann Arbor Press, Ann Arbor, Mich.

Zimmerman, R., R. Gibson, and J. Harrington. 1979. Herbivory and detritivory among gammaridean amphipods from a Florida seagrass community. Mar. Biol. 54: 41-47.

APPENDIX A

Macroalgae epiphytic on <u>Zostera marina</u> (modified from Harlin (1980); Harlin presents literature upon which listing is based).

<u>Acinetospora crinita</u>
<u>Acrochaetium secundatum</u>
<u>A. virgatulum</u>
<u>Anacystis marina</u>
<u>Aphanocapsa littoralis</u>
<u>Ascocyclus magnusii</u>
<u>A. orbicularis</u>
<u>Asperococcus scaber</u>
<u>Callithamnion baileyi</u>
<u>C. byssoideum</u>
<u>C. corymbosum</u>
<u>C. roseum</u>
<u>Calothrix confervicola</u>
<u>C. crustacea</u>
<u>C. scopulorum</u>
<u>Castagnea virescens</u>
<u>C. zosterae</u>
<u>Ceramium byssoideum</u>
<u>C. diaphanum</u>
<u>C. fastigiatum</u>
<u>C. rubrum</u>
<u>C. strictum</u>
<u>C. tenuissimum</u>
<u>Chaetomorpha aerea</u>
<u>C. brachygona</u>
<u>C. gracilis</u>
<u>C. linum</u>
<u>Champia purvula</u>
<u>Chantransia seccundata</u>
<u>C. virgatula</u>
<u>C. baileyana</u>
<u>C. dasypnylla</u>
<u>C. sedifolia</u>
<u>Cladophora crystallina</u>
<u>C. flexusoum</u>
<u>C. gracilis</u>
<u>Cladosiphon occidentalis</u>
<u>C. zosterae</u>
<u>Dasya elegans</u>
<u>Dermatolithon pustulatum</u>

<u>Desmotrichum balticum</u>
<u>D. undulatum</u>
<u>Dictyota dichotoma</u>
<u>Ectocarpus confervoides</u>
<u>E. elachistaeformis</u>
<u>E. fasiculatus</u>
<u>E. penicillatus</u>
<u>E. siliculosus</u>
<u>E. clathrata</u>
<u>E. intestinalis</u>
<u>E. linza</u>
<u>E. plumosa</u>
<u>E. prolifera</u>
<u>Entonema oligosporum</u>
<u>Erythrotrichia bertholdii</u>
<u>E. boryana</u>
<u>E. carnea</u>
<u>E. ceramicola</u>
<u>E. ciliaris</u>
<u>Fosliella farinosa</u>
<u>F. (=Melobesia) lejolisii</u>
<u>Giffordia conifera</u>
<u>G. indica</u>
<u>G. mitchelliae</u>
<u>G. ralfsiae</u>
<u>G. sandriana</u>
<u>Giraudia sphacelariodes</u>
<u>Glaeocystis zostericola</u>
<u>Goniotrichum alsidii</u>
<u>Griffithsia tenuis</u>
<u>Hecatonema foecundum</u>
<u>H. maculans</u>
<u>H. terminalis</u>
<u>Herposiphonia tenella</u>
<u>Heteroderma lejolisii</u>
<u>Hydrocoleum glutinosum</u>
<u>Hypnea musciformia</u>
<u>Kornmannia zostericola</u>
<u>Lomentaria baileyana</u>
<u>Lyngbya majuscula</u>

(continued)

142

Mastigocoleus testarum
Microcoleus lyngbyaceous
Microsyphar zosterae
Myrionema obiculare
M. subglobosum
M. vulgare
Myriotrichia clavaeformis
Oscillatoria lutae
Phaeostroma pusillum
Pogotrichum filiforme
Polysiphonia denudata
P. flaccidissima
P. harveyi
P. nigrescens
P. olneyi
P. scopulorum
P. sphaerocarpa
P. variegata
Porphyra leucosticta

Punctaria latifolia
P. orbiculata
Rhadinocladia farlowii
Rhododermis georgii
R. (=Palmeria) palmata
Schizothriz calcicola
Scytosiphon lomentaria
Seirospora griffithsiana
Smithora (=Porphyra) naiadum
Sphacelaria cirrhosa
S. furcigera
Spirulina subsalsa
Spyridia filamentosa
Stichtyosiphon subsimplex
Stilophora rhizodes
Striaria attenuata
Ulothrix pseudoflacca
U. subflaccida
Ulva lactuca

APPENDIX B

Microalgae epiphytic on _Zostera marina_ (modified from Harlin (1980) who also provides support literature)

Achnanthes brevipes
A. deflexa
A. lanceolata
A. purvula
Actinocyclus barkleyi
Amphipleura micans
A. rutilans
Amphiprora paludosa
Amphora commutata
Anomoeoneis costata
Arachnoidiscus sp.
Chaetoceros sp.
Cocconeis californica
C. costata
C. placentula
C. scutellum
Coscinodiscus sp.
Cymbella turgidula
Diatoma spp.
Diploneis crabro
Diploneis fusca
Exuviella sp.
Fragilaria capucina
F. hyalina
F. striatula
Gomphonema oceanicum
G. parvulum
Grammatophora angulosa
Gyrosigma acuminatum
G. balticum
G. fasciola
G. spenceri
Isthmia sp.
Licmophora sp.
L. gracilis
L. parodoxa
Mastogloia braunii
Melosira moniliformis

M. nummuloides
M. sulcata
Meridion sp.
Navicula directa
N. diserta
N. distans
N. endophytica
N. frauenfeldii
N. fusiformis
N. gregaria
N. grevillei
N. heufleri
N. mutica
N. ostrearia
N. punctulata
N. tumida
Nitzschia aequorea
N. closterium
N. frustulum
N. linnearis
N. longissima
N. lorenziana
N. obtusa
N. oregona
N. pseudohybrida
N. pungens
N. sigmoidea
N. vanhoffenii
Pinnularia spp.
Plagiogramma vanheurckii
P. formosum
P. nicobaricum
Rhabdonema arcuatum
Stauroneis unipunctata
Surirella gemma
S. ovata
Synedra fasciculata
S. formosum

(continued)

144

S. ulna
S. undulata
Tabellaria fenestrata
Thalassionema nitzschioides

Thalassiosira aestivalis
T. salvadoriana
Tropoidoneis lepidoptera
T. vitrea

APPENDIX C

Faunal invertebrates epiphytic on _Zostera marina_ (modified from Harlin (1980) who also supplies support references).

Aiptasiomorpha luciae
Alvania montagui
Amphithoe longimana
Australocochlea sp.
Balanus improvisus
Batea catharinesis
Bittium alternatum
B. varium
Boloceroides mcmmurrichi
Brania clavata
Calliopius laeviusculus
Calliostoma striatum
Campanularia sp.
Caprella geometrica
C. kroyeri
C. penantis
Cirolana cranchi
Clathurella philberti
Clauculus cruciatus
C. jussieui
Clytia edwardsi
C. volubilis
Colomastix sp.
Conus mediterraneus
Corophium acherusicum
C. acutum
C. bonelli
C. cylindricum
C. insidiosum
C. lacustre
C. simile
Crenilabrus ocellatus
Crepidula convexa
Cyathura carinata
Cymadusa compta
Cytherois spp.
Cytherura spp.
Dexamine spinosa
D. thea

Diala vitrea
Doridella obscura
Elasmophus pocillimanus
Elysia catula
Ercolania fuscata
Erichsonella attenuata
Erichthonius difformis
Euplana gracilis
Eusiroides della vallei
Exogone dispar
Gafrarium annulatus
Gammarus locusta
G. mucronatus
G. tigrinus
G. zaddechi
Gibbula adansoni
G. ardens
Glycera tesselata
Grubia crassicornis
Hippolyte gracilis
H. inermis
H. pleuracentha
Hirshamannia viridis
Hyale nilssoni
Hydroides hexagona
Idotea baltica
I. viridis
Jassa falcata
Lacuna pallidula
Leander xiphias
Leptochelila savignyi
Leptomysis sardica
Leucothoe incisa
L. pachycera
L. spinicarpa
Macropipus arcuatus
Maia verrucosa
Melita appendiculata
M. nitida

(Continued)

146

Microdeutopus damnoniensis
M. gryllotalpa
Mitra tricolor
Mitrella gervillei
M. lunata
Molgula manhattensis
Monodenta turbiformis
Neomysis americana
Nereis succinea
Nototropis guttatus
Obelia geniculata
Odontosyllis fulguran
Odostomia bisuturalis
O. impressa
Orhophyxis platycarpa
Panoploea minuta
Paracaprella pusilla
P. tenuis
Paracerceis caudata
Persicula minuta
Phasianella pulla
P. speciosa
Phtisica marina
Pista tetraodon
Platynereis dumerilii
Plumaria strictocarpa

Podarke obscura
Polydora ligni
Pontarachna punctulum
Processa edulis
Rissoa marginata
R. variabilis
R. ventricosa
R. violacea
Rudilemboides sp.
Sabella microphthalma
Scissurella costata
Scorpaena porcus
Sertularella minurensis
Siphonoecetes della vallei
Siriella clausi
Spirorbis foraminosus
Stylochus ellipticus
Syngnathus acus
S. typhle
Tetrastemma elegans
Thoralus cranchi
Triphora nigrocincta
Truncatella subcylindrica
Urosalpinx cinerea
Urothoe elegans
Zygonemertes virescens

50272-101

REPORT DOCUMENTATION PAGE	1. REPORT NO. FWS/OBS-84/02	2.	3. Recipient's Accession No.
4. Title and Subtitle The Ecology of Eelgrass Meadows of the Atlantic Coast: A Community Profile			**5. Report Date** July 1984
			6.
7. Author(s) Gordon W. Thayer[a], W. Judson Kenworthy[a], and Mark S. Fonseca[b]			**8. Performing Organization Rept. No.**
9. Authors' Affiliations [a]National Marine Fisheries Service Southeast Fisheries Center Beaufort, NC 28516 [b]Department of Environmental Sciences University of Virginia Charlottesville, VA 22903			**10. Project/Task/Work Unit No.**
			11. Contract(C) or Grant(G) No. (C) (G)
12. Sponsoring Organization Name and Address National Coastal Ecosystems Team Division of Biological Services Research and Development Fish and Wildlife Service U.S. Department of the Interior Washington, DC 20240			**13. Type of Report & Period Covered**
			14.

15. Supplementary Notes

16. Abstract (Limit: 200 words)

Eelgrass, <u>Zostera marina</u>, dominates the ecologically important but fragile seagrass communities along the east coast of the United States from North Carolina to Nova Scotia. Grasslike leaves and an extensive root and rhizome system enable eelgrass to exist in a shallow aquatic environment subject to waves, tides, and shifting sediments.

Eelgrass meadows are highly productive, frequently rivaling agricultural croplands. They provide shelter and a rich variety of primary and secondary food resources, and form a nursery habitat for the life history stages of numerous fishery organisms. The leaves absorb and release nutrients, provide surfaces for attachment, reduce water current velocity, turbulence and scour, and promote accumulation of detritus. Rhizomes provide protection for benthic infauna and enhance sediment stability. Roots absorb and release nutrients to interstitial waters.

Because of their shallow, subtidal existence, seagrasses are susceptible to perturbations of both the water column and sediments. Eelgrass meadows are impacted by dredging and filling, some commercial fishery harvest techniques, modification of normal temperature and salinity regimes, and addition of chemical wastes. Techniques have been developed to successfully restore eelgrass habitats, but a holistic approach to planning research and environmentally-related decisions is needed to avoid cumulative environmental impacts on these vital nursery areas.

17. Document Analysis   a. Descriptors

Ecology, impact, management, ecological succession, detritus

b. Identifiers/Open-Ended Terms

Seagrasses, nutrient cycling, nursery utilization

c. COSATI Field/Group

18. Availability Statement Unlimited	19. Security Class (This Report) Unclassified	21. No. of Pages 147
	20. Security Class (This Page) Unclassified	22. Price

(See ANSI-Z39.18)

OPTIONAL FORM 272 (4-77)
(Formerly NTIS-35)
Department of Commerce